CHILD CARE MANUAL
FOR
SOCIAL WORKERS

CHILD CARE MANUAL FOR SOCIAL WORKERS

FOURTH EDITION

BY

A. E. LEEDING, D.P.A.

One-time Children's Officer, Warwickshire County Council,
lately Regional Consultant A.B.A.F.A.

LONDON
BUTTERWORTHS
1980

ENGLAND: BUTTERWORTH & CO. (PUBLISHERS) LTD.
LONDON: 88 Kingsway, WC2B 6AB

AUSTRALIA: BUTTERWORTHS PTY. LTD.
SYDNEY: 586 Pacific Highway, Chatswood, NSW 2067
Also at Melbourne, Brisbane, Adelaide and Perth

CANADA: BUTTERWORTH & CO. (CANADA) LTD.
TORONTO: 2265 Midland Avenue, Scarborough
M1P 4S1

NEW ZEALAND: BUTTERWORTHS OF NEW ZEALAND LTD.
WELLINGTON: 77/85 Customhouse Quay

SOUTH AFRICA: BUTTERWORTH & CO. (SOUTH AFRICA) (PTY.) LTD.
DURBAN: 152/154 Gale Street

USA: BUTTERWORTH (PUBLISHERS) INC.
BOSTON: 10 Tower Office Park, Woburn,
Mass. 01810

©

A. E. LEEDING

1980

ISBN 0 406 27003 1

Printed in Great Britain by Billing & Sons Ltd, Guildford, London and Worcester

FOREWORD

This is the 4th edition of Mr. Leeding's Child Care Manual. It concerns itself with a wide spectrum of the social policies and the structure of services in England and Wales relating to children and young persons and their families; the focus is on young people under 18 years of age who are in trouble and in need.

The social policies and background and the relevant law are interwoven. The law of the land is a "body of enacted or customary rules recognised by a community as binding"; this body of rules reflects from generation to generation what is thought to be justice. "The nearest we can get to defining justice" writes the Master of the Rolls, Lord Denning, "is to say that it is what the right minded members of the community—those who have the right spirit within them—believe to be fair. Law and Justice are treated as inseparable."

This is most clearly shown in the oath the Queen herself must take at her Coronation. She is asked by the Archbishop of Canterbury, "Will you, to your power cause LAW and JUSTICE in MERCY to be executed in all your judgments." This applies to all subjects of the realm.

To implement Law, Justice and Mercy it is necessary to understand the social background and origin of a law; it is necessary to be conversant with the law and furthermore to subscribe to the discipline of the law. This Manual provides this knowledge and is therefore commended to parents, Probation Officers, Social Workers, Teachers and Youth and Community Workers, indeed all those dealing and working with children.

An overall picture is given of Preventive Work in relation to families and children experiencing difficulties, the Protection of children, the work of the Courts and the care and control of young people thereafter.

Some of those seeking to help children and young persons in a preventive role perhaps through community activities or through personal relationships, find their role a complex one if and when the child or young person appears before a court. Inevitably there is a change of emphasis in the relationship if Law, Justice and Mercy are to be wisely administered, while, at the same time the helping adult must with sensitive social work skills sustain the relationship with the family and the offender. The care of the individual, the control of the individual and the implementation of Law and Justice with Mercy, are surely not incompatible.

The comprehensive social panorama and the clear, concise and detailed teaching on the law given in this Manual should enable those committed to working for and with children to be better able to carry out their complex task of acting positively in the child's best interests, and at the same time safeguarding the precepts of the law.

The Baroness Faithfull, O.B.E., D.Litt., M.A.
November 1979

PREFACE

The third edition of this book took into account those sections of the Children Act 1975 which were in operation at the beginning of 1976. The last three years have not seen the introduction of a "comprehensive adoption service", or of custodianship, the intended alternative to adoption; but in that time there have been important changes in adoption procedures and in legal provision for children, specially for those in local authority care.

The "welfare principle", though not entirely new, has stressed the importance of the wishes and feelings of any child when a decision is being made about his care. Such a decision can only be made within the bounds of what is lawfully possible. Recognition of this has enabled social workers and their legal advisers to develop a close partnership which has become an outstanding feature of child care practice.

Another outcome of the welfare principle is the realisation that a child may need to be represented in care and similar proceedings by someone other than his natural parents. So far such "separate representation" is severely limited but it may be expected to expand as further sections of the 1975 Act are brought into operation. For social workers this will bring the challenge of working directly with children – of all ages – and of being able to interpret to courts, to colleagues, to solicitors and perhaps to parents what their "wishes and feelings" really are.

I am indebted to the Gloucestershire County Council for permission to quote from their Community Care Programme, and to their Chief Executive for advice in the writing of Chapter 1. My thanks are also due to a number of former colleagues in Gloucestershire who have helped in various ways; and to the Director and staff of the Association of British Adopton and Fostering Agencies for many kindnesses received.

Chalford Hill,   A.E.L.
Glos.
June 1979

CONTENTS

CHAPTER 15—CUSTODIANSHIP AND ADOPTION

APPENDIX

INDEX   285

RESPONSIBILITY FOR CHILD CARE: ENGLAND AND WALES

CHILD CARE AS PART OF PERSONAL SOCIAL SERVICES

In general terms child care may be defined as a blend of legislation and practice which inspires the social care of children and young persons under the age of 18. It has a long history, but the modern concept developed after the Second World War, when the Curtis Committee[1] report was followed by the Children Act of 1948; this established a social service specifically for children who for various reasons were unable to live with their parents under normal home conditions. This service led inevitably but gradually to a concern for the families of such children. That concern helped to shape the concept of the "community based and family oriented" service proposed in the report of the Seebohm Committee.[2] But there is still, in 1979, the International Year of the Child, a recognisable entity known as "child care"; the Children Act of 1975 has given it new significance and importance within the personal social services provided under the Local Authority Social Services Act of 1970. There are three partners in the social service enterprise, the Government, the voluntary organisations and the local authorities.

1. GOVERNMENT

For many years, both before and since 1948, successive governments have been initiating and sponsoring progressive legislation in the interests of children; all child-care functions in England are now carried out under the general oversight of the Secretary of State for Social Services, through the Minister for Personal Social Services and the staff of the Social Work Service based in London and at regional centres throughout the country. The tasks of the Social Work Service are set out in Circular DSWS (79) 1. Child-care functions in Wales are under the general oversight of the Secretary of State for Wales who also has the support of a Social Work Service. The functions of the police, the courts, and the probation and after care service, however, are still within the purview of the Secretary of State for Home Affairs.

2.   VOLUNTARY ORGANISATIONS

Child care was largely pioneered by voluntary organisations, many of which are still very much concerned in it and are making an increasing contribution to the service as a whole. Most of them are in membership of a National Council of Voluntary Child Care Organisations which enables them jointly to consider current problems and to co-operate in many and various ways. A voluntary organisation is defined in the Children Act of 1948 as "a body, the activities of which are carried on otherwise than for profit", but is not "a public or local authority". Clearly, such organisations have no obligation to exist, or to undertake child-care work at all. They are free to provide such services as they think necessary or desirable, and have already initiated new experimental schemes and carried out original research of benefit to the service. For these voluntary organisations, child care is still a specialist service, indeed the only specialist service for children in difficulties; as such, it strengthens and supports the more wide-ranging social services of local authorities.

Although voluntary organisations are independent of both the Minister and local government, some of their activities are subject to the Regulations which apply to local authorities, for instance with regard to the boarding-out of children in their care and the conduct of community homes; the advice of the Social Work Service is available both to voluntary organisations and to local authorities.

3.   LOCAL AUTHORITIES

The duty of implementing social service legislation falls mainly upon local authorities, and there are many statutory requirements which are binding upon them, but not on voluntary organisations. Since local government was re-organised in 1974, there have been seven different types of local authority ranging from parish councils (community councils in Wales) to metropolitan counties. Only four types of local authority have social service responsibility, however, these being the Common Council of the City of London, the London boroughs, the non-metropolitan counties and the metropolitan districts.[3] Of these, the last-named are "all-purpose" authorities, the others being "most-purpose" authorities which do not provide all services. No local authority has power to delegate social service functions to a council of a different type, though there are a number of services in which there is consultation and co-operation between the councils of non-metropolitan counties and non-metropolitan districts. Some of the latter were county boroughs prior to 1974 and as such had full responsibilities for personal services, including child care. Current proposals for "organic change" would restore the former position but have met with considerable opposition. The present structure of local government may not be ideal from a social services point of view but supporters of the *status quo* do not consider that it will be improved by premature and piecemeal change.

Since the personal social services depend so heavily upon local authorities, social workers who are employed in local government should have some general idea of the way in which the affairs of a council are managed, even though they may feel that this subject is rather remote from their day-to-day work. Some understanding in broad outline may help to explain how decisions about the use of resources are likely to be made, and why it is that not all demands for a particular service will be met. The current serious anxieties about the lack of resources for all local authority services (including the social services) have stressed the importance of making the best possible use of the main resources of land, manpower and finance, so that the investment may be of the greatest ultimate benefit to the community as a whole.

A   *Committee Structure*

A local authority consists of a number of people who have been elected by the public to form a council; it is therefore a corporate body. As such, it is ultimately responsible for all the decisions taken in its name, but because of the vast range of its responsibilities, it has traditionally operated through a number of separate committees (most of which were established by statute). Each of these has delegated to it certain powers for the day-to-day performance of the duties of the Council as a whole. As new functions have continued to be entrusted to local authorities, so they have been delegated to the most appropriate committee. In this way there has grown up a concept of a number of specialist committees with sole powers to deal with specific subjects; this has become an accepted part of local government but it has been strongly challenged in recent years.

The specialist concept has been strengthened by the fact that local authorities once had an obligation to appoint a number of specified chief officers—for instance, a clerk, a treasurer, a chief education officer, a director of social services and a surveyor. When such a chief officer was appointed, it was assumed that he should lead a department, even though departments as such have no legal recognition in local government, and consist only of the facilities and staff provided to assist the designated chief officer in his work. It has always been assumed that a chief officer reports not to the Council, but to the committee whose special functions he carries out.

These trends led to a local government pattern of a number of separate committees, each served by a chief officer with his "department", having its own professional skills and expert knowledge, but confined to only one aspect of the Council's overall activities.

It has therefore been very difficult in the past for a local authority to achieve unity in its internal organisation, since instead of co-operation there has been competition for resources; the system has tended to make the committees' interests more important than those of the community they serve.

B   *Corporate Management*

As this has been increasingly recognised, and as local government has spent greater sums of public money, it has become clear that a different approach is essential. If a local authority is to function effectively, it must adopt a corporate scheme of management so that it acts as one entity rather than as a group of loosely allied committees, each with its own chief officer, and each, quite understandably, seeking the maximum resources for its own activities or services. A local authority, unlike a business organisation, cannot demonstrate its effectiveness by the amount of profit it makes, but it must find some other way of measuring the effect of its growing expenditure; in the final analysis this must be done by assessing the impact of its services on the well-being of the community at large.

With this in mind, local authorities have devoted a great deal of attention to management techniques designed to promote a corporate, rather than a committee, approach. These techniques have different names, for instance, M.B.O. (Management by Objective) or P.A.R. (Performance Analysis and Review), and they may have somewhat different methods; but they all have the same purpose, that is, to decide what the overall objectives of the Council are, how they can best be met, and how they are in fact being served by the multifarious activities of the Council's staff in the exercise of statutory powers. These questions naturally give rise to consideration of preference and choice. Which is the best way of meeting this objective? Is proposal A more important than proposal B? Given present resources, what is the Council's order of priority?

Clearly, this management approach cuts across the traditional pattern of entirely separate committees and specialist chief officers. Its implementation has many effects, of which two are mentioned here:

i   Chief Officers under the leadership of the Chief Executive are grouped into a management team, and *in that capacity* should consider the interests and performance of the Council as a whole, rather than merely representing their own service responsibilities.

ii   Committees work more closely to a central Policy and Resources Committee which, as its name implies, first agrees upon the Council's overall objectives and is then responsible to the Council as a whole for the best use of its resources of land, manpower and finance.

From these two innovations many others flow: the importance of research, the pooling of statistical and other information, uniform policies for staff recruitment and training, and methods of periodically reviewing the actual performance of the Council in moving towards the objectives it has adopted.

C *The Local Government Act 1972*

This kind of thinking was going on in a number of the former local authorities before re-organisation and it was realised that the formation of new authorities under the Local Government Act 1972 would present a great opportunity for radically changing the traditional patterns. The Secretary of State for the Environment, together with the then local authority associations, set up a Study Group in May 1971 and in 1972 received its report, entitled *The New Local Authorities: management and structure* (usually known as Bains Report). This contained a number of recommendations which were fitted into the framework of the Local Government Act 1972, operative from 1 April 1974.

As a result of this Act, local authorities now have wider discretion with regard to the appointment of specified committees and designated chief officers, but, contrary to the Bains recommendations, are still required to appoint a *Social Services Committee* and a *Director of Social Services*. The import of the Act, however, is to give authorities greater freedom in the management of their internal affairs and there is much to encourage the adoption of the corporate approach even though a "special" committee and chief officer must be appointed for social service functions.

Corporate management, however, is not without its problems; a chief officer may have less than full control of such matters as research, staffing, and training of his own staff, because these are looked upon as resource services provided centrally for the whole of the local authority's organisation; in some cases he may not even have ready access to the powerful Committees which determine policy; or he may not understand the reasoning behind their decisions.

D *Standing Orders*

All local authorities make rules, known as Standing Orders, governing the conduct of the Council's affairs, and specially such matters as the appointment of Committees, delegation to them, and to officers, of the Council's powers, procedure at meetings, and the making of Financial Regulations. The Standing Orders are the instrument by which the Council sets out the ways in which it operates within the overall authority of the Local Government Act.

E *Committee Procedure*

The committee procedure in any local authority is a matter for the authority to determine and may, therefore, take different forms. Many local authorities have adopted the recommendations of the first Maud Report with the result that sub-committees have been greatly reduced in number or abolished altogether. In these authorities, day-to-day decisions are taken by the permanent staff of the departments, within a system of delegation. The Committee itself may meet only quarterly, and confine itself to the discussion of policies and principles, including the use of resources allocated to it by the Council. In such authorities, it is unlikely that social workers will attend the meetings of the Committee unless there is some matter of policy arising in connection with a particular case or unless they have been co-opted either personally or as union representatives.

In other authorities, where sub-committees exist, they are usually concerned with a section of the Committee's work, such as the administration of homes, and may receive detailed reports from members of staff who are directly involved with the matters to be discussed or, they may have oversight of a service within a part of the Council's geographical area.

Some Social Services Committees have found it advisable to set up a small standing sub-committee to deal with matters of urgency, complaints from the public, or cases of particular difficulty referred by the staff for detailed consideration.

Officers of the authority are not members of the Committee or of sub-committees; they have the duty of tendering advice to the members and reporting on subjects of interest or concern. Officers cannot therefore vote, or speak to a motion, though they may be asked to give their views on any item on the agenda. Under the Local Government Act 1972, authorities have wide powers for the delegation of responsibility from the Council to committees and from committees to sub-committees or to officers.

F   *Finance*

One of the central functions of a local authority is the approval of an annual budget, by which money is allocated to the various services and objectives. Like any other budget, it is made up of income and expenditure.

Income is derived partly from miscellaneous sources, including the charges made for some of its services, but mainly from the rates levied upon householders, and from the Government Rate Support Grant. This grant amounts at present to over 60% of total income and should in theory enable an authority to make its own decisions about the services it will provide. The government grant is calculated annually and is based on a "needs" element, a "resources" element, and a "domestic" element. It takes into account for each authority various population factors such as age distribution, school-age children, one-parent families, and the number of households lacking basic amenities. While there are a few services which receive a specific amount of grant, the police service for instance, the grant is made primarily in respect of an authority's total services and is not earmarked for particular purposes.

Expenditure can only be properly incurred under the various statutes which lay duties on the Council, and must be kept within the budget, once approved. All expenditure must be certified by the appropriate Chief Officer, and is subject to the authority's Financial Regulations, to internal audit, and to the annual audit of the Government Auditor.

4. OTHER BODIES AND ORGANISATIONS

Although the responsibility of an actual social service for children is shared between the government, voluntary organisations and local authorities, there are other important institutions and bodies which have important relevant powers or duties.

A   The courts, which exist independently of both central and local government, are called upon to make decisions affecting the welfare of minors. At the highest level, the Family Division of the High Court has inherent power to make a minor a ward of the Court itself and having done so may exercise general supervision of his upbringing and of his parent or guardian. This court, together with County Courts and Magistrates' Courts has the power and duty to consider the welfare of children in divorce, custody, guardianship, adoption and matrimonial proceedings, and may in certain circumstances make appropriate orders for custody, care and control. Juvenile courts have a duty to consider the welfare of children and young persons who appear before them in either criminal or civil proceedings.

B   Police authorities, which have a general responsibility for the protection of life, and the prevention, investigation and prosecution of offences. The statutory responsibility for the protection of children and young persons is recognised in legislation, *e.g.* the C. and Y.P. Acts 1933 and 1969.

C   The Probation and After-care Service, administered by local probation committees, serves the courts and shares with local authorities a number of duties involving social enquiries, reports to courts, and supervision of children and young persons under court orders.

D   The National Health Service, through Area Health Authorities, is responsible for the physical and mental care of all children, and there are many situations in which social and medical care are complementary to each other.

E   The education service has general responsibility for the education of children of compulsory school age, and is involved in educational services both for those under the age of 5 and over the age of 16. Here again social factors for some children are of great importance, so that a watertight division between care and education becomes impossible.

F   The Department of Health and Social Security is concerned with the provision of adequate maintenance allowances for families or households and in this way directly contributes to the welfare of large numbers of children, including those who are sometimes in voluntary or statutory care for short periods because of family circumstances.

In addition, there are many organisations which have no statutory powers or duties but which exist to further the interests of all children, or of some special group of them. These organisations are far too numerous to mention, but an exception must be made in the case of the National Children's Bureau because of its concern for every aspect of the care of children, and because of its advocacy of their rights in an adult world. The Bureau has produced a large number of reports on such topics as adoption, foster care, and residential care. Its on-going survey of all children born in one week in 1958 is a major contribution to the study of the needs of all children, whether brought up in their natural families or in some form of substitute care.

Lastly there are various bodies concerned with research and the formulation of policy for the whole of the personal social services, including those for children. In view of the tremendous range of interest, it was considered essential that there should be an independent forum with the duty of advising the responsible minister and of developing resources and training for the promotion of an effective service. To meet this need, the Personal Social Services Council was established on the recommendation of the Seebohm Committee; one of its priorities is the bringing about of greater consumer participation in policy making. The first report of this Council, containing a wealth of comment and information, was published in August 1975.[4] In addition to factual data about the financing of the social services, the report contains a number of statements made to members of the Council while they were visiting different parts of the country seeking opinion. These statements were made by Directors of Social Services, councillors, social workers and others in local government and in the voluntary social services. They provide views, not necessarily shared by the Personal Social Services Council itself, on the general position after several years' experience of the working of the Local Authority Social Services Act 1970.

In addition, the Social Work Service (mentioned on p. 2) itself issues frequent reports on various aspects of service provision; there have been other important studies of the place of the "fieldworker" within the organisational structure; and a great deal of research has been solely concerned with the practice of "child care". Later chapters will refer to some of the more significant of these publications.

NOTES

1. Report of Committee on the Care of Children, 1946 Cmnd. 6922.
2. Report of the Committee on Local Authority and Allied Personal Social Services, 1968 Cmnd. 3703.
3. Local Authority Social Services Act 1970, s. 1, amended by Local Government Act 1972, s. 195.
4. First Report of the Personal Social Services Council 1975.

Chapter 2

LOCAL AUTHORITIES

SUMMARY

THE SOCIAL SERVICES COMMITTEE

The Local Authority Social Services Act 1970 is based on the Seebohm
Report (Cmnd. 3703) which recommended that the local authority welfare
and children's services, together with some of the former local authority
health services, should be unified within each local authority into one
personal social service.

Every local authority which has the duty of implementing this Act must
establish a committee with direct responsibility for the service to be
provided, but two or more local authorities may establish a joint committee
for this purpose if they wish. The usefulness of this provision diminished
when small local authorities disappeared in the 1974 re-organisation, but
could again emerge if "organic change" results in the creation of more
small "social services" authorities. The features of the committee may be
listed as follows.

A The Committee must have referred to it by the local authority all
matters relating to the exercise by the authority of its functions
under the legislation concerned.

B Having referred these matters to the Committee, the local authority
may delegate the functions themselves to the Committee.

C Before itself exercising functions under the legislation, the local
authority must, unless the matter is urgent, consider a report of the
Committee.

D Except with the consent of the Secretary of State, the local authority
may not require the Committee to deal with any matters other than

those which stand referred to it. Consent has been given for the Committee to play its part in the corporate management of the whole authority.

E   Any matter which stands referred to the Committee, but which also relates to a general service of the authority, may be referred to another Committee of the authority, but only after a report by the responsible Committee has been considered.

F   The Committee may appoint sub-committees, and may delegate to them any of the functions of the Committee itself.

G   The Committees of two or more local authorities may establish joint sub-committees and may delegate to them any of the functions of either or any of the Committees themselves.

H   The Committee may co-opt persons who are not members of the authority provided that a majority of members of the Committee are also members of the local authority.

I   Sub-Committees and joint sub-committees may include persons who are not members of the authority, or authorities, concerned, provided that at least one member of each of the authorities is a member of the sub-committee.[1]

ROLE OF COUNCILLORS

The Seebohm Report made a number of other far-reaching recommendations for the improvement of the existing services, but as the Act confines itself to organisational changes only, the translation of the Seebohm ideals into reality rests primarily in the hands of the councillors who serve on the statutory Committee.[2]

Since councillors are elected to represent the community as a whole, they are well placed to be aware of social needs, not only of the elderly, the handicapped and the lonely, but also of the homeless, the mentally ill, the "problem family" and children in difficulties. It is the councillors who are best in a position to shape the authority's social policy and to forge close links between all the committees and other agencies which contribute towards the care of the community. It is they who can ensure that services are not only provided, but that they readily reach those who need them, and it is they who are called upon to evaluate the effectiveness of services and to make difficult choices of priority within the local authority's corporate management structure.[3]

Whether or not committees decide to use their power to co-opt, they have many opportunities of obtaining the views of "consumer groups" or social workers by means of working parties on particular subjects or through specially constituted local consultative groups. If social workers feel that the views of the people they serve are not sufficiently considered, they should develop an understanding of the system of local government; they should realise that the vital decisions are made by councillors in Committee, and take appropriate steps to ensure that they have the necessary information.

CHIEF OFFICER

In addition to establishing a Committee to administer the Act, the local authority must appoint a Director of Social Services. The Secretary of State may prescribe the qualifications required for appointment, but until such time as he does so, (for England and Wales) he must be given particulars of the persons who are being considered for appointment, as he has the power of veto. Once appointed, the Director may not be employed by the authority in any other capacity unless the Secretary of State consents. Consent has been given for the Director to take part in the general management process of the local authority. The Act requires the authority to ensure that the Director, as the statutory chief officer, has adequate staff to assist him in his duties.[4]

FUNCTIONS

The function of the Social Services Committee is to administer all the legislation listed in the Schedule to the Local Authority Social Services Act 1970 (as since extended and amended). Some of the Statutes deal mainly with services for groups such as the elderly, or the mentally ill, but some are of more general application. There are, however, a number of Statutes and Rules or Regulations which deal specifically with children and young persons; these were at one time administered by a separate local authority Children's Department which provided what was known as a "Child Care Service".

The Act does not require the Committee to use its functions under the legislation as the foundation of a "community based and family oriented" service; but this was the intention and recommendation of the Seebohm Committee and it has to some extent been fulfilled. For this reason the former child care service cannot be clearly identified, but its functions still exist within the framework of the overall service; and it has helped to inspire the concept of each individual as a member of a family.

But in terms of the corporate approach mentioned in the previous chapter, a local authority cannot just describe its social objective in such words as "strengthening family life", without stating how it intends to work to that end. Instead, it must design a whole "programme area", which consists of an overall objective served by first-level objectives; these are in turn served by second-level objectives. All the many and varied activities of the service in its day-to-day operation may then be set out in such a way as to show which second-level objective they serve. Activities should not be carried out without a realisation of their true purpose; this applies whether they are "statutory" in the sense of being precisely controlled by statute or regulation, or "permissive" in that they are carried out under enabling legislation but only to the extent determined by the local authority. Whatever the type of activity, it should be possible for its true cost to be measured against its effectiveness in bringing about the stated objective. It should then be possible to decide that one activity is preferable to another in given circumstances. In times of economic pressure (which, for the social services, is always), such decisions can be used to alter the investment of staff and resources as between one activity or one part of the programme area and another. It is obviously difficult to conceive of a social service in these terms, because its effectiveness must ultimately be measured in terms of human happiness, but social care is now one of the most costly of an authority's total services, and cannot escape the challenge of effective management at every level.

There are various ways of describing objectives, but the outline programme shown on p. 13 may serve as an illustration.

This particular example suggests that the local authority using it would have a high regard for personal freedom and choice and would look upon *long-term* care or treatment as a last resort. While it would be prepared to provide good long-term care when it was needed, and wanted, it would use its resources in such a way as to enable people to retain their independence for as long as possible, and it would provide different kinds of long-term care, not all residential.

If the authority had accepted that as a deliberate policy, it would follow that each separate activity and service would be seen to be serving one of the sub-objectives and thus ultimately the overall objective itself.

The activities and services need not be limited to those of a particular service. The first-level objective A, for instance, would obviously be mainly carried out by planners, though social services should be involved in it. The same objective would also be served by a number of the activities of the education service, playgroups, for example, or adventure playgrounds or community centres.

This is because under the corporate approach to local authority management, all objectives are those of the authority as a whole, and they need not therefore correspond exactly with the contents of service provision. In Community Care, for instance, the bulk of the activities are provided by the Social Services Committee, but other committees also provide services which to some extent serve the stated objective.

So far as children are concerned, this concept was envisaged as long ago as 1963 when the Children and Young Persons Act of that year laid on the local authority the duty to "make available such advice, guidance and assistance as may promote the welfare of children by diminishing the need to receive them into care or keep them in care, or bring them before a juvenile court". The Act also, for the first time, gave the authority power to use resources of staff and material or financial aid for this purpose.

Although the duty was laid upon the authority as a whole, and stood referred to the Children's Committee of those days, there was no restriction as to the ways in which the advice, guidance and assistance could be provided; but because the existing committees and departments were directed towards services rather than towards children and their families, the opportunity was not grasped. Efforts were made to achieve progress by various forms of "co-ordination" but these rested on attempts to deploy together different separated services which all had their own diverse and specialist objectives.

The integration of some services under the Local Authority Social

COMMUNITY CARE PROGRAMME

OVERALL OBJECTIVE

To build up a community of
families and individuals able
to lead a full personal life,
supported, when required, by
appropriate social measures

FIRST-LEVEL OBJECTIVES

A
To contribute
towards the
creation of a
physical and
social
environment
favourable
to human
development

B

C
To provide,
and deploy,
resources
to minimise
long-term
dependence
on community
care

D

E
To provide
general
administration
and support
services

To detect
those families
and
individuals
who are at
risk of
becoming
dependent
upon the
community

To provide
long-term
care or
treatment
for those
families
and
individuals
who need it

SECOND-LEVEL OBJECTIVES

A. 1-6 | B. 1-2 | C. 1-10 | D. 1-4 | D. 1-4

The second-level objectives are served by a large number of ACTIVITIES which are detailed in Appendix A.

Services Act goes some way towards making co-ordination a reality, but of course there are still other local authority services such as housing and education which have a strong social element. This was recognised by the Seebohm Committee which recommended that housing welfare functions, and the education welfare service should be transferred to the proposed Social Service Department. The Act, while making this possible, did not require it to be done, but left the decision to individual local authorities. The future of the educational welfare service, in particular, has been discussed in this context for many years. Many educational welfare officers saw themselves as social workers within the educational system rather than in the community as a whole, and the Ralphs Report of 1973 encouraged this concept. Very few authorities have yet carried out the Seebohm recommendation, but Directors of Social Services are still urging the importance of "social work services for children in school" as an integral part of the wider social services. At the same time, headmasters are reported as regretting the diversion of teachers into pastoral work within the school setting.

In the absence of general agreement on such issues, corporate management offers some prospect of ensuring that the services provided by Committees other than the statutory Committee will none the less serve the authority's overall objectives, one of which is Community Care.

Although there is no longer a separate "child care" service as such, all children are individuals in the community, and their families are families within the community. The whole of the outline programme set out above can therefore be applied to them and can be used as a framework into which all the authority's social services for children, as for adults, can be fitted with meaning and purpose. It is of course possible to set out objectives in other ways, for instance by East Sussex.[5] But the essential point is that there should be specific goals, rather than generalised aims, and some method of assessing how far they are being met.

RESOURCES

The resources available to the Committee consist basically of voluntary workers, buildings, staff and finance.

VOLUNTARY WORKERS

Chapter XVI of the Seebohm Report[2] examines the concept of "welfare through community" and makes a number of recommendations about the participation of the public in the planning, organisation and provision of the personal social services. It then goes on to state clearly that the increased demands on the local authority services will be so great that it will be unable to meet them without enlisting "large numbers of volunteers" to supplement the statutory services. Though the Report refrains from suggesting exactly how this should be done, it recommends that the members of Social Service Committees, who are themselves volunteers in a way, should, with their Chief Officer, find ways of including both voluntary organisations and individual volunteers in their plans for the administration of the service.

In 1969, a report *The Voluntary Worker and the Social Services* (the Aves Report) examined the subject in great detail, and made a number of specific recommendations relating to the recruitment and training of volunteers, their relationship to full-time social workers, the organisation of their work and such administrative matters as the payment of expenses, insurance cover and authorisation by an appropriate form of certificate.

The conclusions of the Aves Report follow that of Seebohm, that voluntary workers have an *essential* part to play in the provision of personal social services, and that this should be fully recognised. They should not, however, be expected to undertake duties which require "professional" training. Since Aves, the voluntary sector has been much in evidence. The Personal Social Services Council in 1976 issued a document called "Voluntary Social Service-Manpower Resources", suggesting that voluntary service may be seen as a substitute or a supplement or a complement to statutory services. Then in 1977 came the Wolfendon Report on "The Future of Voluntary Organisations". This recommended government financial support for local intermediary bodies, mainly Councils for Voluntary Services and Rural Community Councils, and was followed by a National Council of Social Service scheme for developing a partnership between local authorities and local voluntary agencies.

Another indication of the growing importance of the voluntary contribution to the welfare state is given by the Government call for "Good Neighbour" schemes; but these fall short of the idea that volunteers may be able to provide a genuine alternative to social workers in some cases, rather than being used to supplement official effort. The Community Service Volunteers have begun to operate on a "one to one" basis, as well as taking part in team projects, though usually requiring the support of the local authority or a responsible voluntary agency. And there are no doubt many men and women, outside any such scheme, who are willing to serve, but need some stimulus and direction.

People who have a sense of community and feel a responsibility for their neighbours and friends, or for the district in which they live, are capable of doing more than digging old people's gardens, washing their windows, driving them from home to a day centre, or taking part in fund-raising activities. Their qualities of compassion, understanding, and concern can all be used in a much more liberal way, and, given some basic training in essentials, can go some way to easing the burden on full-time social workers, while at the same time giving practical expression to community concern.

The Seebohm Report envisaged a "large untapped supply" of such people willing to give their time to voluntary social work, provided that they are treated as responsible, that they are given worthwhile tasks, and that they feel that their help is relevant and is needed. If there is such a reservoir of help available, it could be seen as potentially a most important resource to any Social Services Committee which really wishes to develop the involvement of the community in its work, but it is still an uncertain quantity because it has not yet been fully developed.

Traditionally, voluntary effort so far has been provided by a large number of "specialist" voluntary societies, and by more general bodies such as W.R.V.S., Citizen's Advice Bureaux, Councils of Social Service, the Samaritans and church organisations. The most obvious individual volunteers are those who actually deliver meals to the homes of elderly and handicapped people; foster parents; prison and hospital visitors, members of "good neighbour" schemes or "Fish" schemes which have developed in small localities.

There must be many more ways in which people of commitment could help in the provision of services, but if community involvement is to become a reality, it should be borne in mind that to any citizen, his real community is quite small: a hamlet, or part of a village, or, in a town, perhaps two or three streets, or a block of flats.

The voluntary organisations can provide support over a wide area, but the individual volunteer is more likely to be effective in his immediate neighbourhood, and not only in caring for the elderly. The private foster parent, the child minder and the play group leader are all examples of personal voluntary services for the young.

BUILDINGS

Some of the Committee's functions require buildings as a base for advice or services. Such buildings house:

Administrative services;
area social work offices, or sub-offices, administering the Home Help Service, the Meals Service and general social work;
day nurseries for younger children;
workshops for handicapped people;
playgroups;
community services (including facilities for "intermediate treatment");
day centres and clubs for the elderly or handicapped;
day centres and clubs for the mentally or physically handicapped under 65;
adult training centres, or clubs, for the mentally handicapped over 16.

Some of these services may be provided in one and the same building (multipurpose day centres are being developed in some areas). Some of the buildings may be directly provided by the local authority, others by voluntary or community groups or private individuals, or by the Area Health Authority.

Other functions can only be carried out in buildings where people can live either temporarily or on a more permanent basis. These consist of residential accommodation for:

Elderly persons (over 65) and/or younger physically handicapped persons;

mentally handicapped adults;
mentally handicapped children;
mentally ill persons;
mothers and babies;
special groups such as alcoholics, single homeless people, families
needing temporary accommodation, young people of working age,
young children;

children of school age, who are in care;

children and young persons placed for assessment and observation or
under voluntary or statutory supervision;

children and young persons in care who require education training and
care.

Here again, the authority may either provide such accommodation
itself, or may use homes which have been provided by private persons or
by voluntary organisations. So far as children and young persons are
concerned, all the types of accommodation bracketed together, consisting of
both local authority and voluntary provision, are provided under what is
known as a Regional Plan, which, as it applies to a group of local
authorities, and not to one only, requires some brief explanation.

REGIONAL PLANNING

Every local authority has been designated by the Secretary of State for
inclusion in a large geographical region of up to five or six million
population; the authorities within each of these regions are required
jointly to establish a Regional Planning Committee, to obtain information
about all the various establishments within the region and assess the total
needs of the constituent authorities for the accommodation of children and
young persons in their care.

Each Regional Planning Committee was required to prepare and
submit a regional plan for the provision and maintenance of homes to be
known generally as "community homes". These include homes formerly
provided by the constitutent authorities and any voluntary homes *which
elected to be included in the plan* on the understanding that a local
authority will take part in its management. In this context, the phrase
"voluntary homes" includes those former approved schools which were not
provided and maintained by local authorities, together with the former
probation homes and hostels for young persons under the age of 17. Such a
voluntary home must be designated as a *controlled* community home, in
which case it will be managed, equipped and maintained by a specified
local authority, or an *assisted* community home, in which event it will be
managed, equipped and maintained by a voluntary organisation, though a
specified local authority will appoint one-third of the members of the
managing body.

The Regional Plan proposes the nature and purpose of each community
home and in particular sets out proposals for the provision of observation
and assessment facilities for children in the care of the constituent

authorities. The detailed provisions relating to the Regional Planning Committees are to be found under ss. 35 to 48 of the Children and Young Persons Act 1969. Once completed, the plan is subject to review and modification from time to time.

It is important to note that the Regional Planning Committee is concerned solely with planning for the region. It does not manage, maintain or provide any establishment nor directly employ any staff for such establishments. Their staff is provided by the local authority or the voluntary organisation as the case may be. Those community homes which were formerly approved schools are usually referred to as "community homes with education on the premises" or, by the staff, as "community schools". Others are known as observation and assessment units, as that is their primary function. The extent to which each authority has access to each establishment for its children is determined by the plan which requires the approval of the Secretary of State. Special attention now has to be given to the provision of "secure accommodation" within the region.

The Secretary of State himself has power to provide other homes for specially disturbed children who cannot reasonably be accommodated within the community home system.[6] This is a resource in the sense that places in the homes may be provided, but only on application to the Secretary of State. (Such homes are not yet available to the expected extent.)

Another function of the Regional Planning Committee is to plan facilities which can be used in conjunction with supervision orders made by the Courts. It is intended that these facilities will eventually replace attendance centres and detention centres as a means of providing activity and control for those children and young persons who are the subject of supervision orders. The facilities are usually referred to as "intermediate treatment" which will be discussed in detail in the context of supervision orders in Chapter 14. The existence of regional planning opens up a number of possibilities; there is scope for joint arrangements for staff recruitment and training, for research, and for shared schemes of adoption and fostering.

Each Regional Planning Committee originally had a professional adviser for the purpose of drawing up the required plans; this adviser would seem to have been well placed to propose co-operative efforts in these other areas of concern, but some of the Regional Planning Committees have now dispensed with their advisers, on grounds of economy, and will be seeking other ways of promoting inter-authority co-operation.

OTHER LOCAL AUTHORITY RESOURCES

In addition to centralised services, such as those of the Solicitor, Treasurer and Architect, a local authority provides other resources which may be available to its Social Services Committee, especially in the context of overall corporate management. Such resources, while under the administration of another committee and not therefore a resource of the

Social Services Committee as such, play a vital part in forwarding the community care objective of the whole authority.

There are many such resources, two of the most important being:

A   the social service element of the education service, including such matters as provision of free school meals, clothing and maintenance grants and the services of educational welfare officers, who are now recognised as providing a social work service to the schools administered by the authority;

B   the provision of housing, accompanied by housing advice and a social work service for tenants. (In non-metropolitan counties, this is a resource not of the county, but of the district councils within its area; elsewhere housing and social services are both the function of one and the same authority.)

Both the police and the probation and after-care services may also be regarded as providing important resources in the promotion of community care, but are only briefly mentioned here because they are not local authority services in the usual sense of the word.

NON-LOCAL AUTHORITY RESOURCES

Two of the most important resources available to the population as a whole have special relevance for the Social Services Committee. One is the Health Service, now separated from local government, which is organised in such a way as to recognise the special needs of patients; the other is the Department of Health and Social Security's system of welfare rights and benefits, with its recognition of the special needs of particular groups of people, such as the handicapped and one-parent families.

STAFF

The Committee's staff is the most essential resource, since without it none of the other resources, not even volunteers, can operate. For this reason, staffing costs account for about 60% of all the expenditure of a Social Services Committee; hence the concern for the effective management of man-power referred to in the previous chapter.

It will be clear from the range of its functions and resources that the Committee must provide its Chief Officer with a wide variety of staff in accordance with s. 6 of the Act.

These will include:

1. Senior management staff for the conduct of what is a very large enterprise.
2. Administrative and clerical staff for the servicing of the Committee, dealing with finance, supplies, personnel, research, forward-planning, training, records, assessments, and general support work.
3. Liaison staff for effective contact with other committees, Area Health Authority, D.H.S.S., district councils, public bodies, volun-

tary organisations, and the community, including voluntary social
workers.

4. Advisory and supervisory social work staff, team leaders, advisers,
   inspectors.
5. Social work staff in contact with the community, carrying out a
   number of statutory and non-statutory duties, social workers
   attached to general practices, or in hospitals and clinics, specialist
   social workers for the blind, the deaf and other groups, such as
   child-minded children, foster parents and prospective adopters.
6. Administrative and clerical support for social work staff.
7. Managers of workshops, training centres, day centres, day nurseries
   and other non-residential services such as the meals and home help
   services.
8. Administrative and clerical support for domiciliary services.
9. Care and domestic staff for the whole range of residential establishments, and teachers in some of the community homes.
10. Administrative and clerical support for the residential services.
11. Home helps (numerically the largest group of all staff).
12. Ancillary staff who are indispensable in the provision of services.

FINANCE

The annual budget of the Social Services Committee of any local
authority will be of the order of millions of pounds and one of the highest
after that of the Education Committee. The amount available for the
provision of services is subject to the constraints mentioned in Chapter 1
and cannot be readily expanded to meet new or unforeseen needs. The
budget therefore plays a key part in the monitoring of expenditure and
income; finance, though an essential resource, is also a limiting factor in
the development of the Committee's services.

GENERAL

In 1972, the Government asked local authorities to provide information
for the preparation of a ten-year-plan of investment in the local social
services. Suggested guidelines were set out for each group of people
considered to require services; the estimated numbers of staff were shown
in terms of those needed for a stated population; similar estimates were
given for the number of "places" in both day and residential establishments, and authorities were asked to use those in an imaginative way in
preparing plans.

So for the first time Social Services Committees were able to form a
realistic and detailed assessment of the goals they should be striving to
approach by the end of the ten-year period, that is, by 1982. This exercise
was very valuable in exposing those areas of need in which there was
either no service at all or one far below the suggested level. It also provided
a means of comparing existing services with the norms set out for
consideration. In general the resources of buildings and staff were found to

be well below the suggested criteria, and the finance which would have been required to bridge the gap has not yet been made available, nor is there any prospect of it.

But as the "norms" themselves were averages, they did not reflect the greatly varying needs of individual authorities. Inner city areas, for instance, have special problems not shared with either rural counties, or suburban new estates. The differences are obvious, but tended to be obscured by the "average" standards to be used in the Ten Year Plan. But even so, the criteria laid down were in general far above the resources of buildings and staff available to authorities as a whole. Government guidance to local councils now takes the form of a three year illustrated prospectus and shows a greater concern for community support services than for buildings. So far as services to children and young persons are concerned, authorities are being urged to develop foster care and "inter-mediate treatment" and at the same time to plan for the introduction of the statutory adoption service foreshadowed in the Children Act of 1975; however, these aims cannot be achieved without reference to any need there may be for the very costly provision of "secure accommodation for children in care".

All forward planning is still constrained by the economic position; so that authorities are obliged to declare their priorities as between one programme area and another, and as between one part of each programme and another. The chart on p. 13 and the specimen programme in Appendix A show what the choices really are for the Community Care programme. They may have something in common with the stark experience of the Inner London Education Authority which has been compelled by legislation to spend large sums on fire precautions and health and safety measures in its schools. The amount involved, it is reported, would have enabled the Authority to provide nursery education for all children under the age of five.

NOTES

1. Local Authority Social Services Act, ss. 1-5.
2. Report of the Committee on Local Authority and Allied Personal Social Services, Cmnd. 3703.
3. *Social Services: the councillor's task* B.A.S.W., 1973.
4. Local Authority Social Services Act, s. 6.
5. *Social Work Today*, 11 October 1977.
6. Children and Young Persons Act 1969, s. 64.

Chapter 3

THE SOCIAL SERVICES
DEPARTMENT: PART I

SUMMARY

TASK

GENERAL

The task of the Seebohm Committee was "to review the organisation and responsibilities of the local authority personal social services and to consider what changes are desirable to secure an effective family service". It was thus precluded from considering any other way in which such a service might be set up; it had to be in the local authority setting. There might have been something to be said for entrusting the task to voluntary organisations, or for creating a National Social and Welfare Service, parallel to the National Health Service. It may now be argued, after nearly a decade of experience, that health and personal social services are inseparable and ought to be administered by one and the same central authority. But the fact is that they are at present distinct, one being under central control, the other under local elected councils which delegate their responsibilities and functions to Social Service Committees. Given the traditional pattern of local government, this means that even under "corporate management" the Committee must work through the agency of a Department.

The Social Services Department consists of the Director and his staff, and exists primarily to carry out the policy of the Social Services Committee in implementing the legislation. The Seebohm Report's recommendations went far beyond the purely organisational approach of the Act and showed particular concern for the ways in which the service should be developed. It may be helpful to set out a few of the ideas in the Report as a reminder of its intentions.

1. The local authority department should provide a community-based and family orientated service which would be available to all. The department should be able to reach out far beyond the discovery and rescue of social casualties; it should enable the greatest possible number of individuals to act reciprocally, giving and receiving service for the well-being of the whole community (Para. 2).[1]

2. Social problems are of tremendous magnitude compared with the resources available. Much more needs to be done, but especially for the under fives, the elderly, the physically and mentally handicapped, and the "neglected flotsam and jetsam of society". Services should be better deployed, and there should be a far greater effort to involve the community in preventing social breakdowns (Para. 139).[1]

3. People must be treated as people, rather than as separate groups divided by age and type (Para. 142).[1]

4. People should no longer be deterred, by the fear of stigma, from seeking help when they need it; on the contrary a positive effort should be made to encourage everyone to learn about the personal social services, and to use them (Para. 145).[1]

5. A service which is community-based will be subject to criticism because of the non-provision or under provision of services; it will also reduce the gap between "givers" and "takers" of services because it will be increasingly realised that all members of a community are "consumers" either directly or indirectly, and pay for services through taxes and rates (Paras. 491-492).[1]

6. Already in some small ways citizens are taking part in providing services either personally, or in planning, or in the formation of special interest groups of many kinds. This is to be encouraged, though there are difficulties to be faced, one of them being the association between popular pressures and traditional democratic processes, and another the possibly conflicting loyalties of social work staff (Paras. 493-494).[1]

The Seebohm Committee realised that its far-reaching proposals for a really effective family social service would need not only the help of the community but also greater resources, especially of manpower. This would depend upon money, training, recognition of needs, and better deployment of staff already available. But the explanatory and financial memorandum of the Local Authority Social Services Bill, which led to the Act, stated that "the Bill is not expected to result in any significant increase in expenditure out of public funds", and "the Bill is not expected to have any appreciable overall effect on public service manpower requirements". Resources have, in fact, been increased, but not yet to the point of enabling Social Service Departments to see the Seebohm recommendations as much more than an ideal to be attained at some far future date. The Act, as we have seen, was confined to creating a new administrative Committee and structure: a skeleton which has yet to be clothed with the flesh of fulfilment.

Since their inception in 1971, most Social Services Departments have been fully occupied in re-organisation, and in the very practical demands it made upon them. All were committed from the outset to the implementation of the better services for the physically handicapped, which were required by the Chronically Sick and Disabled Persons Act of 1970; and to the development of entirely new services for children and young persons arising from the Act of 1969. Within a few months they were faced with the prospect of carrying into effect the White Paper *Better Services for the Mentally Handicapped.*[2] The large number of elderly people in the population was already a cause for concern in 1971, and is still increasing, especially in the older age group (those aged 85 and over).

In every Social Services Department resources are fully occupied in the many activities required to serve the population, but are in no real sense meeting the needs that are known to exist. The activities include direct social work support, personal services, including the provision of practical help, the day-care services and, for a small proportion, residential services. But alongside this personal work, there is the continuing complex of the planning of services in association with other local authority departments, housing authorities or departments, the Area Health Authority and voluntary organisations. There is a continual effort to attain the higher standards which are exhorted by official circulars, or Acts or White Papers.

This is the position in any authority, though naturally there are variations from one to another. In one place there may be an overwhelming proportion of elderly in the population, in another a high incidence of delinquency, or inadequate housing. But in any area the people known and receiving services will form only a small percentage of those who are in need of help of some kind. This is as true for children and young persons under the age of 18 as for the elderly and handicapped.

THE POTENTIAL CHILD-CARE TASK

The statistics for the year ending March 1977, show that there were then 101,000 children in care in England and Wales, representing about 7 in every thousand persons under 18. 25% had been in care for less than one year, 33% for between one and three years, and 42% for over three years.[3] But the bare figures give no idea of the potential need for services to families with children; the position may be gleaned from the National Children's Bureau's survey, *Born to Fail?*[4] This is based on the Bureau's long-term study of all children born in one week in March 1958. Of the 10,504 children concerned, only 64% could be described as having an "ordinary" family background. The other 36% were members of families in which one or more of the following factors were present:

Only one parent
Family of five or more children
Poor housing accommodation
Low income.

In 30% of the cases, one or more of these factors was present, but in 6% all four were found.

There were in fact variations in the incidence of the factors, ranging from 2% in southern England to 10% in Scotland (for all four factors), but the survey clearly indicates that in every local authority area the number of children in care is small compared to the number of those who lack an "ordinary" background and have special problems to meet.

When it is remembered that the figures relate only to the poverty of the physical environment, and leave out other children who may be disadvantaged physically, educationally or emotionally, the total potential problem for any authority is seen to be of daunting proportions. The national scale of disadvantage was set out in detail in Appendix Q of the Seebohm Report (1968).[1]

Similarly the White Paper *Better Services for the Mentally Handicapped* draws attention to the basic needs of mentally handicapped persons including children and urges the development of services which will enable many of them to live in the community and with their own families.[2] This Paper stresses that the people to be helped are not only the handicapped themselves, but the families who care for them often under great difficulties and who need all kinds of support to help them. This is the meaning of "the effective family service".

There are thus very large demands for services for children of whom something is known either because they are registered in a certain category, or because the department has actually been involved with them or their families in some connection. To these demands must be added the pressure from self-help groups, voluntary bodies concerned with specific needs, other local authority services, the courts, the health service, schools and a host of other agencies who may all bring families or individuals to the notice of the Department so that appropriate help can be offered.

Some of these referrals will call for simple advice, some for fuller investigation and some for long-term help which may continue over a period of years.

ORGANISATION

In a department with so many varied functions and such considerable resources, even though they are always likely to be inadequate, first-class management is essential. The Seebohm Report recognised this very clearly, but in making recommendations about the qualities required in a Director it laid equal emphasis on management ability and social work qualification or experience (Para. 620).[1] Whether or not as a result of this, social work and administration have become entangled in a structure which appears to value the skills of management more highly than those of social work. As a result many experienced social workers have left the work they were doing to take up more highly paid advisory, supervisory and managerial posts for which they might not be so well equipped. But in transferring themselves into "administration" some found it hard to give up the use of the special skill and knowledge they took with them. One consequence of this was to weaken the personal responsibility and accountability of "front line" social workers, both in the field and in the residential sector. This subject was fully discussed in the report of the B.A.S.W. Working Party on Career Grades (for social workers) which broadly suggested, among other things, that the two elements should be entirely separated as in the health service, with administration providing the resources and the social workers using them.

Though the principle of the career grade has now been widely accepted it came too late to stop the flow of practitioners into the higher status, and rewards, of management. Nor, generally speaking, does a career grade take social workers, at whatever level, out of the control of a managerial system, which many of them deplore. There is a continuing tension between the values of a large and publicly accountable Department, and those of the social workers who feel that they are personably accountable for their own work and standards of practice. This conflict lies at the heart of the confusion and lack of confidence which features in several research findings and reports. Yet it is not new. It was not unforeseen. It arises directly from the nature and structure of the organisation.[5]

STRUCTURE

The Act of 1970 gave no guidance as to ways in which the Director should organise his staff, and it was only to be expected that in local government a traditional hierarchy would develop. In its most simple form, this could have been done by allowing the three former services to continue functioning as they were at both central and area level, with the Director acting as unquestioned co-ordinator, with the control of integrated records, forward planning, statistics and other management resources, as illustrated below:

A similar structure could have been imposed for each of the area staff and services in the community, so that social workers and existing domiciliary services, and day and residential services would have operated as before, even in separate offices, except that there would have been overall co-ordination by someone appointed as Area Officer. There might then have been time for adjustments to be made in the size and shape of areas, and for the area staff to find out from the community whether the traditional services were wanted, whether they were used, and whether there might be real alternatives which would be more acceptable.

However, this was not generally done. In an effort to bring about some form of integration of services the pattern usually became:

There were various permutations of this, but essentially the general principle was to have several assistant directors each dealing with a specific aspect of the work, and with or without a deputy director.

The former separated existing area offices were amalgamated under an Area Officer, who had usually no control over the support and residential services in his area. These were still controlled from the centre, so that area staff could only recommend that people should receive a service; they could not supply it directly.

By incorporation into the local government setting, Social Services Departments from the first tended to be bureaucratic, on the lines of an industrial concern. They were expected to "deliver" services to some of their customers, while telling others that there was a shortage of stock, but that delivery might be possible later. They also had the task of delivering some services which people might not want, such as supervision under a court order, or long term residential care or treatment. This reality was, of course, very different from the Seebohm concept set out at the beginning of this chapter. Services were not only to be given to the community, but also received from it.[1]

SURVEY OF SOCIAL SERVICES DEPARTMENTS, 1973

As things are, the "delivery" of services, both wanted and unwanted, still occupy a great deal of the attention of any Department, which is simultaneously involved in servicing the Social Services Committee, trying to assess the potential demand for existing services, dealing with the day-to-day problems of personnel, buildings, allocation of finance, statistics, controlling the service through managers and advisers at various levels, and developing systems of communication between the fragmented areas of responsibility. The difficulties of Social Services Departments as they were in 1973 is well described in a D.H.S.S. publication covering thirty-four different representative authorities.[6] Some of these departments had made progress in delegating from the centre, but rather less in making communication and monitoring effective. In others, specialists of the former separate departments, such as home help organisers and occupational therapists were still working more or less in isolation from social workers, while in yet others there was a marked dearth of special staff for dealing with the needs of handicapped people and with difficult adolescents. In a number of authorities, separate registers of groups of people were still being maintained because integrated record systems had not been established. In these authorities the area staff were having to rely on a "living memory bank" due to the lack of continuous inclusive written case papers.

The D.H.S.S. Report was prepared before local government re-organisation in 1974, and expressed the hope that some of these matters would be put right by the new authorities. It drew special attention to the need for better overall management, with particular reference to:

1.   Improved management of work loads. This entails an adequate record of work being undertaken, together with a realistic appraisal of what must be done, what can be done, and what cannot be done at all. This is largely the responsibility of the leaders of social work teams.

2.   Better ways of providing resources to teams without lengthy and complicated lines of decision-making.

3.   Efficient administrative record-keeping systems. In what aims to be a family orientated service, records should be kept on a family basis, rather than on a basis of individuals known to the department because of different services, so that the whole family picture can be seen immediately. Separated records do not easily reveal that an elderly blind person is otherwise physically or mentally handicapped, or that a mentally ill mother has children in a private foster home, or that she has her own mother living with her. This type of total information can be incorporated into a suitable case paper, and some kind of integration of the sort would seem essential if work is to be family based. Some progress is being made in the recording of family information on a computer, but this development can only be built on the facts as supplied, usually, by a social worker. (There would be much to be said for a form of case record recommended for use by all local authorities, but so far this has not materialised.)

Similarly the assessment of charges for the variety of services should be integrated, rather than being dealt with on a piecemeal basis according to the services provided, even if the assessment is "nil", as it often is. If efforts are being made to support a family for instance by providing a home help and placing one child in a day nursery, there is no point in making two separate assessments, or, as is possible, making yet a third because another child may be in care already, or because the mother has been given a recuperative holiday. There is also a constructive side to the question of assessment. If all the necessary financial facts are collated, it is then possible to advise the family about its rights to a wide range of benefits available from both the D.H.S.S. and the local authority (rent and rate rebates, school meals and clothing). There would not seem to be any reason why a Social Services Department should not put the principle into effect.

4. The quality of service. This may imply that within a Department there is a need for a group of staff acting as inspectors, each with specialist knowledge in some sphere of social work, and all having the authority to investigate and report upon the standard of practice throughout the whole of the departmental activities. Such a group of staff would link with inspection a helpful response to requests from social workers for advice in specific cases, which would probably be more acceptable than the more usual method of pushing cases up through several tiers of staff for a decision.

All these points, however, are internal to the organisation; they do not really touch upon the Seebohm ideal of a Social Services Department "working effectively through area teams, drawing strength from the community they serve, and with a substantial measure of delegated authority ..." (Para. 594).[1] Some progress has been made in this direction. Some departments have established local advisory or consultative groups or panels which represent the community, being composed of members of district councils, members of the Social Services Committee living locally, members of voluntary organisations, and some individual citizens chosen for personal interest and qualities, though not representing any particular section of the community.

Such a panel certainly gives a community some opportunity of stating its view and criticisms, or making complaints, but it is still some way from real involvement, and does not do very much to provide "strength" to the department. If the community is to be involved it must have rather more understanding of the social services than it has at present. A study in South Wales and Southampton in 1969-72 disclosed a marked lack of knowledge of the functions of the various groups of social workers, with the exception of the Probation Service, the N.S.P.C.C. and the Citizens' Advice Bureaux. The study also describes public attitudes towards the people who receive services, current ideas about the extent to which stated needs were unmet, and an indication of the kinds of social situation in which "self help" is seen as the answer, and those in which the people being questioned would *themselves* be prepared to help.[7] If the level of understanding is to be improved, and if there is to be any prospect of taking up the offers of "community help" it would seem essential that social workers should be based in the community, as was indeed the Seebohm concept. But progress may be slow. The study by the National Institute for Social Work, carried out in Southampton in 1972, and again in 1975 seems to indicate that despite the opening of area offices the pattern of referrals had not changed between those two years. The study was confined to people who actually came to the Department, and was not a general study of public awareness. But of those who came for help or advice, about two thirds were referred by some other agency, the exception being prospective foster parents and adopters—who came primarily to give rather than to receive.[8]

THE SOCIAL WORK TEAM

For towns, the Report envisaged a team of social workers in an area office serving a population of 50-100,000 (Para. 590)[1] but pointed out in Para. 593 that this population would also need to be served by teams in specific sub-areas, neighbourhoods and communities. These paragraphs indicate that the *team* is the basic unit, and that its size and composition will need to vary according to a number of factors.

The word "area" seems sometimes to have been taken as applying to the former areas of the Children's and Welfare Departments which, in counties, often had a population far bigger than 50-100,000. In the first instance, therefore, some departments set up area offices for very large populations and it was only later on that they began to establish teams in smaller neighbourhoods and districts. On the other hand, Islington prepared a scheme for siting team offices in the borough on the basis of maximum accessibility. Their approach to the task is set out in "Social Priority Areas and Seebohm".[9]

Where area offices for a large area were set up first, and team areas were later evolved, the area teams tended to be regarded as still forming part of the area office, which with its Area Director and administrative and supervisory staff, could easily become a miniature central headquarters, though lacking the authority to provide resources for the teams. Even the files and record of referrals might still be retained by the area office so that the teams in the new sub-offices were without their own administrative and clerical support.

By contrast, in the Seebohm Report, the team is seen as comprising social workers, occupational therapist and home help organiser (who might also generally promote voluntary service). Such a team would have its own clerical staff and records, would operate independently within its own small community, and would make its own decisions apart from those involving the use of resources controlled from headquarters, or divisional or area offices. In this way, the lines of communication would be shortened, the accountability of the team and of the social workers would be easily apparent, the team leader would perforce act as an effective manager, and the social workers themselves would increasingly identify themselves with the community.

The introduction of the inspecting staff mentioned earlier would help the team to avoid any feeling of isolation, but in any event the individual members of the team would probably be able to undertake part-time attachment to other community bases, such as schools, health centres, courts, and hospitals, and in this way widen their horizons and at the same time develop a special interest in some aspect of social work, while remaining firmly based within the team.

To some extent events have overtaken the Seebohm idea of attachment. Schools have insisted on retaining their own social work service, provided by educational welfare officers, counsellors, or "pastoral" teachers, while the social workers in hospitals, after some resistance, joined their colleagues in Social Work Departments. There is still scope however, for attachment from a team to a court, or to a primary health care team in the locality.

There has been a lengthy debate on the position of local authority social workers in child guidance clinics; some remain, traditionally, in the employment of the Education Committee, while others have transferred to Social Services Departments. Like social workers in hospitals they continue to work in their own specialist setting, but are well placed to broaden the guidance "clinic" into a guidance "service" available to children and their families, however they may have been referred.

The ideal of the autonomous social work team has in recent years been modified by the emergence of "standby teams" intended to deal with urgent situations out of office hours. A number of influences have been responsible for this development and it remains to be seen whether the heavy investment of skilled social work time is justified by the results.

Social Services Departments have not yet solved their organisational problems. They cannot help but be large organisations, needing on the one hand order and effectiveness, on the other, enough disorderliness to encourage creative activity. The first characteristic is embodied in centralisation, the second in decentralisation. Between the two is conflict and tension, which cannot be resolved by compromise; ways must be found for both to exist together. To quote E. F. Schumacher, "The fundamental task is to achieve smallness, *within* large organisations".[10]

This is of course not easy to achieve when once a departmental organisation has been set up on hierarchical lines. But existing patterns are always liable to challenge, for instance by new legislation such as the Children Act 1975. Part I of this Statute calls for a comprehensive adoption service, as an integral part of child-care provision; a study by Dr. Roger Bacon and Jane Rowe, in region 5, demonstrates the effect of organisation on the quality of present practice. Determining factors are the level at which decisions are made, the differences between advisory and executive functions, and the status of centrally held posts in relation to area or team staff.[11] In this aspect of social work, as in others, there is no simple answer. As the D.H.S.S. *Guide to Foster Care Practice* puts the problem: "Owing to the variety of departmental structures that exist, and the differing capabilities of the staff, it is not possible to suggest any blueprint for an ideal organisation. In any case, it is important that once local attempts at solution are made, they should be allowed to develop as people and circumstances change."[12]

TEAM MANAGEMENT

Whatever overall structure a Department may have adopted, its social work operations are likely to be carried out by teams. These may be either "generic" or in some way specialist but in either case the total demands of "child care" will be considerable. Social workers themselves would say that a large part of their time and effort is spent on this, rather than on other aspects of their work. Estimates vary but probably average about 65%. By child care they usually mean all those cases in which there are children, whether in care or under supervision and also those in which a family has been offered social work support on a voluntary basis under s. 1 of the 1963 Act, possibly coupled with material assistance of some kind. (Such cases seem to constitute a good deal of the child care caseload, and tend to be suddenly closed when a social worker leaves a department or team.)

There is reason to suppose that child care in this broad sense is more attractive than other forms of social work, so that under the generic concept it receives possibly more attention than it should. The effect of this on the work of one Department can be seen in a report of a study of the integration of services, which was carried out in 1972.[7] This report also reveals the attitudes of some social workers to specialisation and their attitudes to the many problems brought about by the Seebohm changes. It questions assumptions lying behind the concept of "casework" and "caseloads", and the ways in which work is allocated, kept under review, and terminated; and it calls for more clearly defined aims and a better use by social workers of manpower resources other than themselves. A follow-up study was carried out in the same Department in 1975;[13] it is interesting to find that while the general attitude to integration had improved the preference for work with children and families was unchanged. Social workers were still concerned about such issues as communication with management, defining priorities, specialisation and the continuing pressure of the demands made upon the teams.

These points merit even more attention now, in a climate of economic restraint, when if pressures are to be reduced, the only option lies in better management of present resources. To bring this about, there must be a re-appraisal of attitudes towards "volunteers", social work assistants and unqualified social workers who far outnumber the qualified. There must also be a recognition of residential social workers, especially in child care, as partners who can be relied upon to maintain and strengthen family ties which, as we have seen, are weak in too many cases. And there must be a willingness on the part of social workers to accept that clerical and administrative duties are important in their own right, not to be regarded with hostility as irrelevant and bureaucratic.

The failure to recognise that social work and administration can be distinguished from each other has led very often to an ineffective use of social workers' time and skills. As Andrew Leigh has pointed out, whenever anything goes wrong—as in several well-publicised cases—the effectiveness of administrative and clerical procedures is the first thing to be put under the microscope. The failure of some simple clerical process can have tragic consequences.

In a well-known case of many years ago it was rumoured that a report calling for urgent attention did not receive it because the report itself was accidentally attached to other papers in a paper clip and filed away. Whether or not this was true, simple errors of the kind do occur, but even these are more understandable than a failure to make and record statutory visits, or to arrange for a medical examination at the right time, or to notify a discharge from care, to quote only three examples of bad practice. Clearly such matters have implications for the training of all staff, not only social workers. But they are primarily the concern of management, and especially of the management of a social work team.

It has been said that every qualified social worker is a manager and should be capable of using time and skill to the best advantage. While this may be true, the burden in present organisations falls most heavily on the team leader, as is evident from the kind of job description which is currently in vogue. This usually refers to the "management of a team, including social workers, clerical staff and staff such as occupational therapists, the allocation of referrals and work, case consultation, control and oversight of visits and report writing, preparation of statistics" and to more generalised administrative or community duties, which may include an element of training, or research.

Descriptions of this kind, which may vary in detail from one authority to another certainly seem to make the team leader "accountable" in the management sense of the word; he cannot escape the responsibility for what each and every member of the team does, or fails to do. The supervisory element—though it may be unwelcome—is ineluctable. This is even more the case now that the Social Work Service has modified its inspectorial role, while Social Services Departments in general have not yet introduced inspectorates of their own.

Because of the wide range and complexity of social work, quite apart from child care, it seems likely that local inspection must come. It might well result in the removal of several layers of control, leaving the individual social worker as personally accountable, and the team leader free to advise and support rather than to supervise and direct.

The present dilemmas of management in social work are not new, though they now concern a wider field of operation. In essence they were all present in the former separate departments. So far as child care was concerned, the growth of the old children's departments and the setting up of area teams had focused attention on the changed position of the many social workers who had become managers, almost by accident. In 1965, a special course was mounted for senior child care officers, and some of the papers were published under the title *Administration and Staff Supervision in the Child Care Service.* This booklet contains much that is relevant in the context of the work of a team in a Social Services Department. More recently there have been studies of the expectations required of senior social workers, or team leaders, as members of middle management within the traditional departmental structure.[14]

RESEARCH

Social workers in teams are probably aware that in their departments there are research staff, and may wonder what they do, or whether their work has any connection with the problems "in the field". Generally speaking research is concerned at present with what the Seebohm Report called "good housekeeping". As there had been little research into social work before 1970, there has been a great interest in what has in fact been happening and a great deal has been learned. Inevitably, departmental research staff have been involved in the corporate management approach to the use of resources by the authority as a whole, and are in a position to relate the practice of social work to objectives as set out in programmes such as that in Appendix A.

In previous chapters there have been several references to fact-finding reports of recent years. These illustrate the extent of general ignorance of the facts until they are properly examined; if the reports are read it will be found that they quote a number of references to previous work on the topics concerned. There are a number of bodies now conducting research on a national scale, while locally most Social Services Departments are looking at various areas of work and sharing the results through their Research Association.

Research in a sense is something which all social workers should share with research staff. Almost all the information comes from social workers, and it is to be hoped and expected that a great deal of helpful work can be done within the teams, perhaps under the general guidance of research staff. There is perhaps no area of work which does not need scrutiny, and it is encouraging to see that social workers themselves are either suggesting subjects for research, or are carrying it out themselves. What could be more interesting and startling, for instance, than interviewing a number of children in residential care, and their parents to find out how they see the situation? Or in encouraging young people in care to meet with sympathetic adults to state their views on the lines of the N.C.B.'s project *Who Cares?*[15] The scope for learning is enormous, and knowledge personally gained is likely to result in better practice among the very many pressures which surround the social worker of today.

These pressures have themselves been the subject of research by Professor Olive Stevenson and Professor Phyllida Parsloe whose report has recently been published;[16] it has been welcomed as the most important publication of the last ten years in social work. In another connection, A.B.A.F.A. is carrying out research into the use of some of the newer provisions of the Children Act 1975. There is no shortage of research reports today; but there is still resistance to making the changes which would be required by its implementation.

NOTES

1. Report of the Committee on Local Authority and Allied Personal Social Services (The Seebohm Report, Cmnd. 3703).
2. Better Services for the Mentally Handicapped, Cmnd. 4683.
3. *Children in Care*, 31 March 1977, H.M.S.O.
4. *Born to Fail*, National Children's Bureau.
5. "Conflict and the Social Service Department", Kevin Heal, *Social Work Today*, February 1971.
6. *Social Work Service*, No. 6.

7. "Community perceptions of social work", *Policy and Politics*, March 1973; and "Reactions to Integration", *Social Work Today*, November 1973.
8. "Post Seebohm Social Services, Consumers' Viewpoint", *Social Work Today*, November 1976.
9. *Social Work Today*, September 1970.
10. *Small is Beautiful*, E. F. Schumacher, 1973.
11. *A Study of Needs and Resources for Substitute Family Care*, A.B.A.F.A.
12. *Guide to Foster Care Practice*, p. 382, D.H.S.S.
13. "Post Seebohm Social Services, the Social Worker's Viewpoint", *Social Work Today*, November 1976.
14. See for instance "The Senior Social worker within the Area Structure", A. H. Jones, *Social Work Today*, May 1977, and "Report on a Method of Workload Management and Weighting", Ruth Prime, *Social Work Today*, December 1977.
15. *Who Cares?*, National Children's Bureau, and "Caring", Meg Keyte, *Social Work Today*, April 1974.
16. *Social Services Teams: The Practitioner's View*, H.M.S.O. See also *Social Work Today*, 20 February 1979.

Chapter 4

THE SOCIAL SERVICES DEPARTMENT: PART II

THE PUBLIC AS "CONSUMERS"

As we have seen, the ideal contained in the Seebohm Report is that the Social Services Department should provide services which are available to "everybody" (Para. 32).[1] This is implicit in the emphasis on the whole community, but in fact only a minority of the population so far actually either receives or gives services. Those who receive them became known as "clients", because social work aspired to being a profession; but more recently they are becoming known as "consumers", and as such have opinions which are important to those who supply the services. So far, not enough attention has been paid to finding out what these opinions are, though there have been several books and a number of articles, together with a fair amount of local research.[2] *Social Work Today* has published several down to earth reports on what it feels like to be a consumer, and it is cheering to find that not all the comments are unfavourable; some show a great appreciation both of departments and of social workers.[3] When the comments are unfavourable they point the need for departments to realise that in the eyes of the consumer they barely exist; or, rather, they exist only in the person who represents them, whether this is a social worker in the community, or in an establishment, or any other member of staff who for the moment *is* the department.

As opposed to individuals, a group of "consumers" is in a very different position. There are many such groups comprising well-known organisations such as the Claimants' Union, Shelter, the Child Poverty Action

Group, and Gingerbread, which operate on a national or local scale, with the aim of influencing policy.

The general run of social service consumers, however, is usually less articulate than a group and has not yet formed, or been formed, into an association, though the day may not be far distant. But whatever may be done by such groups, or by the Personal Social Services Council and other influential bodies, a department should ensure that there are ways in which views can be openly expressed, as a means of challenging existing organisation or patterns of work. Possibly this can be done through the local consultative groups, already mentioned, if they are representative enough, or through group meetings or joint working parties. There is a growing trend towards the full and proper consideration of the views of "consumers"—expressed, for instance, in the Children Act 1975—and this has important implications for all members of the staff of a Social Services Department, in whatever capacity they may be employed.

THE SOCIAL WORK STAFF

The staff of a Social Services Department is its fundamental resource. In the specimen Community Care Programme in Appendix A, the sub-programmes A, B and E are relevant to administrative provision and staff, while sub-programme C puts *counselling* as an integral part of the use and deployment of all services. In sub-programme D there are many activities either in the community or in residential establishments which clearly contain a counselling element. So that, in this example, all social services depend upon social work, but "social work" itself has particular functions which may, or may not, be needed in association with the provision of a "service".

But if "social work" is defined as what a social worker does, there are many people who may claim that in the course of their other duties they are at times social workers. Police, for example, clergy, local councillors or Members of Parliament, marriage guidance counsellors, health visitors, prison visitors and the many other volunteers in agencies may consider that at times they are "doing social work". Indeed it may be argued that families and closely knit neighbourhoods are the basic sources of all "social work", in so far as they "have their roots in social philosophies and ethical values"—to quote the B.A.S.W. paper "The Inalienable Element in Social Work".[4]

This paper was an attempt to describe social work, not what social workers do, but it may have helped to promote the idea of professionalism, which until recently has been equated with "qualification". To some extent it still is, but the British Association of Social Workers has now accepted the fact that a high proportion of social workers are "unqualified". It has opened its membership to all engaged in work which should be undertaken by a social worker. It is however rightly pursuing with other bodies the attainment of excellence through a scheme of "accreditation".

For many years, and especially since 1971, there has been an over-whelming outpouring of books, periodicals, journals, magazines and articles concerned with social work; if anyone had the time to read them all, it is certain that he would not have time to attend the many courses, conferences, seminars and discussion groups he would learn about during his reading. The ordinary person who wants to follow events and even to sense what is going on in social work usually has to confine himself to one or at most two periodicals, perhaps with the addition of one publication relating to some sphere in which he is particularly interested. (*Adoption and Fostering*, the quarterly journal of the Association of British Adoption and Fostering Agencies is particularly helpful for social workers working mainly with children and their families; its contents deal with the whole range of care, and include legal notes on recently decided cases.)

The amount of literature may be some measure of the uncertainty which both social workers and administrators feel. It gives the impression that very often some vaunted development of last year was totally mistaken, that there is little agreement on the very nature of social work, and that though there are theories to account for what social workers do, there is still no definition of what they are. Some of the confusions are examined at some length in a report by the Professional Development and Practice Committee of B.A.S.W. called *The Social Work Task*.[5] Though *Social Work Today* deserves credit for opening its columns to all shades of opinion, on this and many other issues, it seems that at present not even B.A.S.W. can speak with unchallenged authority on fundamental issues. The standpoint of individual members varies from the committed "pro-fessional" to the advocate of love and good works, though there are of course many whose position is between these two extremes.

This is not surprising in view of the many strands which went to make up the Association, and of the many other strands which were originally left out of it; but the present lack of certainty is confusing to those already in Social Services Departments, and to those who seek to enter them. It also exercises a powerful influence in the training world, as Margaret Richards has shown in an article "What shall we teach next year?"[6] After looking at some of the conflicting issues, this paper states:

"Increasingly evidence is being produced to reinforce what we have always suspected, that it is the *quality of person* which makes the difference in any helping relationship, and not any specific theories the 'helper' may subscribe to. This is not to say that knowledge and skills are not worth pursuing but rather that what the learner brings will heavily influence what he perceives as relevant to be learned, and that in his subsequent contact with clients what will be important is how he as a *person* exerts personal influence rather than how as an expert he acquires techniques."

Present uncertainty centres around several salient questions which can be stated briefly, but cannot be answered satisfactorily.

THE IDENTITY OF THE SOCIAL WORKER

Local government now has a near monopoly of social workers, the only alternative openings being in some child guidance clinics, or in government and voluntary societies. There is little prospect of earning a living in private practice or in industry. The great majority of social workers are therefore employed by local authorities; they receive the benefits of local government employment and are subject to the conditions of service, and contracts of employment, which usually require them to carry out certain statutory responsibilities, and to perform tasks assigned to them by the Chief Officer. Many of them will also have a written authorisation enabling them to take action on behalf of the employing authority, such as appearing in court in some court proceedings, or visiting specified premises.

So according to one view, the social worker in a local authority draws his right to practise from the authority, which itself draws its powers from statute and from the law itself. It is difficult to escape the conclusion that he is primarily a local government officer especially since the emergence of union power, though within the community he will generally be seen as being part of "the welfare". In many situations he is also exercising his right to practise on the basis of the permission of the person being helped, since there is no power to impose help except when it is done with statutory authority.

But a "professional" social worker may think that his first loyalty lies towards his profession, or to the people he helps rather than to his employing authority; this may lead him into conflict if he feels that the authority is not serving the best interests of the community, or a part of it. He may find it necessary to take part in social action intended to change the departmental structure or policy, or to bring about the allocation of resources to a specific group of people. This is one illustration of the ways in which conflict between "order" and "freedom" becomes real, unless the department and the social worker have identical goals. For a fuller discussion of this issue, see *Social Action and Social Work*, the report of a B.A.S.W. Working Party on the subject,[7] and *A Code of Ethics for Social Work*.[8]

There is yet another school of thought which, presumably in reaction against the large scale local government organisation, regards social workers as employees within what is called the "welfare industry".

The conflict between these different images of social work and social workers has been much in evidence during the widespread industrial action of 1978 and 1979. This has led to further efforts to clarify the Code of Ethics, which begins with the bold assertion "Social work is a professional activity" and goes on to state a number of Principles of Practice to be followed by all social workers.

SPECIALISMS

As in the realm of organisation, there seems, on this subject, to have

been some misunderstanding of the Seebohm Report, resulting in an idea
that social workers were in future to be "generic" as opposed to being
specialists in adoption, mental health or work with homeless families, for
instance. The Report refers in para. 555[1] to *already existing* generic
training, but this was confined to the principles and methods common to
all types of social casework, and did not refer to the application of this
central core to all individuals and families, whatever their problems.
Chapter XVII of the Report[1] dealt with the question of specialisation in
social work, and concluded that it needed to be radically altered. It also
suggested that as far as possible a family or individual should be served by
one social worker, who should alone decide whether other social workers
should be involved to deal with specific needs. But the Report recognised
that each social worker would be more effective in some fields of work
than in others, because of temperament or inclination, and that this should
be taken into account (para. 522).[1] The whole principle of the suggested
attachment of social workers to various social institutions gives further
recognition to the fact of specialisation by reason of interest. It is true that
the Report saw the end of the rigid specialism of the former separate
departments, including child care, but it pointed out that new specialisms
would arise; this has been borne out by the formation of special teams for
intake work, home finding, advocacy of welfare rights, and other
innovations for specialist work "across the board", regardless of age or
other categories.

There was in the early days a tendency to regard all social workers as
"generic", but it is more and more realised that though the service and the
teams are generic, the individual social worker himself is not. This point is
clearly made in the report of the Working Party on Social Work Support
for the Health Service (The Birch Report).

"It therefore needs stressing that it is a misunderstanding of the
Seebohm Report to suppose that the creation of an integrated social
service department entailed the integration of social work skills to such
a degree that specialisms must disappear."

It now seems that "child care" not only survives as a client group
specialism, but that more specific specialisms have developed within it.
Some authorities encourage the formation of "child care teams", while
others appoint specialists in adoption and fostering, or work with damaged
children, or the planning of long term care, assessment, or "intermediate
treatment".

Child care in general is a preferred activity for many social workers, for
reasons of what Seebohm called temperament or inclination, and com-
mands a high priority in any department. This was demonstrated by the
Southampton study, referred to in the previous chapter, and again more
recently by Olive Stevenson and Phyllida Parsloe in *Social Service Teams:
The Practitioner's View* which is based on a study not of one department,
but of thirty-one teams in eight different areas.

METHODS OF WORK

Traditionally social workers have worked with individuals and families on the well-known one-to-one basis, but in recent years more attention has been paid to the importance of working with groups of, for instance, foster parents, young people under court supervision orders, mothers of young families, the elderly, and many more. Such groups need not be "in the community", since there is also much scope for this method in residential or day establishments as a part of the process of enabling people who are receiving help to participate in providing it. This form of social work may be derived from social casework, or from statutory duties, but it is a different concept which has its own literature.

In the same way, various methods of working within a whole community have been developed over the past few years. In some places a team of social workers may have operated in a particular district without letting themselves be publicly identified with their department. In others, the team may have been publicly identified but acting as an interpreter of local needs to the local authority. Here again there is a considerable literature.[9]

All that needs to be said here is that there are different methods of social work. The question often at issue is whether each of the methods comprises a separate specialism, or whether all social workers can, or should, be using them all at different times in the course of their daily work. The latter course is only likely to be followed when a social work team is based entirely in the community it serves and has removed the barriers between itself and the people it exists to serve. This presupposes a very small team serving a very local area and there are serious problems, for instance, in accountability as between the team and the whole department. These problems can only be solved by the organisation of work in such a way that the Seebohm ideal can be achieved.

There has instead, generally speaking, been a tendency to preserve the "casework" approach but to define it in terms of new "techniques", such as "task-centred work", "crisis intervention", and "contract with clients". These have all been the subject of many articles and pamphlets, but the Stevenson and Parsloe study indicates that few social workers consciously used these methods or analysed what they were doing in their work with clients on an individual basis.

FRAMEWORK OF ACTIVITIES

Social Service Teams: The Practitioner's View is an important factual examination of the three issues briefly dealt with in this chapter, the identity of the social worker, the pros and cons of specialisation, and the ways in which social work is actually carried out in the teams which were studied. It indicates the complexity of the social work task, bounded as it is by law and by society in the shape of the local authority, the community, and the people in search of services. All social workers whether in the community or in establishments or administration need to be as well informed as they can be on basic principles. The Central Council for Training and Education in Social Work has drawn attention to training requirements in some of the more important aspects, one of which is law, since it is felt that this subject has not always and everywhere been accepted as essential for social workers. In its paper *Legal Studies in Social Work Education*,[10] the Council points out that legal studies form a necessary part of training for all social workers, and adds that they can be very interesting if seen in the context of day-to-day work. The Report outlines four areas in which law affects the social worker:

Professional law (which is related to practice in special fields);
General law (which affects the lives of all citizens);
Administration of law (the legal profession, legal aid, the courts and tribunals);
Law and society (the need for a legal system and its positive qualities)

The last three aspects have been covered in *Social Workers, their Clients and the Law*.[11] This gives a simple outline of the legal system, and deals with the many points of law which arise for most people at some stage in their lives. Professional law is naturally more specialised and covers the legislation which affects the Social Services Department and was mentioned on p. 11. Those statutes which relate to Children and Young Persons give precise and detailed guidance for what is probably the widest range of work in the whole department.

The standard work is Clark Hall and Morrison's *Law Relating to Children and Young Persons*[12] but there are many other works dealing with specialised subjects, such as adoption, or legislation like the Children Act of 1975. There are also a number of periodicals containing articles and details of decided cases arising from the legislation; the legal content of "child care" is now very considerable and there has been a marked increase in collaboration between local authority social workers and solicitors in using the law for the benefit of children.[13]

This present work is not therefore so much a book on law as an attempt to relate the law to practice in a Social Services Department's wide range of work with children and young persons and their families. There are some situations which arise only rarely and which may need specialist advice; this book is concerned more with points which often have to be dealt with, and tries to show that a proper understanding and use of legislation and regulations can help to ensure a high standard of practice in the sensitive area still known as "child care".

Not everyone may accept the suggestion, made above, that the social work task is carried out within a framework of the law and of society in its various forms. The concept may not be very exciting, but it can perhaps offer some kind of base at a time when social work is continually being described as being "at the crossroads". It cannot stay there indefinitely.

NOTES

1. The Seebohm Report, Cmnd. 3703.
2. For example *The Client Speaks*, Mayer and Timms, London, Routledge, 1970; and *Social Work Today*, 6 March 1975.
3. "Community Perceptions in Social Work", *Policy and Politics*, March 1973.
4. B.A.S.W. February 1973.
5. *Social Work Today*, June 1977.
6. *Social Work Today*, 11 April 1978.
7. B.A.S.W. Publication, No. 6.
8. B.A.S.W. Discussion Paper, No. 2 (later revised).
9. For example *Community Work, Theory and Practice*, edited Philip Evens, Alistair Shornach Ltd., P.O. Box 70, Headington, Oxon., and C.C.E.T.S.W. Paper No. 8, *Teaching of Community Work*.
10. C.C.E.T.S.W. Paper, No. 4.
11. Michael Zander, London, Sweet and Maxwell, 1974.
12. London, Butterworths, Ninth ed. 1977.
13. "The Relationship of Social Worker and Lawyer", Richard White, *Adoption and Fostering*, 1976.

CHILDREN AND YOUNG PERSONS

SUMMARY

DEFINITION OF "CHILD" AND "YOUNG PERSON"

Among the people who are dealt with by Social Services Departments are many children and young persons, who are usually members of a nuclear family. Within the overall objectives of the department they are no more important than other people, but they are more vulnerable, and because of their immaturity need protection from many surrounding pressures which do not affect older people so strongly.

There is no definition of "child" in social service terms, but the word usually means a minor (*i.e.* under the age of 18). This is the meaning in the Children Acts of 1948, 1958 and 1975, but in the other major Acts (the Children and Young Persons Acts from 1933 to 1969), it normally means a person aged under 14. But in looking at the Act of 1969, special care must be taken because the Secretary of State has power to define from time to time the upper age of childhood. Similarly a person aged 14 to 17th birthday is normally in the Children and Young Persons Acts a "young person", but owing to the Secretary of State's power under s. 34 of the 1969 Act the age limit is below 14.[1] There are special reasons for this, which will be dealt with later, but it is important to realise that "child" or "young persons" when they appear in the Act of 1969 do not always refer to those under 14 and those over 14 respectively.

Of all the Social Services Departments' responsibilities, that towards these two groups attracts by far the greatest public attention and concern. If young children are ill-treated by adults there is quite rightly an immediate outcry; if social workers are in any way involved, or it is thought that they should have been involved, there is public indignation. A number of tragic cases have been the subject of official enquiries whose reports, when published, urge the need for improvement of services, better communication between social agencies, a higher degree of skill in detecting children at risk of injury or neglect, and more emphasis on the protection of helpless children.

Quite apart from these well-known cases, much attention has been paid for some years to the problem of child abuse, or the "battered baby syndrome"; all social agencies are well aware of the danger signals, and have established various ways of forestalling injury, or of taking appropriate action when non-accidental injury by parents or others is suspected. The ill-treatment of children is nothing new and is not confined to physical injury, but certainly much more attention is now given to it and it has assumed larger proportions altogether.

Young persons, those between, say, 12 and 17, attract almost equal attention but usually for very different reasons. Some of them commit extremely serious crimes against property and against the person, they arouse condemnation by attacking and robbing houses or people, who may be elderly and handicapped, and they often forfeit any public sympathy they might once have had because of their "unfortunate backgrounds", whether these exist or not; others commit less serious offences but commit them frequently and are often defiant and aggressive towards authority and society.

This again is no new phenomenon, as we learn from *A Winter's Tale* written by Shakespeare in 1610:

"I would there were no age between sixteen and three and twenty or that youth would sleep out the rest; for there is nothing in the between but getting wenches with child, wronging the ancientry, stealing, fighting."

Nothing has changed much except that the age group is rather younger, corresponding to the lower age of majority at 18.

But although both these problems of childhood and youth are of very long standing, and are still with us, this does not mean that they have been ignored in the mean time. Over the years there has been a steady stream of legislation designed to provide help for both the groups usually called "the deprived" and "the depraved", with the result that Social Services Departments now have heavy responsibilities towards both, even if they are not in local authority care. Those who actually enter care create another dimension of responsibility, which again comes under the searchlight of public opinion if anything goes wrong.

Since 1974 any member of the public who claims "to have sustained injustice in consequence of maladministration in connection with action taken by or on behalf of a (local) authority" may make a complaint to the Commission for Local Administration (the ombudsman). This right of members of the public has been exercised in recent years in several instances concerning children, either directly or indirectly, and some of the complaints have been upheld. The existence of the Commissions (one for England, the other for Wales) provides a relatively new safeguard against the misuse of the local authority's considerable powers, specially in such matters as the deprivation of the liberty of a child or young person.

CHILDREN AND YOUNG PERSONS ACT 1969

Before the Children Act 1975, the last piece of legislation was the Children and Young Persons Act of 1969, which has been in partial operation since 1971, and which has caused so much concern that it has been considered by the Expenditure Committee of the House of Commons and was amended by The Criminal Law Act 1977. This Act rests upon the philosophy that, broadly speaking, the young child at risk of injury or neglect, the child in care and the young offender have basically the same social needs and may be suitably provided for in similar ways. There are however some situations in which the protection of the public must be taken into account, as well as the interests of the child or young person concerned. This Act will be considered in more detail later, but it may be helpful at this stage to set out the modified philosophy, then the various sections of the Act in which the philosophy can be seen, and finally the effect the Act has had so far. Following this are some generalised summaries of comments which have been made by police, magistrates and the British Association of Social Workers during discussions. These show that while there may be broad acceptance of the principles of the Act, there is some conflict between those who wish to see it amended in some way, and those who wish to see it implemented more fully.

PHILOSOPHY

The Act does not stand by itself, but is the last step in a progressive modification of the criminal law in its application to children and young people. Starting with the Departmental Committee on Young Offenders (1927), this theme has run through the Children and Young Persons Acts of 1933-63, the Ingleby Committee Report on Children and Young Persons (1960), the White Paper, *The Child, the Family and the Young Offender* (1965), and the further White Paper *Children in Trouble* (1968).[2] The Act itself stems largely from this last mentioned White Paper.

What is the philosophy?

For many years there had been debate about juvenile delinquency as though it were something which in itself could be "prevented". During the 1960s the figures were always increasing, and in particular there were marked failures in the methods then in operation. Of all children discharged from approved schools 80% committed further offences within three years of discharge, 68% of all those released from borstal and 61% of all released from detention centres were known to have committed subsequent offences. It seemed that, whatever their merits, these measures were not outstandingly successful.

The philosophy of the White Paper attaches much less importance to the distinction between "good" and "bad" children, and much more to the kind of treatment which is necessary, irrespective of the cause of the "trouble", which may or may not manifest itself in delinquency. Very few people have grown up without committing acts which could be called offences, and allowance must be made for the differing rates at which young people grow up into personal responsibility. Moreover, and this may be lost sight of, the upbringing of a child is the prime responsibility of his parents and if they need help in this obligation, it must be provided by society as a whole. The intention, therefore, is that in taking action to deal with a child who comes to notice, full regard must be paid to his family and wider social backgrounds with a view to drawing out whatever strengths are to be found there.

Formal procedure, such as appearance in court, should be reserved for those situations where intervention is necessary in the interests of the child, or of society. Firm and consistent discipline is a part of upbringing; if parents cannot provide it, society must do so.

The methods of providing for all children in trouble must be flexible, and not geared solely, as in the past, to their particular problems, e.g. delinquency, non school attendance etc.

In general, this philosophy has not been seriously challenged, but there are differing views on the age at which young people arrive at personal responsibility; there is also doubt in some quarters about the principle of relying so heavily on the support of family and community when either or both of these influences may in fact be tolerant or even encouraging towards deviance from acceptable behaviour. Above all, there is a good deal of reluctance to accept that a child in need of care should be dealt with in the same way as one who needs control, and *vice versa*.

THE PHILOSOPHY AS EXPRESSED IN THE 1969 ACT[3]
(As applied to juvenile offenders against the law.)

		Effect
1. Recognition of varying rates of personal development.	s. 4 No child under 14 to be charged with an offence, except homicide.	Neither s. 4 nor s. 5 is in operation yet. There is however a good deal of co-operation between police and Social Service Departments, by which the latter
	s. 5 No young person to be charged with an offence (except homicide and other serious offences to be specified by the Secretary of State), unless it is considered that the	are notified of children and young persons who have come to police notice, and have the opportunity of making their own enquiries into personal and social background, so that full information can be

Effect

case cannot be dealt with in some other way, after consultation with the local authority. | exchanged with the police. Because of the large numbers of such cases they receive far too little attention.

2. Recognition of the desirability of dealing with young people without taking criminal proceedings.

s. 1 (2) (f)
A child or young person who has committed an offence (except homicide) may be brought before the court as being in need of care or control, instead of being charged with the offence.

As a result of the joint discussions children may be offered services by the social workers, or may be cautioned by the police, or may be summoned to appear before the juvenile court. The use of police cautions varies widely from one part of the country to another, so that the number of court appearances is misleading.

3. Recognition of the need to involve the family and other influences on a basis of voluntary co-operation.

It is not enough in such cases for the offence to be proved or admitted. It must also be proved that an order of the court is required if the necessary care or control is to be provided. (In other words full enquiry and possible voluntary help must reveal that compulsion is needed.)

This procedure seems to be very little used. Only a handful of young offenders are dealt with in this way, most, if they appear in court at all, being charged with an offence, rather than being brought as in need of care or control.

4. Recognition of the need to replace punitive measures.

s. 7 (1)
Minimum age for committal to Borstal to be raised from 15 progressively to 17.

This section is not operative. Borstal committals have increased from 818 in 1969 to 1,935 in 1977.

s. 7 (3)
Detention centres and attendance centres to be phased out.

Detention centres and attendance centres are still in use, and a greatly increased number of young persons go there. Custodial sentences in all have increased, contrary to the intention of the Act, 2,228 Detention Centre orders in 1969 increased to 5,757 in 1977.

Effect

5. Recognition of the need for a flexible variety of provision, not related to the reason for appearance in the court.

s. 7
Probation orders, approved school orders, and orders of committal to a remand home abolished, to be replaced by care orders, supervision orders, and remand to the care of the local authority.

In operation.

6. Recognition that the social needs of delinquents are similar to those of other children in trouble, and may be met in similar ways.

ss. 11/12
Supervision under order of the court removed from the probation concept. Unlike probation orders, supervision orders are not dependent on consent. They may not contain any condition about residing at a particular place. They may however contain general conditions to assist the supervisor, some about maintaining contact, others about various activities usually referred to as intermediate treatment, *i.e.* intermediate between supervision without any conditions, and removal from home. The supervisor however chooses whether or not to apply the conditions. There are no statutory rules for the exercise of supervision by local authority social workers.[4]

Supervision orders are being made in considerably fewer cases than were formerly dealt with under probation orders in criminal proceedings. There was a decline of 3,500 between 1969 and 1977. Committal to borstal, detention centres and attendance centres increased in inverse proportion.[5]

The ninety-day residence under an intermediate treatment order was intended to replace a period at a detention centre; other provisions were intended to replace attendance centre orders. The facilities were to be planned by the Regional Planning Committee, but not until after the residential provision had been planned. Facilities so far made available are disappointing and unimaginative—there is little scope for any form of community service, for example. The development of these facilities depend upon the appointment of a specialist member of staff, it is said, but not enough authorities have taken this step.

Effect

Dissatisfaction with the effectiveness of the supervision order in criminal proceedings has now led to the introduction, in the Criminal Law Act 1977, which is now in force, of additional conditions which may be imposed by the juvenile court; without giving the supervisor discretion as to their use. As action may be taken for "breach" of these requirements, the supervision order in criminal proceedings can be seen as reverting largely to the former probation order. There are also new provisions for the enforcement of payment of fines, and some variations of the conditions to be included in such orders. These will be considered in Chapter 14.

s. 20
Courts may commit a child or young person to care of a local authority, which then has certain powers and duties. It must decide upon and provide suitable accommodation (which may be the child's own home), must exercise its powers in the best interests of the child, but must also take into account the protection of the public (ss. 24, 27).

It must review each case every six months to ensure that the care order is still necessary. There is no time limit regarding a placement

Though the use of supervision has declined, care orders appear to be increasing.[5] One-third of all care orders were made without any previous noncustodial orders. It appears that care orders are often used as a first resort.

The Act contains provision for dealing with the persistent offender who may in fact be in custodial care for longer (if he is under 15) than was the case under an approved school order. There are however other factors besides the decision of the care authority, notably the lack of facilities for highly disturbed young people, and the powers of heads of establishments to decide which cases they will and will not accept.

Effect

at a particular place, except that of age for the expiry of the care order.

There has been much criticism of local authorities who have placed at home children who are subject to care orders. This has led to a call for courts to be able to make care orders stipulating that children should be placed in custodial care. While courts have not been given these powers, the Magistrates' Association and the local authority Associations have worked out a code of practice, which is commended to all local authorities. This Code makes it clear that when a court makes a care order it presumes that the child or young person will be placed in a foster home or in residential care, rather than being placed with his own parents—unless there are exceptional circumstances. The Code is meant for local authorities, as such, and the British Association of Social Workers has commented that it does not alter the fact that the placement of a child is, in their view, a matter for the "professional" judgment of the social worker concerned.

7. Recognition of the need for residential provision.

ss. 35–48
All approved schools, observation centres, nurseries, local authority homes and hostels and some voluntary homes, to be merged into a community homes system, administered in regions. Regional Planning Committees set up, but not to provide facilities, only

In operation.
Pressure is being exerted to obtain sanction for more secure accommodation—representing another movement away from the concept of treatment in the community. It has been estimated that one-third of the children in long-term residential care could be better provided for by facilities developed under the intermediate treatment

	Effect
to advise authorities as to regional needs, *e.g.* on the extent of required secure accommodation.	concept of partial care with supervision.

8. Recognition of the need for special provision for children outside the community homes system.	s. 64 The Secretary of State has power to provide homes for children needing special facilities and services which are unlikely to be available within the community homes, however varied and specialised they may be.	In operation. Total provision of such homes is, and will remain, small, as it is intended that the great majority of children however disturbed will be contained in Community Homes.

GENERAL COMMENTS ON THE WORKING OF THE ACT[3]

Police	*Magistrates*	*British Association of Social Workers*
It is important that early preventive action is taken and co-operation with Social Services Departments has been developed. But there are difficulties when these measures have not been effective, and young people continue to commit offences. What positive action can be taken after a care order has been made and a further offence is committed?[2]	Regret losing powers to order remand to a special place and now use remand centres, for those young people too refractory for Local Authorities care. Regret loss of power to select cases for long-term residential treatment. Are often dealing with young people who have already been under supervision orders, and care orders, and feel unable	This Act by itself will not and cannot bring about a reduction in juvenile crime. If this is to be done, it will be by better policy in health, housing, education and poverty relief agencies, *e.g.* the recognition of needs as shown by the Finer Report. Important parts of the Act have not been brought into operation. Community care by preventive measures has still not been provided as proposed under the Act of 1963, but the Act of 1969 is based on the assumption that these are to be available. Plans for intermediate treatment have low priority in local authority departments. They should be developed before plans for residential care and should contain provision for short-term placements with a constructive purpose.

Police	*Magistrates*	*British Association of Social Workers*
When neither care orders, attendance centre orders, or detention centre orders are made, as in some assault cases, fines are useless, as they are virtually unenforceable until age of 17. Attachment of Earnings Orders only useful if there are any earnings.	to make any other order which will be effective.	Though there is an increase in crimes committed by juveniles, this must be seen in the context of an increase in crimes committed by persons of all ages.
	Supervision by local authorities less effective than supervision by probation officers, who are directly responsible to the court.	Of all indictable offences in 1970, 23·7% were committed by persons under 17. By 1973 the percentage had increased to 24·6%. In the last quarter of 1974, adult crime showed an increase of 18%, but juvenile crime by 15%.
(The Criminal Law Act 1977 implements a recommendation of the Eleventh Report of the Expenditure Committee that juvenile courts should be empowered to enforce fines on juveniles. This criticism has thus been met.)	Suggest that the Act was brought into operation before facilities and staff were available.	While all these increases are to be deplored, it can hardly be said that they are directly due to the operation of the Act.
		Because of lack of resources children are not receiving the help they need. Community homes are not in the right locations, many being quite separate from the surrounding community. There are not enough qualified or skilled residential staff; there is a need for much more provision for observation and assessment of children coming to notice.
		While secure accommodation is not seen as desirable in itself, there is a need for more, so that it can be used constructively to deal with the more highly disturbed young people who are committed to care.

The Social Work Service itself carried out a survey of the working of the Act towards the end of 1971, when the new provisions had been in effect for rather less than one year. The results are contained in a memorandum issued with D.H.S.S. Circular 29/72 of 26 July 1972.[5] The Act has since then been under continuous examination and there is much concern that whether its philosophy is sound or not, there are more young people in various forms of incarceration than ever before. It will be seen from the foregoing notes that already the philosophy is being modified by legislation, but it seems quite certain from research that yet more residential care may be quite ineffective and may confirm delinquents in their styles of life. We must look elsewhere for any real improvement in the situation.

The Children Act 1975, referred to earlier, deals with rather different aspects of child care and will be referred to in appropriate chapters. Its provisions will have little immediate effect on the Act of 1969, or on the treatment of young offenders.

Clearly, children and young persons make very large demands on Social Services Departments and their staffs, not only because of the potential numbers involved, but also because of the wide range of needs and services for delinquents and other children "in trouble". In considering these, and the legislation which governs them, it may be helpful to relate comment to the specimen community care programme at Appendix A, which of course applies to all "consumers" irrespective of age, social difficulties or kind of service provided. In this way it may be easier to study details while at the same time keeping in mind the ultimate goal, which is the well-being of all individuals and families in the community.

NOTES

1. *Guide to Part I of the 1969 Act*, paras. 249-251, London, H.M.S.O., 1975.
2. Cmnd. 3601, 1968.
3. "B.A.S.W. states the case", *Social Work Today*, 20 February 1975 and a further paper from B.A.S.W. in June 1977.
4. The Children Act 1975 contains powers for such Rules to be made.
5. For a fuller examination of the Act and its working, see the Eleventh Report of the Expenditure Committee of the House of Commons, July 1975, H.M.S.O.; and the White Paper, Cmnd. 6494 of May 1976, setting out the Government's observations on the Eleventh Report. This sees the philosophy as fundamentally sound but calls for a better use of community resources and a greater acceptance of "parental responsibility". Also see *A Study of the Implementation of the Children and Young Persons Act 1969 (from 1969 to 1975)*, D. Thorpe, University of Lancaster.

Chapter 6

PREVENTIVE WORK

In Social Services, as in medicine, the main thrust of effort is towards "prevention". This applies not only to the elderly, the disabled and the mentally handicapped, but also, and perhaps more significantly, to children and young persons. It may be helpful to consider what is really meant by preventive work. It is certainly much more than the mere prevention of the admission of children to care, as this can be done in an entirely negative way.

By "prevention" is meant a positive promotion of the welfare of children and young persons by meeting their social needs whatever they may appear to be, so that only when there is no alternative will long-term care or treatment be provided.

This concept has been mentioned in many reports during this century, culminating in the White Paper "Children in Trouble" of 1968; the fundamental basis is that the prime responsibility for the welfare and upbringing of children belongs to their parents. Social services exist to help parents to carry out this duty and to enrich the lives of their children. When help of this kind has not been forthcoming in the past some families have disintegrated, the individual children have suffered, some have become delinquents and of those a number have joined the well-trodden road from supervision through various forms of care to enforced and repeated detention in borstal or prison, or, sometimes, mental hospital.

The aim of the Director of Social Services and his staff must, therefore, be to prevent the unnecessary separation of children from their families by taking every possible action to help parents and to look upon this as the first priority. But it is only the unnecessary separation which is to be discouraged. The purpose of s. 1 of the Act of 1963 is not "to diminish the need for children to be admitted to care, or to appear before a juvenile court ...". It is to "promote the welfare of children". This may be done by preventing admission or committal to care, but equally in some cases it may be done by actively ensuring admission or committal to care.

STAGES

As suggested by the Ingleby Report[1] (which preceded the Children and Young Persons Act 1963) preventive work should be thought of in terms of the four following separate stages, not be confused with each other:

1. DISCOVERY AND REFERRAL

The former Children's Departments were providing advice, guidance and assistance in 1963 or even earlier; in consequence, the machinery for discovery and referral was well established, prior to 1970, though capable of improvement and development.

Almost all families containing children are known to the Health Service or to the schools and education welfare service; both these services are well placed to learn of families and children who are in difficulties and to refer them to the Director of Social Services when specialist social work help is needed. Other "general" referring agencies include clergy and ministers, family doctors, members of the public and parents or children themselves.

There are, in addition, a number of agencies of various kinds which may become aware of difficulties of a specialist nature, such as:

Housing Departments	Arrears of rent, unsatisfactory care of children, threat of eviction.
County Courts	Debts, threat of eviction from tied houses or houses being purchased on mortgage.
Police N.S.P.C.C.	Children and young persons receiving unsatisfactory care or control or in physical or moral danger, or being ill-treated.
Department of Health and Social Security	Families in financial difficulties.
Citizens' Advice Bureaux	Family problems.
Probation Officers	Problems affecting families or individual children.

It is unlikely that any family or child in need of social help can long escape discovery by one or other of these agencies, and the Director of Social Services will need to ensure that when a situation is discovered, it is referred as soon as it becomes clear that social work help, which cannot perhaps be given by the referring agency, is needed (see specimen Community Care Programme C 1 in Appendix A).

2. RECORDING

The efficient recording of all referrals is a task which is vital to the Department as a whole. There must first be a policy as to what does and what does not constitute a referral: is it a case not dealt with before? Is there any previous record? Is it merely a request for advice? Does it need investigation? If so, to what extent? It is also important to record the source of the referral (to check on the effectiveness of the "discovery" procedures) and on the presenting problem, even though this may later prove to be less important than some other factor. Referrals are likely to provide useful material for the Department's research staff, so that there is a lot to be said for noting in each case the home area, within a defined small area, such as village, hamlet, or, in towns, enumeration district (which can be allocated from the appropriate map). Information about each individual or family must also be recorded, whether there are children concerned, family structure and other agencies known to be involved. This information may be either very simple or, if it is to be used for compiling a case history, more detailed, but this will depend upon the administrative pattern adopted. Lastly there should be some easy means of recording each referral in such a way that it will be easy to see what degree of work it entailed, how long it took to deal with it, and whether it is completed, as a referral, or whether it is still outstanding.

This aspect of a department's work is obviously most important, and takes up so much time, effort and skill that the concept of "intake work" has developed as one of the new specialisms, at least in larger urban districts. Social Services Departments have developed more positive methods of encouraging referral, rather than waiting for a crisis situation to arise. This is an administrative task as explained[2] in sub-programme B which involves two functions:

A Encouraging the possibility for people to refer themselves, either to the Department itself or to other referral points, such as probation officers, hospitals (where some social work teams are based), Citizens' Advice Bureaux or Councils of Social Service. Where this policy is adopted, there must be enough centres of this kind, they must be publicised, and the needs of remote areas must not be forgotten. In this context, the Department has to make decisions about the number and location of its team offices and calling offices, the use of its other establishments which are not social work offices, the possibility of mobile office units, and the provision of an "on-call" service, and its method of operation.

B The setting-up of a series of "early warning" systems, by which other agencies may know how and when to refer people to the Department.

The extent to which referrals are encouraged in both these ways will of course depend on the relative value placed on this activity as against others, such as the provision of services. If there are far more referrals than can be dealt with effectively, accessibility may have to be reduced, but there is some choice between functions A and B.

The idea of specialist intake teams[3] is at first sight attractive, as one of its purposes is to relieve part of the social work staff from the continual "bombardment" of new work of all kinds; another purpose of course is to improve the quality of this first contact with people who may be in a state of stress. But the method is not a panacea for all ills, and gives rise to particular problems. It needs very careful planning, a clear delineation of the area of referrals to be dealt with, and a precise understanding as to when a referral is to be passed over for long-term work. It is also essential that staff carrying out this task should be committed to it, should perceive its relevance to the rest of the work of the team, and should not be allowed to become depressed by the constant pressure of demand and the lack of adequate resources. It is generally felt that social workers should only specialise in intake work for a limited time, during which they will gain invaluable experience. The control of intake teams is a management problem since the way in which the team works has a profound effect on the whole team, or groups of teams in the area. The National Institute of Social Work's study in 1977[3] indicates that a high proportion of new referrals need only a short period of intensive work. It is necessary to know enough about the facts to be able to decide how many staff should be allocated to long-term work, and how many to "intake". There might well be a case for intake staff to outnumber long-term staff, possibly by two to one, in some districts but the question then arises—If so many referrals can be either referred elsewhere, or be dealt with on a short-term basis, is this work for highly skilled trained social workers? Or should it be entrusted to, say, social work assistants?

Many social work teams, specially those operating on a small patch will probably not be able to develop this specialism, however, and may have to rely on the conventional method of making good reception arrangements, either by using an experienced reception clerk, or social worker, or by operating a system of duty roster. Whatever method is preferred, there is likely to be a constant stream of referrals coming in by telephone, letter, form, or personal call and dealing with these is an important social work task. Referrals are likely to fall into the three classical groups contained in the phrase "advice, guidance and assistance" or into some combination of these.[4]

"Advice" may be taken to include the many requests which are made for information, for instance, about whether some service such as child-minding is available. It will also include requests for advice about departmental or external services, and may be dealt with simply by referring the enquiry to the appropriate agency. But the aims of the department will be far better met if, in addition to this, accurate advice can be given immediately. The range of requests will be extremely wide and advice can only be given if the team has available up-to-date literature on the many questions which arise. A number will call for basic knowledge of legal aid, simple law on a number of family situations such as rent, eviction, matrimonial disputes, child care, and welfare rights or benefits. Many of these can be dealt with directly and simply if the appropriate books and booklets are available.[5] Help in a wide range of legal questions is available from Citizens' Advice Bureaux. A rural team, especially, ought to be in close touch with the nearest C.A.B. which may in fact be in a distant town, though it will no doubt answer questions by telephone if necessary when there is a good contact with the team.

"Guidance" can take the form of either one interview or a series of interviews about more personal problems which may exist quite apart from the need for factual advice. There may often be a need for the factual advice as well, but guidance is something rather separate, and should only be offered when it is requested as a rule.

"Assistance" is the most complex of the three factors, because it may well contain the other two. The aim should be to help the enquirer to deal with his own problems as far as this is feasible: he can be helped to fill in a form of claim for some benefit to which he is entitled, or be offered personal support before a tribunal, or in dealing with a housing authority. There is a wide area of help of this kind which is certainly assistance, but which does not necessarily involve social casework, or any form of on-going support. In some instances, however, it will be apparent that there is a need for something more than practical advice, guidance and assistance; this should lead to the offer of referral for social work support. From this has grown the idea of the "contract", by which a mutual agreement is made for the offer and acceptance of some form of social work help, individually or by group, or community, for an agreed time, during which it is intended to achieve some stated goal. Whether this contract is to be carried out by the intake team, or duty officer, or whether this is the stage at which the case is passed on for longer-term work, will depend on the pattern adopted by the team or department concerned.[3] Some studies have shown that misunderstanding or even conflict may arise between an intake team and a long-term team on this very point.

3. INVESTIGATION

As a first stage, it will be necessary to enquire whether the family is willing to accept assistance; this cannot be imposed, but it is unlikely from previous experience that it will be refused. Investigation should normally be carried out by one social worker and may be the beginning of "a casework relationship" unless, of course, this relationship already exists by reason of a previous referral. The immediate reason for the referral will be taken into account but will need to be considered in the whole context of the case. A request for reception of a child into care for instance, may stem from some other underlying problem within the family, which may become apparent during the enquiry and which needs to be identified as a basic social need. Investigation calls for great skill on the part of the social worker and should be given the highest priority on account of the effects which flow from it. In some cases investigation will be sufficient; in others there may be a need for assessment.

4. ASSESSMENT

Assessment has a long history and literature, especially in relation to children and young persons. As long ago as 1948, local authorities were obliged to provide accommodation for the observation and assessment of children who were admitted to care. Remand homes existed partly to "assess" children who had appeared before the courts, so that they could make recommendations for "treatment". At the same time there were separate child guidance clinics for the assessment of children with emotional difficulties, diagnostic units for physically handicapped children, and the school psychological service for assessing children with educational or mental handicaps. Recent discussions about the future of the child guidance service have once again highlighted the present complicated network of assessment agencies concerned with children and young persons. There are many sources of referral which usually take a pre-determined course, for instance, police to social services, school to school psychologist, doctor to child guidance clinic and so on. Assessment by the chosen agency is carried out without reference to the others, which might have relevant knowledge, and recommendations often only take into account one part of the total available resources. In this way, children who come to the notice of the Social Services Department initially because they are to appear in court may have had no formal assessment, or some form of special assessment, but no overall assessment of their needs. All too often this is finally supplied when they have been before the court and have spent some time at a special assessment unit; by then it may be too late to be of help. Comprehensive assessment for children was being urged as long ago as 1968,[6] but has not yet been brought about. However, the corporate approach of local authorities, which are providing the various forms of assessment in their own departments, may lead to the intro- duction of a central *referral unit*, or units, which will be for all children, whatever their apparent difficulties. There are practical problems to be overcome, but thought is being given to the possibility, and at the very least there should be more effective exchange of information about children, however and wherever they are referred.

In the former Children's Departments "assessment" was thought of too much in terms of residential assessment. This was perhaps due to the fact that there were establishments which carried out most of the task; and though remand homes as such no longer exist, there is still a kind of hierarchy of establishments from the small reception home to the sophisticated assessment units with highly skilled staff, which receive children and young persons for observation, and report upon them to the Social Services Department which placed them. Even now, however, there is a tendency for children who have been before the court for offences, especially boys, to be sent to the sophisticated units; other children who come to the notice of the department rarely receive that kind of com- prehensive assessment and probably only few need it. Highly sophisticated residential assessment is open to a number of criticisms: it requires the removal of the child from his own surroundings, perhaps paying too little attention to his wishes and feelings; it then looks at him as a "case" in isolation, and proceeds to diagnose a condition and prescribe a treatment which may in fact not be available. It is very expensive in terms of staff time, and accommodation, and there is some doubt as to whether the clinical reports produced play much part in the life of the child in care over the ensuing years.[6]

But there are other forms of assessment which ought to be used more than they are. A number of ideas were contained in a booklet[7] issued by the Ministry in connection with the Children and Young Persons Act 1969. Here assessment facilities were seen as absolutely vital to the working of the Act, and to the whole range of children who were expected to come to notice. As will be seen in Chapter 9, for instance, no child should come into care in any way without *investigation*. This booklet stresses the fact that in some cases this will not be enough; it should be followed by assessment.

However, we need not think of assessment as being carried out solely in a residential setting. The following methods are available and the most suitable should be used in each case:

1. Assessment of a child in his own home before removal by a social worker aided where necessary by others, such as educational psychologists, etc.
2. Daily attendance at an assessment centre near the child's home, foster home or other children's home where he usually lives.
3. Placement in an assessment centre providing a specialist consultation.
4. Assessment of a child wherever he may be by visiting specialists from an available assessment centre.
5. Placement in a highly specialised assessment centre with full facilities, including the provision of secure accommodation.

There should therefore be a graduation of assessment procedures to be chosen solely in relation to the child's need; with the exception of (5) above all these procedures should be directly within the Authority's control. The purpose and content of the assessment should however in all cases be the same. Moreover, assessment will not always be a once and for all requirement and must be available at all times during a child's period in care.

Assessment in its simplest form is used almost daily by a social worker. It is, or should be, a basic skill. The other forms of assessment involve other services which should be used only when necessary, if they are not to be placed under too much strain. The type of referral *unit* mentioned earlier on should bring about a greater comprehensive use of whatever facilities are available.

Something of this kind has already emerged in the detailed schemes of consultation which have been worked out for dealing with referrals of battered children, whoever receives the first intimation. The mounting concern about these cases has been strong enough to overcome most of the problems in co-operative consultation. But these children, important though they are, form only a small proportion of those who would benefit from the same kind of careful, ordered assessment of their history and background.

5. TREATMENT

It is only after proper investigation, that treatment can begin.

Treatment is the bringing together of the identified social problem and the resources which are available to meet it. An essential part is the acceptance by the family of the social worker and his acceptance of the family; whatever else may be provided or done it is usually necessary that some one person shall be seen by the members of a family as being concerned for them and being the means of bringing the right resources to bear on their difficulties.

The first and most important resource is the continuing support and interest and concern of the social worker himself.

Over and above this, there is no limit to the amount of help which can be given, except any limit imposed by the local authority as regards finance and staff. The resources available to the Director need to be applied in such a way as to promote the welfare of all children referred, by providing constructive help when it appears that in the short term or long term there is a likelihood that a child or children of a family may need to be admitted to care or committed to care for one of many reasons. These "reasons" are indicated in the annual statistics for England and ·Wales, now rounded up to the nearest hundred; those for the year 1976-77 being as follows:

Admitted to Care under Section 1 of the Children Act 1948	*1000s*
A Short-term illness of parent or guardian	11.5
B Long-term illness or incapacity of parent or guardian	1.0
C Confinement of mother	1.7
D Family homeless (eviction or other cause)	1.2
E Parents dead (no guardian)	0.2
F Abandoned or lost	1.2
G Death of parent, other parent unable to provide care	0.7
H Deserted by parent, other parent unable to provide care (including child illegitimate, mother unable to provide)	5.3
I Parent or guardian in prison or remanded in custody	0.9
J Unsatisfactory home conditions	5.8
K Other reasons	7.3
Care Orders under Children and Young Persons Act 1969	
L In care proceedings	3.6
M In criminal proceedings	2.9
N Not specified	0.3
Temporary Care Orders	
Interim care orders	4.5
Remand orders	3.5
Committals to Care under Other Legislation	0.5
Total	52.1

These statistics[8] show for the first time not the number of children admitted, but the number of episodes of admission, which is 5,500 greater. As each episode relates to a continuous period of care, irrespective of "category", it appears that many children entered care twice or more during the year. The new style figures repay close study, especially for the light they shed on the duration of each care episode. 71% of all admissions were under Section 1 of the Children Act 1948, 15% on interim care orders or remand, and only 14% as a result of committal by courts under all the relevant legislation. Yet of the largest group—the 1948 Act admissions—55% of the care episodes lasted for less than 8 weeks, and 70% for less than 6 months. On the other hand, of the children who had remained in care for 5 years or more, over half had been admitted under the 1948 Act, not on court orders of any kind.

A comparison of admissions for 1976/7 with those of previous years is not straightforward due to some slight changes of classifications under the Children Act 1948, but it appears that there was a decline in admissions because of short-term illness of a parent, and homelessness, but an increase in children "abandoned or lost", those with one parent who was unable to provide, and those suffering "unsatisfactory home conditions". There was also an increase in the number of committals under the 1969 Act, including temporary orders, over the number for a previous specimen year, 1973/4.

The "reasons" for admission are taken from the returns made by each local authority; the returns are based on the information supplied by social workers responsible for the admissions. Whenever admission is as a result of an order of court, the legislation and the section is precisely stated, together with the sub-section in cases under the 1969 Act. In contrast, the far larger number of admissions under the 1948 Act all appear as having been made under Section 1 of that Act, though they are sub-divided into groups in which a certain "reason" is presumed to exist. Although there are a number of "reasons"—one of which ought to be selected as relevant—over a third of all admissions are described as being due to "unsatisfactory home conditions" or "other reasons". At one time "unsatisfactory home conditions" covered cases in which the home was physically unsatisfactory but it seems doubtful that this should apply in no less than 5,800 episodes of admission. 7,300 children were admitted for "other reasons", that is for reasons other than those set out in the statistics. It is unfortunate that so far local authorities, and social workers, have not been asked to specify what these "reasons" are. It may be found that there may have been a good reason for admission to care, but that it would have been more appropriately dealt with through the court.

However, as admission, or committal, to care was the form of treatment which was in fact applied in these thousands of cases, it must be assumed that it was preceded by investigation, or even assessment. Leaving aside those committed by courts, the local authorities made 36,800 decisions to admit a child or young person to care, for a variety of reasons amounting to family misfortunes, many of which might affect anyone.

Many people have short-term illnesses, many parents desert their partners, or have unsatisfactory home conditions. Why do some cope with their own problems, while others come to the Social Services Department for help? This question becomes even more pertinent in view of the fact that a great many voluntary admissions to care are as the statistics show, for a short period only.

This subject was studied some years ago by a method involving a comparison of 100 child-care families with a control group of 100 other families who made their own arrangements for children during a mother's confinement.[9] One of the conclusions was that the application for care was rarely the result of practical difficulties. It often arose because of a basic weakness in the family life, with poor family relationships and a disregard of the effects that separation would have on the lives of the children. Even short-term admission to care, then, is probably only an indication of the need for prolonged support, and continuous assessment. Other aspects of this report will be discussed in Chapter 9.

There is clearly every reason why a local authority should develop new resources and new preventive services designed to support social workers in their dealings with families and children. It is in this area of social work that the many voluntary organisations and services may be able and willing to pioneer schemes to meet particular situations, either alone or in co-operation with the local authority. But the time has come for less reliance on the casework method—the "one to one" approach which makes enormous demands on limited resources of time and skill. More stress should be laid on stimulating and encouraging group work, neighbourhood work, and community development. Using these methods, it may be found that the people of any given neighbourhood can themselves make a great contribution to the solution of their own problems and difficulties, especially those which spring from isolation and a sense of inadequacy. The greatly needed corporate approach by the whole local authority to the promotion of the welfare of children by the use of existing services has so far not been much in evidence. Day care, even for children under five, is inadequate, and for older children even more so. It needs to be planned as an integral part of a caring service, and as akin to daily fostering. The Humberside scheme, for the under fives only, is described in *Social Work Service* for May 1977. Even social workers often think of preventive work in terms which do not go beyond using money provided under s. 1 of the 1963 Act to pay overdue electricity or gas bills, rent arrears, debts or other embarrassing liabilities, on the grounds that payment will "keep children out of care, and be much cheaper". The power to use money *in exceptional circumstances* which was given by this Act was intended to enable social workers to assist a family with counselling, knowing that finance would be available if it was needed in that context. It was never intended to provide money without the counselling that went with it. It the event, payments under the 1963 Act have gone far beyond the intention of the Circular 204/1963 and are being used largely to subvent or replace supplementary benefits.[10, 11] This raises once again the question of a social worker's awareness of the field of welfare rights; the principles of social work practice are outlined in a B.A.S.W. publication *Cash Code for Social Workers, 1977.*

In the context of preventive work, it must be remembered that among the cases of families and children referred from many official and unofficial sources, there will be some which demand primarily the *protection* of a child or young person. There will be others to which preventive measures and voluntary support have already been applied without success. It is essential that the social worker should recognise these situations and should be able to take appropriate steps to provide either the *protection* or the *care* which is seen in any particular case to be necessary for the child. This is a hard decision, and the failure to make it lies at the heart of much controversy and conflict about the rights of a child as against those of his parents, or other adults. All through the process of discovery, referral, investigation and assessment the rights of the child as a person are at issue and at no stage can they be ignored.

NOTES

1. Report of the Committee on Children and Young Persons 1960, Cmnd. 1191.
2. Specimen Community Care Programme, Appendix A.
3. "Work in a Social Services Department—intake", *Social Work Service*, No. 5, December 1974; and *Towards Accountability in Social Work*, National Institute for Social Work, 1977.
4. "Family Advice Service", Leissner—B.H.J. 17 January 1969.
5. For instance, *Social Workers their Clients and the Law*, Zander; *Family Benefits and Pensions*, D.H.S.S.; *Exceptional Needs Payments*, London, H.M.S.O., 1973; *National Welfare Benefits Handbook*, Child Poverty Action Group; *Legal Aid*, B.A.S.W.; *The Rent Act 1974*, Shelter, 86 The Strand, London, WC2R 0EQ; *Small Claims in the County Court*, free from Lord Chancellor's Department.
6. See for instance Chris Payne in *Social Work Today*, 10 May 1977.
7. *Community Homes Project: assessment* (1969).
8. Children in Care, 31 March 1977.
9. *Child Care and the Family*, Schaffer, London, Bell 1968.
10. "Section One Money: a survey of use", *Social Work Today*, 3 April 1975.
11. "The Problem of Disconnected Electricity Supplies", *Social Work Today*, 15 May 1975. See also a code of practice drawn up with the Gas and Electricity Boards, January 1978, and the Memorandum of November 1976 on "Assistance in Cash"; and *Money Payments, Social Work and Supplementary Benefits*, Michael Hill and Peter Laing, University of Bristol, 1978.

Chapter 7

PROTECTION

SUMMARY

IMMEDIATE PROTECTION

One of the important functions of a Social Services Department is that of acting as a sentinel, especially as regards children and young persons under seventeen. The word implies constant vigilance and readiness to take action when danger threatens. Among the referrals coming to a department, either in or out of office hours, there will be some which primarily call for immediate steps to safeguard a child who needs either care or control, which must now be defined.

DEFINITION OF "CARE OR CONTROL"

At one time the Children and Young Persons Act 1933 provided ways of dealing with those who were found to be in need of *care or protection*. That Act also allowed parents to bring their children before the court as being *beyond parental control*. The Act of 1963 took away this direct right from parents but provided means of dealing with children who were in need of *care, protection or control*. The Act of 1969 refers only to children in need of *care or control* but states that care includes protection, and control includes discipline.[1] The circumstances in which a child or young person may need either care (including protection) or control (including discipline) are set out in the primary conditions described in s. 1(2), as amended by the Children Act 1975, as follows:

A   his proper development is being avoidably prevented or neglected or his health is being avoidably impaired or neglected or he is being ill-treated; or

B   it is probable that the condition set out in the preceding paragraph will be satisfied in his case, having regard to the fact that the court or another court has found that that condition is or was satisfied in the case of another child or young person who is or was a member of the household to which he belongs; or

BB   having regard to the fact that a person convicted of a First Schedule offence is, or may become, a member of the same household as the child; or

C   he is exposed to moral danger; or

D   he is beyond the control of his parent or guardian; or

E   he is of compulsory school age within the meaning of the Education Act 1944, and is not receiving efficient full-time education suitable to his age, ability and aptitude; or

F   he is guilty of an offence, excluding homicide.

Of these, condition A is most likely to call for immediate protective action; s. 40 of the Children and Young Persons Act 1933 lays down a procedure which may be followed, even if the identity of the child is not known. The section authorises any person to take the action, and it has been held that "anyone" includes a parent who might for instance want to protect his own child who for some reason is in the charge and control of another party. Only a "suspicion" that condition A exists is justification for the use of this section; as we shall see later the condition is presumed to exist if there is an unreasonable refusal on the part of a householder to allow the visiting of a child in the household who is either a "private" foster child or a "protected child" under the Adoption Act 1958.

CHILDREN AND YOUNG PERSONS ACT 1933, S. 40

Anyone acting in the interests of a child or young person and suspecting that:

A   the child or young person has been or is being assaulted, ill-treated, or neglected in any place within the jurisdiction of the justice, in a manner likely to cause him unnecessary suffering, or injury to health; or

B   that any offence mentioned in the First Schedule to the Act of 1933 (cruelty, ill-treatment, assault, etc.) has been or is being committed in respect of the child or young person,

may lay *information on oath* to that effect before a justice of the peace who may issue a warrant authorising a constable to search for the child or young person, who need not be named, and to take him to a place of safety if the information is found to be correct.

For this purpose the constable may enter a house or building, by force if necessary, and may remove the child or young person from it. Although the warrant may only be addressed to and executed by a constable, the justice may direct that the constable shall be accompanied by a medical practitioner; the person laying the information may also go with the constable unless prohibited by the justice.

This section sets out the lawful way of gaining entry to a house by force if need be. It mainly concerns the police, acting under the authority of a J.P. and may also involve a doctor, and the complainant whether a social worker or not. In the generality of cases however such dramatic action will not be necessary because the name of the child is known, and there is no reason to assume that entrance to the house or other premises will be refused.

THE DUTY TO INVESTIGATE

The local authority has the prime duty of investigating any case in which it receives information suggesting that any of these conditions A to F apply to any child or young person residing or found in its area, unless it is satisfied that such enquiries are unnecessary.[2] A parent may still ask the local authority (in writing) to bring his child before the court, as being beyond parental control, subject however to s. 3 of the Children and Young Persons Act 1963.

Furthermore, the authority has the duty of bringing care proceedings if they are justified by the enquiry, unless satisfied that it is not in the child's interests or the public interest to do so, or that some other person is about to bring proceedings.[3] (The "other person" would be a police officer or an officer of an authorised society, the National Society for the Prevention of Cruelty to Children; or in cases described in E above, the local Education Authority.[4]) Information received by a local authority may refer to a number of situations some of which may appear to require the removal of the child or young person from the persons who have his care or control for the time being, whether parents or not. Such an emergency situation could arise, for instance, if there is imminent danger to an unwanted stepchild or adopted child, a child who is rejected by one or both parents, anyone under 17 found to be suffering from unexplained injuries, a child or young person who has been punished excessively by a physical attack or by being locked in a room, or a child or young person who is "beyond control" to the extent that he may have been turned out from his own home. A local authority social worker employed in a hospital may be the first person to have contact with an injured child; in this event, he has the duty of either making the necessary enquiries himself, or ensuring that they are made by another social worker in a local team, or perhaps on stand-by duties. It does not follow of course, that care proceedings *will* be taken in every case; indeed it is intended that they will not; but there are some instances in which it might be thought essential that the child or young person should be removed for the time being to a place of safety.

Social workers sometimes try to deal with this situation by using voluntary admission to care, and then placing the child in a foster home or children's home. This is of doubtful legality, and is often futile. If the first need of a child is for protection, even for a short time, this will not be achieved by admission to care under the Children Act 1948 since the parent can at present remove the child at will, leaving the position much as it was before the admission.

DETENTION IN PLACE OF SAFETY

If the need for safety is obvious, the proper course is removal to a place of safety where the child can be *detained* under proper authority. Being detained is not the same as being in care and is more akin to a form of arrest, though for purely protective reasons, and may be arranged in one of two ways.

1. Any *constable* may detain a child or young person if he has reasonable cause to believe that any of the above conditions A to D is satisfied or that condition B would be found to be satisfied by an appropriate court or that a juvenile is being taken from place to place by a vagrant. (A constable has no power to detain a child or young person in respect of condition E as failure to attend school does not itself warrant immediate removal. He would, therefore, have to consider in such cases whether any of the conditions A to D is satisfied.) In detaining the child or young person or arresting him without warrant, the constable must take such steps as are possible to inform the parent or guardian of the detention and the reason for it.[5] The constable must then ensure that the case is enquired into by a police officer not below the rank of inspector; that officer shall, after completing the enquiry, release the child or young person, or if he thinks fit, arrange for his *detention in a place of safety*, informing him and his parent or guardian of his right to apply to a justice for his release. The child or young person may lawfully be detained in the place of safety for a period of only eight days from the beginning of the detention. If, during that period, the child or young person or his parent or guardian, applies to a justice for release, the justice must direct that he be released unless he considers that further detention is necessary in the interests of the child or young person.[6] In this event, further detention would be authorised under an interim order.

2. *Any other person*, for example, but not necessarily, an officer of a local authority or Inspector of the N.S.P.C.C., wishing to *detain* a child or young person and take him to a place of safety, must apply to a justice, who may grant the application if he is satisfied that the applicant has reasonable cause to believe that:

A   any of the conditions set out in A to E above is satisfied; or

B   an appropriate court would find condition B satisfied; or

C   the child or young person is about to leave the United Kingdom in contravention of s. 25 of the Children and Young Persons Act 1933, which relates to persons under 18 going abroad for the purpose of performing for profit.

On the authority of the justice, a child or young person may then be detained in a place of safety for a period not exceeding twenty-eight days.

Here again, the child or young person and the parent or guardian must be informed of the detention and the reason for it,[7] but not of the right to apply for release. Whichever method of detention is intended, it is only necessary for there to be "reasonable cause" for belief that a child's circumstances fall within the conditions set out in s. 1 of the Act. Proof is not required at this stage, but may be sought later.

The main differences between the two methods are:

A   The constable may detain on the authority of a police inspector, without obtaining a justice's order, but any one else must obtain an order.

B   The constable can only detain for a maximum of eight days, whereas a justice's order authorises detention for up to twenty-eight days.

C   When a child is detained by a constable, he or his parents on his behalf may apply to a justice for release, but this does not apply when a child is detained by an order made by a justice. There is no direct appeal against such an order, but use may be made of sub-s. (6). This provides that any person detained whether by a constable or under a place of safety order may apply to a magistrate's (juvenile) court or a justice for an interim order. Such an order must be made or refused, and in the latter event the court or justice may direct that the child should be released. (This sub-section seems to have been intended to allow a local authority to apply for an interim order before the expiry of the detention in a place of safety; but it was held in *R. v. Lincoln (Kesteven) Juvenile Court*, [1976] 1 All E.R. 490 that a parent is not precluded from making such an application, and in some cases this has happened.)

A place of safety is defined as "a community home provided by a local authority or a controlled community home, any police station or any hospital, surgery or any other suitable place, the occupier of which is willing temporarily to receive a child or young person".[8] The place of safety need not therefore be a place within the control of the local authority and can, for instance, be a private house.

The D.H.S.S. Memorandum on Child Abuse, recommends that the first essential step in dealing with a child suspected of being damaged by non-accidental injury is immediate admission to hospital. A hospital may of course be used as a place of safety, and is defined as such, but mere admission to it does not necessarily provide protection. The parents may, as the report suggests, attempt a panic withdrawal of the child while investigations are going on. If this is likely, it is advisable for the admission to be made on the authority of a place of safety order obtained in the usual way. A note on the content and use of the order will be found in Appendix B. Either the local authority or the N.S.P.C.C., will usually be concerned in a case, and has the power to apply for a place of safety order. The police do not need one. Another point about detention in a place of safety is that it need not continue for the full period of eight or twenty-eight days as the case may be. The detention can be brought to an end by an application under sub-s. (5) or (6), or by care proceedings, or by reception into care.

INTERIM ORDERS

While a child or young person is detained whether by a constable for a period of eight days or under the authority of a justice's order for a period of up to twenty-eight days, an application may be made to either a magistrates' court or to a justice of the peace for an interim order to be made. On such an application the interim order must either be made or refused; the application cannot be adjourned. If the order is refused, the court or justice may direct that the child or young person be released forthwith. An interim order may only be made if the child is present, unless he is under the age of 5 or cannot be present because of illness or accident. An interim order commits the child or young person for a period of not more than twenty-eight days to the care of the local authority in whose area the person resides or where the circumstances arose, the decision as to which being at the discretion of the court or the justice.[9] It may be necessary to obtain further interim orders in some cases, but those can only be made by a juvenile court and not by a single Justice of the Peace.

The order lays upon the local authority a duty to bring the child or young person before the court on the expiration of the order or such earlier time as the court may require; but if the child is under 5 or unable to appear by reason of illness or accident, the court need not require his attendance; it may make a further interim order for a period of twenty-eight days.[10] In the case of a male young person over the age of 14, if the court or justice certifies that he is too unruly to be safely committed to the care of the local authority under an interim order and if there is a remand centre available to the court, the court or justice may commit him by warrant to the remand centre for twenty-eight days or for a less period. If an interim order is already in force, such a warrant may only be issued on the application of the local authority, and may not in any case run beyond the date fixed for the expiry of the interim order. On the issue of such a warrant an interim order will cease to have effect.[11] (A female young person (under 17) may no longer be committed to a remand centre or to prison; she may only be committed to the care of the local authority unless, in the case of a young offender, released on bail, or committed to a Crown Court with a view to a sentence of Borstal detention (C. and Y.P. Act 1969, Modification of Part I Order 1978).)

A person in respect of whom an interim order has been made may apply to the High Court for the order to be discharged and the High Court may discharge the order on such conditions as it thinks fit. If, however, the High Court refuses to discharge the order, the local authority to whose care the child or young person is committed may not allow the parent or any other person to be in charge of him without the consent of the High Court and in accordance with any directions which the court may give.[12]

There are, therefore, provisions for removing children and young persons from actual or suspected perils with the authority of the law and there are safeguards for their appearance before a court within a specified time unless it is more in their interests for them to be released. These provisions apply to all children and young persons under the age of 17 who are believed to fall into any of the categories (a) to (d) of s. 1 of the Children and Young Persons Act 1969. Among these are those children originally referred to as "battered babies", though frequently they are not literally babies and may be aged 3 or 4 or even older. Concern about such children has led to the establishment of what amounts to specialised treatment and consideration under the title Child Abuse, or Non-Accidental Injury to Children (N.A.I.), which has been the subject of much enquiry and report in recent years. The Children and Young Persons Act of 1933 recognises the special nature of offences against children—as opposed to offences against people in general—and it follows from this that a criminal act against a child may well justify a prosecution, apart from whatever action is taken to protect the child.

In such a situation there is a conflict between the relative claims of the law, social considerations and either physical or mental health, or both. Efforts to resolve the conflict have led to the development of a highly structured system for dealing with cases in which there is a suspicion of N.A.I.; the management of the system now takes up a growing proportion of social work time and skill.

The basis of the management is the D.H.S.S. Memorandum "Non-Accidental Injury to Children" (April 1974). This has resulted in the establishment in each local authority area of an Area Review Committee, with overall responsibility, and the setting up of Case Conferences as a means of bringing together all those agencies, including the police as a rule, who are concerned in a particular case. It has also led to a number of criteria to be used in deciding to enter the name of a child in a Register, in one of several categories according to the adjudged seriousness of the allegation. Case conferences usually appoint one of their number as the "key worker" who is responsible for co-ordination of effort and for ensuring that no member of the case conference takes unilateral action, since it is intended that decisions shall be taken jointly.

N.A.I., as it is known, is a tremendous subject; it has a great deal of literature and was dealt with at some length, for instance, in *Social Work Today* of March 1978. One of the articles there by David Jones and John Hawke, of an N.S.P.C.C. special unit, includes a list of relevant books and publications. Concern and anxiety mount with each successive case in which an injured child is reported on by the Press; it is not surprising that in their recently published survey Olive Stevenson and Phyllida Parsloe think it possible that social workers are made fearful by the dominance of circulars, conferences and memoranda on this most painful subject.

Some from time to time have expressed their concern that preoccupation with conferences and registers may be a hindrance in dealing with the real issues involved. There is for instance a danger that the names of children will be recorded in a Register without the knowledge of the parents, or that, having been entered, there is no procedure for removal. Where practices of this type exist, it will be difficult for a social worker to promote the kind of relationship advocated in the text books.

GENERAL PROTECTIVE FUNCTIONS

These apply in a number of cases where there may not be any element of crisis or danger, but none the less protection (by supervision) is provided for children and young persons who, for various reasons, are living either entirely or partly with people who are not of their own family. The two principal Acts concerned are the Children Act 1958 (Part I) as regards "foster" children, and the Adoption Act 1958 (Part IV) as regards "protected" children. There is no provision in either of these two Acts for regulations to be made by the Minister, as for example in the Children Act, concerning the boarding out of children, though the Children Act 1975 (s. 95(3)) empowers the Secretary of State to make Regulations governing the visitation of "foster children" under the Children Act 1958. The two Acts have many similarities and for this reason the following notes have been set out in two columns for convenience of comparison. *The numbers in the margins refer to the sections of the appropriate Act.* This method makes the functions appear legalistic, but the details are important even if they are uninteresting. Very briefly, there are certain ways in which people who are looking after other people's children have to notify various events to the Social Services Department. (There are a number of exceptions which are all set out.) The Department has duties towards these children because they all need protection, though not all to the same degree. It also has powers which it can exercise over the people who are providing the care for the children. It has powers to prohibit placing in stated circumstances, and can take steps to remove children by stated procedures, when this is in their interests. Other comments follow after the summary of the two Acts.

SUMMARY

CHILDREN ACT 1958— (AS AMENDED) FOSTER CHILDREN	ADOPTION ACT 1958— PROTECTED CHILDREN
Introduction	
1. The work undertaken by local authorities under this Act is referred to generally as "Child Protection" and was previously known as "Child Life Protection". The Infant Life Protection Act 1897, laid down a maximum age of 5	1. Local authorities have various duties in connection with children who are to be legally adopted but in this chapter we are dealing with the supervision of children being cared for by persons who are proposing to adopt them.

years for children with whom the Act was concerned and this age was raised to 7 years by the Children Act 1908; to 9 years by the Children and Young Persons Act 1932, and to the upper limit of compulsory school age by the Children Act 1948.

The whole question was discussed by the Curtis Committee who recommended in 1946 that these children should fall under supervision in the same way as foster children who were at that time fostered for reward.

Legislation

2. The principal Act is the Children Act 1958, as extensively amended with effect from 1 January 1970 by the Children and Young Persons Act 1969 (ss. 51-57) and by the Children Act 1975.

2. The necessary legislation was effected in the Adoption Act 1950, and was re-enacted in Part IV of the Adoption Act 1958. Part IV of the Adoption Act 1958, bears a resemblance to Part I of the Children Act 1958, and details will not be repeated in the case of provisions which are identical in both Acts. As a result of amendments in the 1969 Act, however, the Adoption Act 1958 is concerned only with children specifically placed for adoption.

Definition

3. *Meaning of "foster child"*— A foster child is defined as a child below the upper limit of compulsory school age whose care and maintenance are undertaken by a person who is not a relative, guardian or custodian of the child; the child becomes a foster child as soon as the person who has given the undertaking receives him. There is no definition in the Act of the term "guardian" or "custodian". But see list of exemptions at 4 below.

2   3. *Meaning of "protected child".*

A The powers and duties of local authorities in this part of the Adoption Act relate only to "protected children" so that it is important to establish precisely the meaning of the term.

B There are two main categories of protected children. In the first category are those children below school-leaving age who are placed in the actual custody of persons who are not parents, guardians or relatives of the child (but who propose to adopt him),   37 under arrangements made *by* another person not being the parent or guardian of the child. There is sometimes doubt as to whether or not a person has in fact taken part in arrangements for the placing of a child with another person and in this connection it is helpful to refer to s. 57(2) of the Act which sets out quite clearly that taking part in the arrangements includes entering into, or making any agreement or arrangement for, or for facilitating, the adoption of the child by any other person whether the adoption is effected, in pursuance of an adoption order or otherwise. It also includes agreements or arrangements for, or for facilitating, the placing of the child in the care and possession of another person. The section goes on to say that if the third party initiates or takes part in any negotiations of which the purpose or effect is the conclusion of an agreement or the making of any arrangement for the purpose of adoption or if he causes another to do so, then he has taken part in the arrangements for the placing of the child within the meaning of s. 37 and the child will be a protected child. A child who is placed by a local authority or voluntary organisation in whose care he is does not become a "protected child" by virtue of the placing.

C In the second category are 37

children in respect of whom notification of intention to apply for an adoption order has been given to the local authority under s. 3(2) of the Act. An adoption order cannot be made unless such a notification has been given in respect of the child, except where the applicants or one of the applicants is a parent of the child, or where the child is over compulsory school age at the time. (When s. 18 of the Children Act 1975 comes into operation there will be no exemption from the duty to notify intention, either on the grounds that one of the applicants is a parent of the child, or because the child is over compulsory school age.)

D It follows, therefore, that all the children in the first category will also fall within the second category if and when notification of intention to adopt is given; but there will also be children falling in the second category who have never been in the first, where adoption is arranged by a registered adoption society, a local authority or by direct arrangement between the parent or guardian of the child and the proposed adopter.

E The child will only be a protected child while he is in the actual custody of the person referred to in the first category, or of the person giving the notice in the second category. Rare exceptions to this relate to

children who are not physically living in the household
of the persons who have
actual custody, for instance
because the child is in
hospital (s. 37(3)).

Exemptions

4. Children are not regarded
as foster children within the
meaning of the Act in the
following circumstances:

A While in the care of a local
authority;

2 4. The provisions with regard
to exemptions are very similar
to those contained in the Children Act 1958, in respect of
foster children:

A Children in the care of local
authorities or voluntary
organisations, though not
"protected" at the time of
placing, are not exempt
from becoming protected
children; the obvious case
will be where a child who is
boarded-out becomes the
subject of an application for
an adoption order and the
notice of intention is given
under s. 3(2) of the Ado-
ption Act.

B While in the care of a
voluntary organisation;
C While boarded-out by a
Health Authority;
D While boarded-out by a
local Education Authority;

B The provisions with regard
to exemption at the time of

D placing for protected children are the same as in
para. 4B to D opposite; but

E While in premises in which
any parent, adult relative or
guardian of his is for the
time being residing;
or, in the care of a person—

E A child is not exempt from
becoming a protected child
by virtue of the fact that he
is in the care of any person
in premises in which a
parent or adult relative or
guardian of his is for the
time being residing.

F While in a voluntary home;

G While in any school within
the meaning of the Edu-
cation Acts *in which he is receiving full-time education;*

F The provisions with regard
to exemption for protected

37

H While in a hospital or nur-
sing home registered or
exempted from registration
under the appropriate legislation;

I While in any home or institution not specified above
but maintained by a public
or local authority;

J While in the care of any
person by virtue of a supervision order under the Children and Young Persons
Act 1969;

K While liable to be detained
or subject to guardianship
under the Mental Health
Act 1959, or resident in a
residential home for men-
tally disordered persons
within the meaning of Part
III of that Act;

L While in the care of a person who does not intend to,
and does not in fact, undertake his care and main-
tenance for a continuous
period of more than six
days, or, if that person is
not a "regular foster parent", for a continuous period
of more than twenty-seven
days. The period may be
continuous (even though
broken within the period).
See *Surrey County Council*
v. *Battersby*, [1965] 1 All
E.R. 273. A person is a
"regular foster parent" for
this purpose if she has
during the preceding twelve
months had the care of one
or more children for a period
of three months, or for
periods totalling three
months, or for a least three
continuous periods each of
more than six days. Chil-

K children who would be protected by virtue of a notification are the same as in
para. 4F to K opposite.

"Guardian" now includes a
father who has custody of
an illegitimate child (Children Act 1975, Schedule 3.)

L There is no time limit for
protected children.

dren who are cared for for periods of not more than six days are subject to supervision under the Nurseries and Child Minders Regulation Act 1948. The above provisions regarding persons who are not "regular foster parents" give exemption from supervision in the case of children placed for short holidays or in an emergency.

M While placed with a person who proposes to adopt him under arrangements made by a local authority or registered adoption society, or while he is a protected child. (Such children are, or may become "protected" but cannot be "foster" children.)

Reward

5. It is no longer necessary to establish "reward" in order to bring a child within the definition of a "foster child". (But see 12 below—Insurance.)

5. There is no reference to 50 "reward" in connection with protected children. On the contrary there is a general prohibition of payments in respect of children who are to be adopted, in Part V of the Adoption Act.

Duty of Local Authority

6. Local authorities for the 1 purpose of this Act are non-metropolitan councils and metropolitan district councils and their duties are allocated to the Social Services Committee. The local authority has the duty to ensure the well-being of foster children in its area by causing officers of the authority to visit the children from time to time, at the discretion of the authority and give such advice as to the care

6. Here again, local authori- 28 ties for the purpose of the 38 Adoption Act are the councils of non-metropolitan counties and metropolitan districts and their duties with regard to the visitation of protected children are similar to those in respect of foster children, the difference being that there is no discretion allowed as to visitation; the requirement is that all protected children must be visited from time to time by

and maintenance of the children as appears to be needed. It is for the local authority to decide in each case whether continuous visiting is necessary. Regulations to be made under s. 2A may prescribe the frequency of visits by social workers.

officers of the authority, who must satisfy themselves as to the well-being of the children and give such advice as to their care and maintenance as may appear to be needed.

Notices to Local Authority

7.A A person who proposes to maintain a foster child not already in his care must give *written* notice to the local authority of his intention to do so not less than two weeks and not more than four weeks before he receives the child unless he receives the child in an emergency (undefined). In the case of a child received in an emergency, the person must give *written* notice to the local authority not later than forty-eight hours after he receives the child, and the same provision applies to the case where the person had in his care a child who was not a foster child but who became a foster child while in his care. The notice is to be given to the local authority for the area in which the premises concerned are situated. The notice must give the date of reception, and the address, but as to other information, see para 7F below. The reception of subsequent foster children need not be notified to the local authority provided one or more foster children have been maintained continuously since the first notification was given (but see below).

A person maintaining a

3

7.A The provisions of the Adoption Act with regard to notifications to local authorities are very similar to those required for foster parents under the Children Act 1958. Where, however, arrangements are made for placing children who would come within the first category referred to above, the responsibility for giving the notice to the local authority falls on the third party or agent and not on the person in whose care and possession the child is to be placed, nor by the parent or guardian of the child. There is, however, no need for a local authority or voluntary adoption agency to notify the initial placing of a child, though they frequently do so. See also 7F below.

40

B The requirement for giving

foster child must notify the local authority, in writing, if he changes his address, at least two weeks and not more than four weeks before the change. If the change is made in an emergency then the notification may be made not later than forty-eight hours after the change. If the new address is situated in the area of another local authority, the first mentioned authority must notify the authority concerned and send particulars in respect of the child.

c If a foster child dies, the person having the care of the child must inform the local authority and the person from whom the child was received within 48 hours of the death. Where the child is removed or removes himself the local authority may require notice to be given to them of the name and address of the person into whose care the child has been removed. Such notices must be in writing.

d Although there is no requirement to notify the local authority of the removal of individual foster children, a person who ceases to maintain any foster children at particular premises must notify the local authority thereof in writing within forty-eight hours, unless notice is already required by c above, or unless the person intends to maintain any of the children again within twenty-seven days. If this intention is abandoned, however, or if the child is not received again within⁵ the twenty-seven-day period, not-

written notice of change of address is similar to that required for foster children under the Children Act 1958.

3 c If a protected child dies, the person having the actual custody of the child must notify the local authority in writing within forty-eight hours of the death. There is no provision in the Adoption Act for notification of children being removed or removing themselves as under the Children Act 1958.

d There is no equivalent in the Adoption Act to that contained in the Children Act 1958, in respect of notification of children ceasing to be foster children.

ice must be given. (The Children Act 1975 will amend this section by providing that the removal of each individual child must be notified unless the same child is to be placed again within 27 days.)

E Local authorities no longer have the power to grant exemption from the giving of notices of intention to act as foster parents.

F The local authority *may* require a person maintaining or proposing to maintain a foster child to give the following particulars, *i.e.* the name, sex, date and place of birth of the child and the name and address of every person who is a parent or guardian or acts as a guardian of the child or from whom the child has been or is to be received.

Note: The Secretary of State has powers to make Regulations requiring parents of proposed foster children to notify the local authority (s. 3A).

8. *Power to Inspect Premises, Impose Conditions or Prohibit the Keeping of Foster Children.*

A Any local authority officer who is authorised to visit foster children may inspect any part of premises in the area of the authority in which foster children are to be or are being kept, but before doing so the officer must, if so requested, produce a duly authenticated document saying that he is entitled to visit foster children. If admission to the premises is refused, or

E Local authorities do not have the power to grant exemption from the giving of notices in respect of protected children when this is required by the legislation.

3 F The requirements of the Adoption Act in respect of protected children are identical with those of the Children Act 1958, in respect of foster children, as regards the information to be supplied to the local authority on request.

8. *Power to Inspect Premises, Impose Conditions or Prohibit the Keeping of Protected Children.*

A Officers of a local authority 39 have the same authority to inspect premises as is contained in the Children Act 1958, in respect of foster children. In the event of refusal, note 11 applies.

refusal is expected, or the occupier is temporarily absent, a justice of the peace may on production of sworn information in writing issue a warrant authorising entry to the premises, by force if need be, within forty-eight hours, for the purpose of inspecting the premises. The warrant may only be issued if there is reasonable cause to believe that there is a foster child in the premises. The power to inspect premises must be distinguished from the duty to visit foster children referred to in paragraph 6 above.

B A local authority *may* impose requirements on a person who is keeping or proposes to keep foster children in premises used *wholly or partly* for that purpose. The requirements may relate to the following:

i. The number, age and sex of the foster children who may be kept at any one time in the premises or any part thereof.

ii. The accommodation and equipment to be provided for the children.

iii. The medical arrangements made for protecting the health of the children.

iv. The giving of particulars of the person for the time being in charge of the children.

v. The number, qualifications or experience of the persons employed in looking after the children.

vi. The keeping of records.

4 B There is no power for a local authority to impose requirements in respect of protected children in the same way as is referred to in the paragraph opposite.

vii. The fire precautions to be taken in the premises.

viii. The giving of particulars of any foster child received in the premises and of any change in the number or identity of the foster children kept therein. This requirement is important as it enables local authorities to keep themselves informed of all admissions and discharges of foster children, if they so desire, notwithstanding the last sentence of 7A above.

If the authority so desire, the requirements may only apply when the number of foster children in the premises exceeds a specified number, or may relate to a particular class of foster children only.

C Local authorities may prohibit persons from keeping foster children as follows:

i. If the premises are unsuitable, from keeping any foster children in those premises.

ii. If the person is unsuitable, from keeping any foster children in any premises in their area.

iii. If the premises or the person are unsuitable for a particular child only, from keeping that child in those particular premises.

Any such prohibition may be cancelled by the local authority. The requirements and prohibitions referred to must be imposed by notice in writing addressed to the person concerned. Any person aggrieved by any such

4   C The local authority under the Adoption Act has no *general* power to prohibit children being received in any premises but the local authority may prohibit a person from undertaking the actual custody of *a child* if the authority consider that it would be detrimental to the child to be kept by that person in those particular premises. This power may not, however, be exercised if a Registered Adoption Society or another local authority took part in the arrangements. There is a similar provision for persons aggrieved by any prohibition imposed by the local authority to appeal to a juvenile court.   41 42

requirement or prohibition may appeal to a juvenile court within fourteen days from the date of notification of the requirement. Although[5] the prohibition takes effect at once, a requirement does not take effect while an appeal is pending. Local authorities imposing requirements or prohibitions are required to include in the notice a statement notifying the person concerned of his right to appeal and of the time within which he may do so.

9. *Disqualification for keeping Foster Children.*—A person may not maintain a foster child if:

A An order has been made 6 against him under this Act removing a child from his care.

B A child has been removed from his care after having been found to be in need of care or control under the Children and Young Persons Acts 1933-1969.

C He has been convicted of any offence specified in the First Schedule of the 1933 Act or has been placed on probation or discharged absolutely or conditionally for any such offence.

D His rights and powers with respect to a child have been vested in a local authority under s. 2 of the Children Act 1948.

E A local authority have made an order under sub-s. 4 of s. 1 of the Nurseries and

9. *Disqualification for keeping* 34 *Protected Children.*—There is no provision comparable to that under s. 6 of the Children Act 1958, disqualifying certain persons from keeping foster children. Local authorities receiving a notice of placing under s. 37(1) have the opportunity of making enquiries on these points and, if necessary, of prohibiting the placing (except when it is being made by a local authority or voluntary adoption agency).

Child Minders Regulation
Act 1948, refusing his registration under that Act, or
have made an Order under
s. 5 of that Act cancelling
his registration or the registration of any premises
which he occupies.

F An order has been made
under s. 43 of the Adoption
Act 1958, for the removal of
a protected child who was
being kept or was about to
be received by him:

*unless he has disclosed that
fact to the local authority and
obtained their written consent.*

These disqualifications apply   6
also to every person living or (2)
employed in premises in which
it is proposed to keep foster
children.

10. *Removal of Foster Children kept in Unsuitable
Surroundings.*

A A local authority may com-
plain to a juvenile court that a
foster child is being kept or is
about to be received by any
person unfit to have his care,
or by a person disqualified
under the preceding para-
graphs for keeping foster children, or in any premises or any
environment detrimental or
likely to be detrimental to him,
and if the court, on hearing the
complaint, is satisfied of the
truth of the allegations they
may make an order for his
removal to a place of safety
until he can be restored to a
parent, relative or guardian or
until other arrangements can
be made for him. In cases
where there is imminent danger

10. *Removal of Protected Children kept in Unsuitable
Surroundings.*

A and B the provisions of the 43
Adoption Act with regard to
the removal of protected children kept in unsuitable surroundings are identical with
those for foster children.

to .the health or well-being of the child the application may be made by a person authorised to visit foster children and the order made by a justice of the peace.

B The order referred to in the previous paragraph may be executed by an officer of a local authority or by a constable.

C The order may require the removal of all the foster children in the premises if the ground of the complaint is that a prohibition by a local authority made under s. 4 of the Act has been contravened.

C This does not apply to protected children.

D Any children removed from premises under this paragraph may be received into care by a local authority under s. 1 of the Children Act 1948, whether or not the circumstances fall within s. 1 of the Children Act and the child may appear to be over the age of 17.

D and E The provisions of the Adoption Act with regard to the reception of children on removal into care and the notification to the parent or guardian of the child are identical with those in respect of foster children. 43

E The parent or guardian of any child removed under this paragraph must be notified by the local authority if this is practicable.

Power to Issue Warrants to Search for and Remove a Child

11. This section extends the power under s. 40 of the Children and Young Persons Act 1933, to search for and remove a child under warrant. Under that section the warrant may be issued if it appears from information on oath that there is reasonable cause to suspect that a child has been or is being ill-treated or neglected or is the victim of certain specified offences. This section provides that a refusal to allow the 8

11. This provision is identical with that contained in the Children Act 1958, in respect of foster children. 45

visiting of a foster child or the
inspection of any premises by a
person authorised to visit under
Part I of the Act shall constitute reasonable cause for
such a suspicion and hence for
the issue of a warrant to search
for and remove the child.

Insurance

12. The Life Assurance Act 9
1774, provides *inter alia* that
no insurance may be made
unless the insurer has some
interest in the life of the
insured and that he may not
recover more than the value of
the interest. The section provides that a person who main-
tains a foster child for reward
shall be deemed for the purposes of the Life Assurance Act
1774, to have no interest in the
life of the child.

12. This provision is identical 46
with that contained in the Children Act 1958, in respect of
foster children, except that the
reference to "reward" is
omitted.

Sittings of Juvenile Courts

13. This section relieves juven- 10
ile courts, while they are
dealing with appeals under s. 5
or complaints under s. 7, from
the restrictions imposed by s.
47(2) of the Children and
Young Persons Act 1933, as to
the time and place of sittings
and the persons who may be
present. The appellant or
defendant will be an adult and
the respondent or complainant
will be a local authority. There
is thus no need in such cases
for these special provisions that
govern the work of juvenile
courts when they are dealing
with juveniles.

13. This provision is identical 47
with that contained in the Children Act 1958, in respect of
foster children.

Appeal to the Crown Court

14. There is a right of appeal 11
to the Crown Court from any
order made under Part I of the
Act by a juvenile court or any
other Magistrates' Court
within the meaning of the
Magistrates' Courts Act 1952.
The expression "Magistrates'
Court" is defined as "Any
Justice or Justices of the Peace
acting under any enactment or
by virtue of his or their commission or under the common
law". The effect is to provide a
right of appeal to the Crown
Court against an order made
by a justice of the peace acting
in an emergency under the
provisions of s. 7(1) as well as
from an order made by a
juvenile court under that section or s. 5.

14. This provision is identical 48
with that contained in the Children Act 1958, in respect of
foster children.

Extensions to Certain School Children During Holidays

15.A Where a child resides 12
during school holidays in a
school for a period exceeding
one month, Part I of the Act
shall apply to him, subject to
the following modifications, as
if children in schools were not
excepted from Part I:
B Where the provisions of the
Act in relation to such children
obtain, the duty to give the
local authority on request the
particulars specified in para.
7F above is applied, but instead
of the duties previously referred to, to give notice of intention to maintain a foster child,
to notify change of address and
to notify the death or removal
of a child, there is a duty to
notify the local authority of the
estimated number of children,

15. This paragraph is inap-
plicable to protected children.

if any, who will reside in the school for a period of more than two weeks during the school holiday. The local authority retains the duty to inspect the premises, but not the power to impose requirements or a prohibition under s. 4.

c A local authority may exempt any person from the duty of giving notices under this section either for a specified period or indefinitely and the exemption may be revoked at any time by notice in writing.

dThe schools concerned in this paragraph are schools within the meaning of the Education Acts 1944-53, which are not schools maintained by local education authorities, *i.e.* in effect independent and direct grant boarding schools and non-maintained special schools.

Extensions of Age

16. A foster child on attaining the upper limit of compulsory school age remains a foster child until he reaches the age of 18; or lives elsewhere than with the person with whom he was living when he attained school leaving age; or apart from his age ceases to fall within the definition of a foster child; whichever event occurs first. 13

16. A protected child ceases to be a protected child if a guardian is appointed for him, if the application for an adoption order is withdrawn, or if one of the following orders is made by a court: 37

A an adoption order, not being an interim order;

B an order for care or supervision on the refusal of an adoption order;

C a custodianship order;

D an order for custody or care or supervision under the Matrimonial Causes Act 1973.

Otherwise, he remains a protected child until the age of 18.

Offences

17. The offences under this Act are as follows:

A Failing to give any notices or required information within the time specified or failing to give the information within a reasonable time or knowingly making or causing or procuring any person to make any false or misleading statement in the notice or information.

B Refusing to allow an authorised officer to visit a foster child or to inspect premises, or obstructing an officer entitled to inspect premises by virtue of a warrant issued by a justice of the peace under s. 4(1A) of the Act.

C Failing to comply with any requirements imposed by a local authority or keeping any foster children in any premises in contravention of a prohibition.

D Maintaining a foster child in contravention of s. 6 of the Act, but a person is not guilty of an offence in respect of a person referred to in s. 6(2) if he proves that he did not know and had no reasonable grounds for believing, that a person living or employed in the premises was a person to whom the section applies.

E Refusing to comply with an order for the removal of any child or obstructing any person in the execution of such an order.

The Act provides a maximum penalty on a summary conviction of imprisonment for a

14

17. The definition of offences in this part of the Adoption Act and the penalties on conviction follow very closely those contained in the Children Act 1958, in respect of foster children, except that imprisonment is for a term not exceeding 3 months.

44

term of 6 months or a fine of
£400 or both. In England and
Wales a local authority may
institute proceedings for offences under this section.
(Penalties as amended by the
Children Act 1975, Schedule
3.)

Service of Notices

18. Any notice of information 15
required to be given, may be
given by post.

18. The provision for notices 55
is identical with that contained
in the Children Act 1958, in
respect of foster children.

Authentication of Documents

19. Any notice by a local 16
authority may be signed on
behalf of the authority by the
Clerk of such authority or by
an officer of the authority
authorised in writing to sign
such a notice.

19. The provisions for authen- 49
tication of documents have
been repealed.

Advertising

20.A Advertisements indicating 37
that a person will undertake or
will arrange for the care and
maintenance of a child shall
not be published unless they
truly state the name and
address of the person concerned.
B The Secretary of State has
power to make Regulations
prohibiting advertisements,
including those made by
parents who are seeking foster
parents.
C Any person who causes an
advertisement to be published
in contravention of this para-

20. The restriction upon ad- 51
vertising in the Adoption Act
1958, is stronger than that in
the Children Act 1958. No
advertisement may be pub-
lished indicating that the
parent or guardian of a child
desires to cause the child to be
adopted; or that a person
desires to adopt a child; or that
any person (other than a Registered Adoption Society or a
local authority) is willing to
make arrangements for the
adoption of a child. A person
who publishes an advertisement in contravention of pro-

graph shall be guilty of an offence and will be subject to a fine similar to that referred to in para. 17 above.

D Local authorities may initiate proceedings for offences under this section.

visions or causes such an advertisement to be published, shall be liable on summary conviction to a fine not exceeding £400.

Note: Such advertisements must relate to a living child, not to an expected child. See 122 J.P. 289.

Definitions

21. In both Acts "relative" has the same meaning as set out in Chapter 10. In both Acts, "child" means a person under the age of 18. In both Acts "place of safety" means a community home provided by a local authority, a controlled community home, police station, or any hospital, surgery or other suitable place the occupier of which is willing temporarily to receive a child. In both Acts "compulsory school age" has the same meaning as in the Education Acts and is now up to 16 plus.

Supervision

Dealing first with the children falling under Part IV of the Adoption Act 1958, supervision in many cases does not last long because adoption often follows within a few months of placing or notification. But there are cases in which the notification has been given and accepted, when it was not really valid, and there was no certain prospect of adoption from the start. This situation can arise when the preliminary steps towards adoption have not been properly taken; it leads to so-called "supervision" possibly for many years, and it is not surprising that visiting "from time to time" means hardly ever. Even when visiting is regular and frequent for a few months, it is often rather purposeless, because it is looked on as a prelude to the making of a guardian *ad litem* report to the court; adoption has been thought of as inevitable unless some serious objection to it arises.

Probably the best use to be made of visiting under s. 38 is to "give advice as to care and maintenance" by thoroughly discussing with the prospective adopters their attitude, and that of their relatives, to the natural parents of the child, and to the child, first as a baby, then on entering school or playgroups, later as an adolescent and finally as an adult. The physical care of the child will usually be satisfactory, but in any event advice on health matters will be available from a health visitor, leaving the social worker free to concentrate on the adoptive relationship. (When the Children Act 1975 is fully implemented children placed by adoption agencies will not be "protected" even after notification of intention has been given; there will then be no local authority "welfare supervision" except for such "private" placings as are allowed under ss. 28

and 29 of the 1975 Act. In such cases the quality of supervision will be crucial.)

The privately placed foster children dealt with under the Children Act 1958 do not generally receive the attention they should, especially as there are so many of them. At 31 March 1974, 29,738 children in local authority care were in foster homes, some of them with relatives.[13] At the same date 9,694 children were known to be in private foster homes, but this is only an unknown fraction of the total, because of ignorance of the duty to notify, or failure to do it. Notices in post offices and other public places drawing attention to the law, in simple language, seem to have limited effect.

Little is known about this large group of children, but there has been valuable research on a small scale by Robert Holman.[14] Indications in his sample are that:

1. The children's parents are for the most part overseas students, or unmarried mothers, or deserted fathers.
2. Most children are under the age of 5.
3. Placings take place informally as a result of a meeting, or a notice in a shop window.
4. There is no preparation for the placing.
5. Enquiries into notifications are rarely carried out by Social Services Departments, or if they are, they do not prevent unsuitable foster parents from taking children. Thus there are those who have physical illnesses, or criminal records, or whose own children have been committed to care for neglect.
6. Foster care is often provided by the woman alone, her husband taking little part in it.
7. Many of the children themselves suffer from various defects and difficulties.
8. Private foster parents receive no allowance from the local authority and depend on amounts payable by natural parents at a low rate, with no certainty of receiving even that.
9. Private foster parents have no rights with regard to the children; they rarely know how long they will stay, or whether they will ever go.
10. Visits by social workers are "from time to time" which often means very rarely. During the visits few children are seen "on their own". This stems from the use of the discretion mentioned in s. 1 of the 1958 Act. This discretion may be reduced by Regulations made under the new s. 2A of the 1958 Act. On the other hand, the Social Work Service found in its survey that in some authorities all "foster children" were visited and that no use was being made of the present discretionary powers. In addition all private foster parents were required to notify each new placing and removal in the same way as before the passing of the Act of 1969. This brief report on the position in 1975 contains a useful statement of the importance of proper management of the private fostering service.[15]

On the credit side, many foster parents were far more than "baby-farmers" and had loving attitudes to the children, even when there were serious behaviour problems, with which they received little outside help. Sometimes the genuine attachment to the children was so great, that the fear of their removal at any time, without warning, created strong tensions and anxiety; in extreme cases, it could lead to the offer of bribes to parents to let the children stay, or to the foster parents moving from the district to escape the threat of removal.

If these brief comments are compared with the provisions of the 1958 Act, it will be clear that better practice would lead to a great improvement in the lot of these children and the private foster parents. Whatever else may be said about private fostering, it obviously provides a substantial social service as an alternative to local authority care. Ways could be found to turn it into a major resource in the spirit of community care. The Children Act 1975 will strengthen the position of the private foster parent. After caring for a child for 3 years he or she will be able to apply for a custodianship order under Part II, and after 5 years will be able to apply for an adoption order. In either event a parent will not be able, as at present, to remove the child until the application has been determined. In the case of an application for a custodianship order the welfare of the child will be the first and paramount consideration, as in guardianship. (Applications for custodianship or adoption orders can be made at an earlier stage, provided that there is parental agreement.)

NURSERIES AND CHILD MINDERS REGULATION ACT 1948, AS AMENDED

In addition to foster children and protected children, there are a number of children requiring the protection of the authority because, although they live at home, they are cared for during the day by people other than their parents. Their supervision is governed by the Nurseries and Child Minders Regulation Act of 1948, as amended by s. 60 of the Health Services and Public Health Act 1968.

A   *Introduction*

The need for this Act arose because there were a considerable number of children being cared for in nurseries and in private houses who did not fall under the supervision of the local authority. To come within the scope of the child protection enactments, as previously described, children placed privately by their parents had to be cared for by persons other than relatives who undertook their *care and maintenance for reward*. Owing to the demand for female labour, the practice of placing children with daily minders spread to many parts of the country, and these children did not fall under supervision because they were cared for by the day and were not, therefore, being *maintained* in such a way as to bring them within the scope of child protection. Similarly, children placed by their mothers in nurseries provided by the employers in mills and factories were also outside the definition of foster children for child protection purposes.

B *Registration*

The Act of 1948 introduced a dual system of registration of premises and persons and the distinction between the two is maintained throughout the Act. So far as *premises* are concerned, the obligation to register applies where the premises are used for the reception of children under compulsory school leaving age to be looked after for the day, or for two hours either continuously or in the aggregate each day, or for a period not exceeding six days, whether for reward or not, but does not apply where the premises are used wholly or mainly as private dwellings, or in the case of a home or institution as defined in the Children Act 1958, or a school. The term "wholly or mainly" has no precise meaning and many such children are cared for without the premises being registered. Premises used mainly for the reception of children for a period exceeding six days, to which the child protection provisions of the Children Act 1958 apply, are also exempted from registration under this Act. The registration relates to the premises or buildings and not to the person in charge of the children.

A *person* caring *for reward* for one or more children under 5 years of age to whom she is not related, looking after them for the day or for two hours either continuously or in the aggregate each day, or for a period not exceeding six days, *must* apply for registration.

In both cases changes in circumstances require fresh registration. Failure to register is an offence for which the penalty on summary conviction is a fine up to £50 and for a second or subsequent offence £100 and/or three months' imprisonment. A local authority must issue a Certificate of Registration and may also impose conditions in respect of both *premises* and *persons* concerning the number of children to be kept; the precautions to be taken against exposing the children to infectious disease; the qualifications and number of staff employed; the adequate maintenance and safety of buildings; the diet and feeding arrangements; and the records to be kept. Additional requirements may be laid down for *premises* only in respect of the qualifications of the person in charge and the medical supervision of the children. These requirements may be varied or revoked by the local authority and must be specified in the Certificate of Registration. Local authorities may refuse registration if they are not satisfied with the fitness of the persons who are to look after the children or with the premises in which they are to be kept. Playgroups may be established either in "premises" (*e.g.* church halls) or in private houses and fall to be registered accordingly.

C *Appeal*

Any person aggrieved by the action of the local authority in refusing registration, cancelling registration, or imposing conditions may appeal to a Court of Summary Jurisdiction (s. 6).

D *Inspection*

Local authority inspectors are empowered to enter *premises* used for child-minding to inspect the children, the records and the premises, also the home of a *person* registered as a child-minder. ·

E *Avoidance of dual supervision*

Where *premises* are used both for day-minding and for the care and maintenance of foster children within the meaning of the Children Act 1958, there is provision for the avoidance of dual supervision. If the premises are used mainly for the reception of children falling within the 1958 Act, *i.e.* for a period exceeding six days, then the provisions of the 1958 Act with regard to visitation, entry and inspection apply and the requirements regarding registration in the 1948 Act do not apply.

In the same way, a *person* required to register under the 1948 Act is exempted from registration if she receives one or more children falling to be dealt with under the 1958 Act or subject to supervision as boarded out children under any other Act, ss. 9 and 10.

F *Entry*

Entry when there is reasonable cause to believe that premises or persons are child minding without registration can be effected by obtaining a warrant issued by a Justice of the Peace.

G *Prosecutions*

Proceedings for offences under the 1948 Act may be taken by the local authority.

H *Definitions*

A "local authority" for the purpose of the Nurseries and Child Minders Regulation Act 1948, is the Social Services Committee.

In this Act a "Child" is a person who has not attained the upper limit of compulsory school age; that phrase and "relative" have the same meaning as in the Children Act of 1958.[16]

Comment

Though the Regulations covering child-minding are somewhat confusing (as between premises and personal child-minding), the intention is quite clearly to protect children who are placed by the day in the care of people who are not their parents or relatives. Most of these children are placed in the houses of individual child minders who should be registered and may be visited by social work advisers.

Reports from the Child-Minding Research Unit suggest however that about 57,000 children are placed with registered child minders and a further large number, at least 100,000, with people who are not registered, thus committing an offence against the Act.[17] The standards of care provided, however, do not seem to depend on registration, some of the unregistered persons giving a better service than some of the registered.

When the standards are low, young children may spend many hours a day, sometimes from as early as 6 a.m., sitting in an attic or back room and being kept out of sight of callers and passers-by for fear of detection.

Often there is no stimulus, no play equipment or experience and in some instances children may even be tied to furniture to keep them out of the way.

Compared with more fortunate children who are taken shopping, play in the park, visit friends, and enjoy both books and toys, many day-care children lead an extremely deprived life which will seriously affect their later development. Like the privately placed foster children mentioned earlier, this is another very large group of children who are protected by legislation, but not by the way in which it is implemented.

As long ago as 1968, when the local authority Health Department administered the Act, the Minister of Health issued an excellent memorandum of guidance,[18] with Circular 37-68, on the whole question of the various methods of providing day-care for children under 5, including advice on physical standards of accommodation, recommended equipment, and feeding. It advocated the encouragement of good child-minding, especially for priority groups of children who were defined, and who constitute the kinds of children whose parents for a number of reasons use day-care services. The present position falls very far short of the ideals in the memorandum, even when social workers have been appointed specially to deal with applications for registration and to visit and advise the people actually caring for children. (There is no duty to visit individual children.)

As in the case of private foster parents, child-minders are providing a social service; in this case it is an alternative to the expensive day nursery and, if conditions are good, it can be far better. (In the connected field of nursery schooling, the National Foundation for Education Research has issued a report suggesting that the proposed extension of nursery schools as such, is a "gigantic social hoax", and that nursery education would be more effective if carried out with small groups of children in private houses.[19]) Circular LASSL 78(1) deals with the co-ordination of educational and social services for children under 5, and advocates the recruitment of people to provide day care which, for children under 3, should be with a child-minder, in a normal household. The National Health Service Act 1978 empowers a local authority to make and recover charges for the provision of this service, but charges are not mandatory. This may give impetus to the positive promotion of good child minding services. In some areas, attempts are being made to give child-minders training, to persuade the unregistered to register, to use already existing powers to pay them for their service, and to supply fireguards, toys and play equipment.

In the context of "protection", the Act provides this for those children who are placed with registered child minders; the unregistered are liable to prosecution, but this is unlikely to be as effective as a recognition of the value of the service being provided, together with the use of powers to assist all child-minders to attain the levels required for registration. They are, after all, providing a spontaneous community service which is usually available in the districts where it is needed most. Under suitable direction and encouragement it could be made into a valuable resource, without capital investment, and in the process those child-minders who should not be caring for children would be more readily identified and prohibited.

It is apparent that so far as "approval" is concerned, adoptive parents, local authority foster parents, private foster parents and child-minders have a good deal in common. A suggested method of combining the process of investigation in all cases is set out in Appendix C.

"PROTECTION" OF THE YOUNG OFFENDER

The Act of 1969 was intended ultimately to ensure that children under the age of 14 are dealt with under the same procedure, generally speaking, whether they are offenders or not. The Act is not however to be fully implemented at once and can only be put into operation gradually by the Secretary of State's exercise of powers under the VERY IMPORTANT S. 34. These are used virtually to determine at any particular date who is a "child" and who a "young person", a point which has to be borne in mind in consulting the Act. Section 5, restricting prosecution of children over a minimum age, has not been brought into operation nor does the Government intend to raise the minimum age for prosecution to 12 until they are satisfied that the necessary resources are available. The position, therefore, is that all children become of an age to be prosecuted at 10, which is also the age of criminal responsibility.

For this reason there are still parallel procedures relating to "offenders" and "non-offenders" over the age of 10 years.

Earlier in the chapter we have looked at the procedure for protecting a child or young person when it is considered that one of the primary conditions A to E is satisfied, and that there is need for immediate action. When the condition F (the offence condition) is satisfied, there is a different procedure, set out in s. 29. This provides:

(a) That the person may be arrested without warrant; if so he may be brought before a court at once, or taken to a police station where his case will be enquired into. He must then be released unless it is felt that he should be detained in his own interests, *e.g.*, he cannot at once be handed over to his parents, *or* unless his release would defeat the ends of justice. If he is released a recognisance may be taken for him to report to a police station if required.

(b) Alternatively he may be arrested on a warrant, in which case a recognisance for his attendance at court must be taken.

(c) In all cases of arrest, with or without warrant, the police officer concerned must inform the parent or guardian, and if the child is not released must make arrangements with the local authority for him to be received into care and accommodated in the most suitable way. He must then appear before a court within seventy-two hours, unless this is impossible, *e.g.*, because of illness.

(d) On appearance in court, the court must order release unless the arrest was on warrant, or unless detention is in the interests of the arrested person, or the interests of justice. When the court does not order release, it may remand either on bail, with recognisance, or in custody. In the event of a remand in custody, the accused must be informed of his right to apply to the High Court for bail (Children and Young Persons Act 1969, s. 29(6)).

(e) Remands may be to the custody of a constable for one day only, but will generally be to the care of the local authority with provision for committal to a remand centre or prison of any male person over 14 who is certified to be too unruly of character to be detained in the local authority's care. Certificates of unruliness may only be issued in situations covered by the Certificates of Unruly Character (Conditions) Order of 1977 as expanded by subsequent orders. The conditions include the nature of the offence and the seriousness of absconding or disruption arising in a community home. Applicants must be a police inspector, or, at least, an Assistant Director of Social Services.

There are further measures for what may be called the "protection" of young offenders from criminal proceedings. Although an offender may be arrested and dealt with as above, or may more simply be alleged to have committed an offence, it does not follow that criminal proceedings will be taken against him. As s. 5 is not in operation there is no actual provision in the Act for consultation between police and local authority for the purpose of deciding whether a child or young person should be dealt with by voluntary methods, or by care or criminal proceedings. It is intended, however, that there should be consultation between the two services as there has been since 1964, and that this should be developed and expanded as the resources become available. In each area the police and the Director of Social Services were asked to consider the method and scope of such consultation, as outlined in paras. 92-97 of the "Guide". They should take into account the use of the police caution, the juvenile liaison scheme, where it exists, and other informal arrangements such as the referral of all cases involving persons under the age of 17 to a joint police-local authority bureau for a decision as to whether court proceedings are essential, and if so whether they should be care or criminal proceedings. Generally these consultations affect children up to 14 at present, as social workers would find it impossible to deal in this way with all young persons up to 17. As it is, the inter-service discussion is superficial and does not often include full enquiries, as was the intention. The inability of Social Services Departments to follow the recommendations in the Guide may well account for much of the current concern about young offenders and ways of dealing with the problems they present. A preliminary report on a small scale project in Cheshire gives some indication of the tremendous investment of social work time and effort which is needed to develop an effective relationship with the police in the way envisaged; but more importantly it shows that it is possible to lay the foundations of a comprehensive and flexible service for children (under 14 in this study) using social work methods, but at the same time stressing the appropriate role of the juvenile court.[20]

Although a local authority may itself institute care proceedings on the basis of the offence condition, this does not mean that it should investigate alleged offences as such. This remains a matter for the police, as does the final decision as to whether or not to prosecute for an offence. In coming to this decision regard will be paid to such criteria as the gravity of the offence, the public interest, and the necessity for a court appearance, for instance in certain traffic offences involving a penalty such as disqualification from driving.

A further point about the young offender is that if he is charged with an offence he will be dealt with summarily, generally speaking. This will not be the case if he is charged with homicide or with other grave crimes punishable with a long period of detention which the magistrates consider would be an appropriate sentence but cannot themselves order; or if he is jointly charged with an adult. But even then, if he pleads "not guilty" and his co-defendants plead guilty and are committed for trial or discharged, the court may remit the juvenile to a juvenile court (Criminal Law Act 1977, s. 34).

PROTECTION GENERALLY

The overall protection of children and young persons in court proceedings is provided by the Children and Young Persons Acts 1933-69. These Acts deal with such matters as juvenile court procedure, evidence of children, limitations on publication of reports, and the general principles to be observed by courts in cases involving young people.

Finally, all proceedings both care and criminal are subject to the right of Appeal to the Crown Court against orders made by the court. One such case, *R.* v. *K.* (1977) has raised questions of great importance. In an appeal to the Crown Court against a care order made in criminal proceedings, there was an application for bail pending the Court's determination, but the Judge held that the subject of a care order was not in custody (within the meaning of the Courts Act 1971, s. 13(4)), and that bail could therefore not be granted. In the same case it was held that a care order is a "sentence" (within the meaning of the Magistrates' Courts Act 1952, s. 83) and this is of course justification for an appeal. The decision with regard to bail seems to arise from the mingling of justice and welfare, and is the subject of an article in *Social Work Today*.[21] When a more immediate decision is needed, there is now the right to apply to the High Court for the discharge of an interim order, in care cases, or for bail in criminal cases. In all cases legal aid for children and young persons is available and may be granted by the court. Parents of persons under the age of 16 may be ordered to make a contribution to the cost. Explanatory leaflets have been issued, and all local authority social workers should ensure that both children and their parents or guardians are aware of the right to apply for legal aid at any stage of proceedings in the juvenile courts.

What may be seen as protection for the young offender thus falls into three categories. The last of these is the protection which is extended when he is involved in criminal proceedings. Prior to that stage, there is the potential protection offered by the use of care proceedings involving the offence condition F. But the main protection is, or should be, in the use of local authority and community resources in such a way as to obviate the need for recourse to the courts. This is the real heart of the matter of prevention. Concern about the younger offender, and about the facilities for dealing with him, has now resulted in the formation of a campaign called "New Approaches to Juvenile Crime", which is sponsored by the various social work and probation agencies most deeply involved in the problem. The campaign concedes that there is a small number of young people who pose a serious threat to society and who must be placed in secure accommodation. But there is no evidence that more committals to establishments will halt the rise in crime. There is much more to be gained by work within the community and by the development of local schemes which do not involve formal proceedings or the breaking of family and community ties.

PROTECTION IN EMPLOYMENT

This account of the protective functions of the local authority would not be complete without mention of the duty to protect children and young persons in employment, by controlling the conditions in which they work, regulating their appearances as public performers, prohibiting their exposure to injury, and ensuring that their education is not neglected.

This general function is, however, the province of the local education authority, not of the Director of Social Services. The powers are as set out in the Children and Young Persons Acts of 1933 and 1963 (Part II) and the Children (Performances) Regulations of 1968.

OTHER PROTECTION

The general protective attitude of society towards minors is still being illustrated by legislation of a specific nature. Thus we have the Tattooing of Minors Act, and more recently the Protection of Children Act 1978 which deals with the taking of "indecent" photographs or films of children under the age of 16. The Domestic Violence and Matrimonial Proceedings Act 1976 gave further protective powers to a county court; similar powers will shortly be available to magistrates under the Domestic Proceedings and Magistrates' Courts Act 1978.

NOTES

1. C. and Y.P. Act 1969, s. 70(1).
2. C. and Y.P. Act 1969, s. 2(1).
3. *Ibid.*, s. 2(2).
4. *Ibid.*, s. 2(8).
5. *Ibid.*, ss. 28(2) and 28(3).
6. *Ibid.*, ss. 22(1) and 28(3)-(5).
7. *Ibid.*, s. 28(3).
8. C. and Y.P. Act 1933, s. 107, as amended.
9. C. and Y.P. Act 1969, s. 20(2).

10. *Ibid.*, s. 22(3).
11. *Ibid.*, s. 22(5).
12. *Ibid.*, s. 22(4).
13. *Children in Care*, 31 March 1974, Cmnd. 6147.
14. *Trading in Children*, R. Holman, London, Routledge and Kegan Paul, 1973.
15. "Private Fostering", circular DSWS 77(1) of 29 July 1977.
16. See Paragraph 21 above.
17. Child minding Research Unit "Action Register" 1974.
18. Ministry of Health Circular 36/68 and 37/68, and Memorandum of guidance to local (health) authorities.
19. National Foundation for Educational Research Press Report.
20. "Police, Social Workers and Children in Trouble", Neville Shone and Ruth Christie, *Journal of Social Welfare Law*, March 1979.
21. "Bail for Juvenile Offender", Richard Jones, *Social Work Today*, 1 May 1979.

Chapter 8

INVOKING THE COURT

SUMMARY

There are a number of situations which may put young people into the jurisdiction of the courts. There are first the children of parties to divorce or matrimonial proceedings, who may be placed under supervision or, exceptionally, committed to the custody or care of the local authority. As will be seen in the Table in Chapter 6 (admission to Care) this power has so far been little used, and it must be presumed that in the majority of such cases the courts have been satisfied that responsibility for the children of the family could be given to one or other parent, or to another person, with or without a supervision order. Studies indicate however that courts frequently come to this conclusion without calling for social work or probation welfare reports. Three-quarters of all divorces involve children under the age of 16, the majority being under 11. While some of these children may appear to be unharmed by the divorce of their parents there is no doubt that many are seriously affected in either the long or short term. It is hoped that Family Courts, if and when they are established, will be able to pay special attention to the difficulties of the large and growing number of children whose parents obtain divorces.[1]

The Family Law Reform Act of 1969 empowers courts which have jurisdiction in wardship proceedings to make supervision or committal orders in the same way and under the same conditions as the divorce courts. This is an additional power in respect of young persons who are already wards of the court. It should be remembered that the Family Division of the High Court has inherent powers by which it may make minors "wards of court". An application for wardship can be made by taking out a summons which makes the minor a ward for up to twenty-one days, during which time the court will hear the application and give a preliminary judgment on the merits of the case, though a final decision may be long delayed. There have been many situations in which wardship has been applied for, including those in which there was already in force an order affecting the minor concerned. When a local authority is involved in the case of a child in its care the court will rarely review its decisions, provided that its powers have been properly exercised under the relevant statute. But wardship is available when a local authority is concerned about a child in its care; in several cases judges have encouraged a local authority to invoke the wardship jurisdiction on behalf of a child not in care. This may be advisable when there is concern about a child who appears to be in need of care, but there is insufficient evidence to ensure the making of an order under s. 1 of the Children and Young Persons Act 1969.[2]

Then there are the courts which are concerned with applications under the Guardianship of Minors Act 1971, as expanded by the Guardianship Act 1973, and which have the power to make orders relating to the custody and upbringing of minors. In these domestic situations, proceedings usually start because of disputes between parents or guardians; the children's welfare is therefore endangered and the courts have power to decide the issue. Whatever the original ground of the application may be, the welfare of the child is the first and paramount consideration, and there is now power for the court to make a supervision order or to commit the care of the child to a local authority.

The Children Act 1975, s. 17 gives similar powers to a court when it refuses to make an adoption order. (When Part II of the Act is implemented the court will have a similar power on hearing an application for a custodianship order, or when revoking such an order.) In proceedings under the Act relating to refusal of an adoption order or relating to custodianship, the principle of s. 1 of the Guardianship of Minors Act 1971 will apply, so that the welfare of the child will be the first and paramount consideration. In this way, adults who make an application to the courts in domestic, matrimonial or custody (or similar) proceedings automatically invoke the courts on behalf of the children.

There are many other situations in which it may be necessary for children or young persons to be brought before a court either in their own interests or those of society, or both.

Some social workers tend to mistrust the courts and to look upon the legal system as a punitive and coercive machine which, once it is started, cannot be stopped and is largely concerned with prohibitions. It does not seem to be sufficiently realised that the law and the courts provide many necessary safeguards, especially for children and young persons, against adverse circumstances in which they are helpless. They also provide a defence against the possible abuse by social workers of their very considerable powers. Other social workers accept the courts as an institution but have a particular antipathy to the juvenile court and would like it to be replaced by some kind of welfare council, as in certain other countries. Yet others would abolish the juvenile court, but would separate criminal matters from civil matters and allow all young offenders aged 15 to 17 to be dealt with in the adult courts. Another school of thought wishes to retain the juvenile court, but to separate care and criminal proceedings, and to ensure better legal representation for both children and their parents, especially when a care order is a likely outcome of the proceedings.

Whether or not any of these changes will eventuate, we have at present to accept the existing juvenile court which is, like other courts a legal institution; it can be the firm ally of the social worker when he feels the need for reinforcement of his legitimate aims, or when he has justifiable grounds for thinking that it may be necessary to intervene in some way in the interests of a child or young person. Among recent tragic cases there have been some in which social workers, after taking the best possible professional advice, have been unable to agree on a right course of action and have taken a case before the court for resolution. In other cases, the social workers did not bring their undoubted misgivings before the court, but continued to work on a voluntary basis in circumstances of great risk. In this they were acting without the support of the magistrates as the representatives of society as a whole. Courts are no more perfect than social workers, and will on occasions make mistakes, perhaps by remaining unconvinced of the needs of a child as presented by a social worker or other witness.

All these considerations are specially important in dealing with very young children who have been ill-treated or where there has been ill-treatment of children within the household. The prospect of repetition of assault is high, and unilateral decisions by social workers are fraught with risk as well as being deplored in the D.H.S.S. Memorandum. For discussion and the accepted warning signs, see "Parental abuse on children".[3]

CARE PROCEEDINGS (C. AND Y.P. ACT 1969)

Under s. 1 of the Act, it is necessary for any of the persons authorised to bring care proceedings to have decided that he "reasonably believes that there are grounds for making an order" under the section. Before he can decide this, he must clearly have considered whether there are alternative ways of ensuring that the child or young person receives care or control. This involves consultation, and specially with the local authority which may in turn involve other agencies (see Chapter 7).

Care proceedings may not even be considered of course unless one of the primary conditions, set out in Chapter 7, is satisfied. Paraphrased, these conditions refer to a child who is:

neglected or ill-treated, or is a member of a household in which a child has been ill-treated or neglected, and a court has found that that condition was satisfied;* (See paras. A, B, and BB, page 67.)

---

* Section 1(2)(a) uses the words "is being" and there has been some concern about this when, for instance, a child has been detained in a hospital or other place of safety. While there, can it be said that he "is being" ill-treated or neglected?

exposed to moral danger;†

beyond the control of parent or guardian;

failing to attend school;

believed to have committed an offence other than homicide (which involves criminal proceedings).

If any one of these conditions exists there is a ground for social intervention, which may or may not include invoking the court. As we have seen in the last chapter, when the offence condition is being considered, the police may decide to institute *criminal proceedings* for one of several reasons; if they do not, the offence stands only as a prima facie justification for social intervention in the same way as the other primary conditions mentioned above. The police may decide to issue a formal caution, or to refer the child for joint consultations with social workers or other agencies.

The next stage consists of the decision whether or not to institute *care proceedings*. This is a question which must be considered in the light of what is called the "care or control" test. The person considering the case must ask himself "Can the needs of this child or young person for care or control be met by any of the resources which could be made available on a voluntary basis by any means at all?", and "If proceedings are not taken is this child or young person likely or unlikely to receive the care (including protection and treatment) or the control (including discipline) which he as an individual appears to need?". If the answer, after taking into account all that is known about the total situation, is "unlikely" then care proceedings would be justified.

Put another way, it is no longer enough to know or to be able to prove that a child has been neglected or ill-treated, or is the victim of an offence, or at risk of being neglected, or beyond control, or in moral danger, or that he is not receiving efficient full-time education or that, being over 10, he has committed an offence. While these facts may tend to indicate that the child is in need of either care or control or both, they do not prove it. Nor is it enough to say that the child is not receiving adequate care, protection and guidance from his parents or guardians; the quality of parental care is only one of the factors to be considered. The child's total circumstances,

---

There is reason to suppose that in these circumstances "is being" means "was being" at the time when preventative action was taken. If this were not so, a place of safety order would not lead to protection for the child. "Ill-treatment" does not apply to a child whose parents refuse consent to a life-saving blood transfusion or operation. (See Ministry of Health circular F/P9/1B of 14 April 1967 addressed to Regional Hospital Board, and Home Office Circular 63/1968 of 5 March 1968.)

† A person aged 16 who is or has been married may not be the subject of care proceedings. A girl under the age of 16 may have married lawfully in another country, but is not *for this reason* exposed to moral danger (*Mohamed* v. *Knott*, [1968] 2 All E.R. 563). In any event, it may be felt that much of what used to be regarded as moral danger for girls is now condoned by various means, such as free contraceptive advice to young people under 17. But exposure to moral danger may arise in other ways, for instance by coercion of a child for criminal purposes.

past, present and future, must be examined with a view to deciding whether care or control is *unlikely* to be available if a court order is not made.

A local authority social worker considering care proceedings should enlist the advice and co-operation of the authority's legal staff. A solicitor will be in a position to look at the situation from a legal point of view, and to advise whether there are grounds for an application, and if so which ground is to be preferred. He will also be able to consider whether the desired end can be obtained in some other way, for instance by a s. 2 Resolution if the child is already in care under the Children Act. Or, if there is some other order in existence, such as a supervision order made by the divorce court, he may advise application to that court so that it can exercise its powers in such a way as to make a care order unnecessary. It is at this stage also that the whole range of preventive provision has to be considered, the local authority and voluntary facilities, the informal initiatives known loosely as "intermediate treatment", the possible influence of the wider family, friends, or the local community. Section 1 of the Children and Young Persons Act of 1963 is the base for the exploration of whatever possibilities there may be to promote the welfare of a child by making it unnecessary to have recourse to court proceedings (unless, of course, that is the best available course to take in the interests of the child). It seems rather unfortunate that Intermediate Treatment is thought of in terms of the Act of 1969 instead, though it is less relevant than to the Act of 1963. (See Chapter 14.)

All these considerations are binding on those who are authorised to bring care proceedings, that is a local authority, a constable or the N.S.P.C.C. If the primary condition is non-attendance at school, it is the local education authority which must, after applying all the tests, institute proceedings.

The recent increase in non-attendance at school (and in actual absences from school of adolescents who are officially recorded as being in school) is a cause for great concern.[4] There is a move to make non-attendance (or absence) in itself a ground for care proceedings, without the need for application of the "care or control" test which at present applies. Whether or not this would be justified in the cases of adolescents, for younger children at primary schools the care or control test should remain. This would make it more essential for the widest possible enquiries to be made before care proceedings are used. In the course of these enquiries, education welfare officers and the schools should be brought into contact with the comprehensive assessment process referred to in Chapter 6. In this way the isolation of the School Social Work Service from other social workers and agencies would be diminished, and the needs of at least some of the children should be discovered and met without the need for care proceedings[5] or, alternatively, proceedings might be brought on different grounds.

If the offence condition is the basis of proceedings, they will be taken by the local authority or, more likely, by the police. Proceedings in respect of other primary conditions may be instituted by a local authority or the police, or by the N.S.P.C.C. following consultations.

Once it has been decided to start either *care* or *criminal* proceedings, the local authority must be informed; so must the probation service, in cases concerning children over the age of 13.

The person bringing the proceedings will be responsible for the whole of the evidence as to (a) the satisfaction of the primary condition, and (b) the care or control test, since the court itself has to be fully assured that an order is essential. The whole purpose of the proceedings is to satisfy the court which has the ultimate responsibility of deciding whether or not to make an order, and if so, which of several orders. This means that the court must have evidence of the offence in criminal proceedings or evidence of one of the conditions (a) to (f) in care proceedings. In many cases it will be the social worker who is called upon to provide the evidence—a task which is sometimes undertaken without full understanding of the procedure or of the customs of the court. The position should be better when, as is often the case, a local authority solicitor is involved.

In a straightforward prosecution the court has only to be satisfied on the question of guilt. In care proceedings, including those citing the offence condition (which must be fully proved) proof of the facts is not enough. There has to be proof that a court order for "care" or "control" is necessary; this again may involve a social worker in giving evidence on which there may be cross-examination.

Since it is the court which must be satisfied that the care or control test has been applied, magistrates themselves may not be convinced by the evidence and may themselves suggest preventive measures, such as adjournment, or interim care orders. One court for instance has aroused controversy by repeatedly adjourning cases brought under condition (d) (non-attendance at school) and has claimed a high rate of success in obtaining compliance. Social workers have been critical of this action, stating that it wastes time, and that definite orders should be made so that the court would not appear to be collaborating with the education authority. Conflicts of this type underline the need for regular and continuous co-operation between social workers and juvenile court magistrates, as advocated in the Home Office Guide, para. 107.

The "Guide"[6] deals fully with other forms of consultation, provision of information for the courts, the types of orders which the court may make in care and criminal proceedings, and Part I of the Act generally. As the Guide is available to courts and practitioners it does not seem necessary to cover the same ground in detail in this book, except in so far as the general duties of the Social Services Department are concerned, but the general effect and the salient points are set out here for easy reference to the Guide, which in turn refers to the appropriate sections of the Acts as amended by the Criminal Justice Act 1972.

As a result of the 1969 Act, and the wider use of preventive powers, less young people appear before the juvenile courts, but at the same time the local authority should be much more vitally concerned in the work of the courts than previously, and may well find it essential to be regularly

represented at court sittings, if this is not the case already. There is much
to be said for the appointment of a specialist social worker in busy courts.[7]

The general effect of the procedures under the 1969 Act is to simplify
the whole of the proceedings, and to make it clear that although the local
authority may have wider powers than before, the rights of children are to
be safeguarded by the courts and by the availability of *legal aid in all
proceedings under the Act.* Legal aid is not, however, available to parents
in all situations, and even for children it may not be always capable of
challenging the opinions, as opposed to the evidence, of social workers. It
is being increasingly felt in some quarters that both children and their
parents sometimes need the help of an independent social worker, and
several organisations are already working on these lines. The need for
independent social work involvement is at present recognised only in
adoption work, and in a small number of care proceedings (see Chapter
13), but there is provision for more in care proceedings (Children and
Young Persons Act 1969, s. 32A and 32B, only partly implemented, and
Children Act 1948, s. 4B—not in force). The need therefore seems to be
recognised, but is at present being met by voluntary means.

The method of taking immediate action, by arrest or detention, followed
by consultation as appropriate, has already been dealt with. When this
stage is followed by a decision to institute either criminal or care
proceedings, the following questions may arise for consideration. (Where
numbers are quoted they relate to the paragraphs in the Guide.)

COMPARISON WITH CRIMINAL PROCEEDINGS

	Criminal Proceedings	*Care Proceedings*
How will process begin?	By summons or charge (216).	By notice, or summons or warrant if necessary to secure attendance (176).
May parents be required to attend?	Yes. C. and Y.P. Act 1933, s. 34.	Yes (179).
Who will institute proceedings?	Police.	Police or local authority if offence condition alleged, education authority if non-attendance alleged; in other primary conditions A to D either police, local authority or N.S.P.C.C.
In respect of children of what age?	10, and over from 1/1/71. Age may be raised under s. 34, except for charge of homicide (4).	Any age up to 17, unless over the age of 16 and has been married.
In which court?	Juvenile, or magistrate's court for area where offence committed.	A juvenile court anywhere (189–190).

	Criminal Proceedings	*Care Proceedings*
When would the magistrate's court be concerned?	If juvenile jointly charged with person over 17 (C. and Y.P. Act 1933, s. 46). But this means jointly charged with the same offence not with a different offence arising from the same circumstances. (Magistrate's court may remit to juvenile court however under Criminal Law Act 1977, s. 34.)	Not at all, unless child is a witness. If the court convicts a person of offences against a child, it may not now direct that the child be brought before a juvenile court, as it cannot apply the care or control test. It may, however, draw the case to the notice of the police or local authority (26). *But* in school attendance cases only, the court may direct that the child be brought before a juvenile court (37).
Has a juvenile the right to elect to go for trial?	No.	
May he be sent for trial?	Yes, in certain circumstances (217 and 218) but written statements must be taken (C.J. Act 1972, s. 44).	
Can a magistrate's court deal with a case in any other way than committal for trial?	Yes, by fine, compensation, binding over of parent, discharge, or traffic offence penalty. Otherwise must remit to the juvenile court for juvenile's home area (228/9).	
What happens if the original court is not that for the juvenile's home area?	If magistrate's court, as above. If a juvenile court, may try the case, and make an order, *or* remit to court for home area (C. and Y.P. Act 1933, s. 56).	Juvenile court must either dismiss case, or direct that juvenile be brought before court for home area. *But* if offence condition alleged may hear evidence before deciding whether to dismiss or remit (191/2).
If a court remits to court for home area, what happens in the meantime?	Release on bail or remand procedure under s. 23, *i.e.*, remand to care of local authority usually (229, 220–227) unless	May allow child to return home and inform local authority for home area, or make interim care order committing to

	Criminal Proceedings	*Care Proceedings*
	"unruly" certificate is issued (See Chapter 7.)	care of more appropriate authority (193–195).
Who takes action in the home area court?	Police.	Usually local authority for home area, within 21 days. Could be the education authority in respect of condition E.
Who produces evidence?	Police.	Person bringing proceedings (50).
What is the burden of proof?	As in criminal proceedings.	As for civil proceedings (42). But if condition F is alleged, offence condition, and is denied, burden of proof must be as in criminal proceedings. If court not satisfied, it must dismiss the case. If satisfied, there will be separate civil proceedings, with evidence in respect of care or control test (45 and 46). For education cases, see paragraph 44.
How will social reports be supplied to the court?	Police will notify local authority and probation service. Social service dept is primarily responsible for supplying all local authority information but if probation service normally deals with home surroundings aspect it may continue to do so (99, 100, 103) until the age for prosecution is raised under s. 34. But even if the home surroundings report is prepared by the probation service, local authority has a duty to supply any information it has which will assist the court (103).	Person bringing the proceedings will notify local authority and probation service. Local authority responsible for all reports in respect of children under 13, and normally in respect of any child brought before the court by the local authority itself (104). Education authority similarly responsible in cases it brings itself (102). Probation service will still supply reports relating to children over 13 who are not brought before the court by the local authority or education authority, and may in any event be asked for

Criminal Proceedings	Care Proceedings
	a report in a case of any kind (104/5). (The age of 13 may be raised under s. 34.)
After reports, what are the considerations relating to the use of the court's powers? What orders can the juvenile court make?	The welfare of the child and his need for education and training (C. and Y.P. Act 1933, s. 44). "Welfare" is not the first and paramount consideration.
These are set out in para. 77 and detailed below.	These are set out in para. 51 and paras. 58–63 detailed below.

————————————Care Order————————
————————————Supervision Order—————————

Containing requirements set out in C. and Y.P. Act 1969, s. 12.

Containing additional
requirements set out in
Criminal Law Act
1977, s. 37. (If so
decided by the court.)

Care orders are dealt with in Chapter 9, and supervision orders in Chapter 14.

These are the two orders which most closely concern the social worker, but it should be remembered that there are other orders which the court may make under the 1969 Act as now amended by the Criminal Law Act 1977.[8]

OTHER ORDERS

A.   In care proceedings (including those in which the offence condition is the ground of the application to court).

1.   *Recognisance by the parent to exercise proper care and control in the sum of £200* (C. and Y.P. Act 1969, s. 1 3)). This seems to be little used, possibly because of a reluctance to follow the philosophy that the primary responsibility for the upbringing of children rests on their parents. Or it may be that parents are unwilling to accept the responsibility.

2.   *Hospital or guardianship order* (s. 1(3)(d), (e)). These can only be used when mental health provisions under the Act of 1959 apply.

3.   *Recognisance by the* young person *before the court in a sum of up to £50 for his own good behaviour* (s. 3(7)). This order can only be made with consent, and there is therefore no appeal against it.

4.   *Order for compensation,* up to £100 which *may* be payable by

parent or guardian if he has conduced to the commission of the offence
(s. 3(6)), and if he has been informed of the intention to make such an
order.

B.   In criminal proceedings, where the child or young person is charged
      with an offence, as such.

    1.   *Binding over parents or guardian with their consent* (s. 7(7)) (see A
1 above).
    2.   *Binding over the offender himself, with his consent* (Common
Law).
    3.   *Absolute or conditional discharge* (Powers of Criminal Courts Act
1973).
    4.   *Hospital or guardianship order* (see A 2 above).
    5.   *Fine up to £200 for a young person, £50 for a child.* Fines have
been virtually unenforceable but now in default of payment the court may
make an attendance centre order (if a centre is available to the court) and
may also require a parent, with his consent, to enter into a recognisance to
ensure that the defaulter pays any arrears of a fine imposed. It also has the
power to transfer any unpaid arrears to a parent or guardian, but not a
foster parent, and to recover the sum outstanding as though the fine were
unpaid by the parent or guardian. There is however a right of appeal.
    In dealing with enforcement of fine payments in these ways the court
must be satisfied that the defaulter has had the means to pay but has
neglected or refused to do so.
    6.   *Compensation, £400,* otherwise as in care proceedings, above. For
the application of the above to a local authority having parental rights and
duties, or powers and duties, see Chapter 11.
    7.   *Attendance centre order.* This order can only be made if the court
concerned has an attendance centre within reasonable reach. Such a centre
should not be more than ten miles or forty-five minutes' travelling time
from the home of the young offender.
    8.   *Detention centre order.* Junior detention centres are for young
offenders aged 14-17. Ideally they should not be used for first offenders,
but in fact are. Nor should they be used for persons who have previously
been sent to a detention centre, or have been in a community home under a
care order, or have previously been in borstal. As will be seen in the
comments on the use of the Children and Young Persons Act 1969 in
Chapter 5, the detention centre order is being made increasingly in recent
years. Attendance centre and detention centre orders can only be made
where the offence is punishable with imprisonment. Both types of centre
are part of the penal system and are not administered by local authorities.
There is considerable conflict of opinion as to their purpose, and especially
as to whether they are punitive, or reformative; and in consequence the
regime varies from one centre to another. It was originally intended that both
would be phased out and replaced by other provisions under the 1969 Act,
but there seems little immediate prospect of this.

9. *Borstal detention.* A juvenile court can only order committal to borstal for anyone already in care and placed in a community home (see Chapter 11). It can however commit a young offender to the Crown Court with a view to borstal training. The minimum age is still 15, as s. 7(1) is not in force and both boys and girls over that age committed to Crown Court may be certified as of too unruly a character to be remanded in local authority care. (See Chapter 7.) (Home Office Circular 213/1978.)

As was mentioned in Chapter 5 the number of young offenders under 17 in borstal is increasing.

10. *Deferment of sentence.* Under the Criminal Justice Act 1972, s. 22, a juvenile court may defer sentence for a period of up to six months, without making a remand order.

11. *Deprivation of property.* Under s. 23 of the same Act, a juvenile court may deprive an offender of property which has been used, or was intended to be used, for criminal purposes.

12. A higher court may on convicting a child or young person order Borstal detention, if aged over 15, or detention under the Children and Young Persons Act 1933, s. 53 (punishment of certain grave crimes).

General comment. Before a young person is sentenced to a period of borstal training, or detention (either of which will deprive him of liberty for an appreciable time), the court must ensure that he has legal aid, or that he has had the opportunity of having it. There is no such requirement before the making of a care order, which may also entail loss of liberty. Social workers may well wish to consider whether they ought to ensure that the provision of legal aid is understood by any young person likely to be made the subject of a care order, and by his parents.

NOTES

1. National Children's Bureau, Highlight No. 13.
2. See "The local authority and the ward of court", *Social Work Today*, 29 November 1977.
3. Joan Gibson, *Social Work Today*, 18 April 1974.
4. "The Many Problems of R.O.S.L.A.", *Social Services*, 13 July 1974.
5. "The E.W.O., Truancy and School Phobia", *Social Work Today*, 30 May 1974.
6. *Part I of the Children and Young Persons Act 1969* (A guide for courts and practitioners), London, H.M.S.O., 1970.
7. "The Social Worker and the Courts", Brian Harris and Geoff Sage, C.C.E.T.S.W. Paper 7.
8. For fuller treatment of this subject, see *The Law Relating to Children*, H. K. Bevan, London, Butterworths, 1973, and *The Legal Context of Social Work*, J. D. McClean, London, Butterworths, 1975.

GENERAL NOTE ON CARE PROCEEDINGS

D.H.S.S. Local Authority Circular (75)18 of 25 November 1975 urges local authorities to bring care proceedings when they feel that there is a case for protecting a child. The circular arises from the judgment of the Court of Appeal in *Surrey County Council* v. *S.* concerning the meaning of s. 1(2)(b) of the Children and Young Persons Act 1969.

Chapter 9

ADMISSION TO CARE

SUMMARY

It was explained in Chapter 6 that the local authority receives information about families or children "in trouble" of many different kinds; it has wide powers to improve these situations by the use of the family support service and must direct its energies to assisting parents to undertake their responsibilities in so far as they are able and willing to accept such help.

It is inevitable, therefore, that local authority social workers are increasingly working with families and children with their consent. If a family accepts this kind of voluntary support for itself or for one of its members, it may be said to be receiving *care*, in the most natural and constructive way within the family setting. Support of this kind may include the use of any kind of service which the authority has or may develop, for instance, the child guidance service, attendance of children at play-groups, adventure weekends, group sessions for mothers, and in fact anything which can be said to enrich and broaden life experience, while encouraging parents to provide adequate care for their children.

Involvement of social workers with families in this way is "care" and the former concept of a child either being *in care* or *not in care* at any particular time has become somewhat blurred, except perhaps for statistical purposes.

There are, however, situations in which it is difficult or undesirable for a child to be cared for by his own parent or parents (because of their present circumstances) or by members of the wider family, and the question of admission of the child to local authority care has to be considered. Whether or not to admit to this form of care is one of the most important decisions a social worker will be called upon to make, especially in a case newly referred, in which there may have been no previous contact with the family.

The statistics for the years 1972-77 show that though admissions under the 1948 Act have fallen from 43.5 thousand to 36.8 thousand in 1977, they constituted 71% of the total admissions. The prevalence of short stay cases, and the vagueness of the "reasons" were referred to in Chapter 6.

These short-stay admissions appear to be arranged somewhat casually, despite the various studies which indicate that even a short separation of a child from a caring family can cause him deep distress.[1] Nor is that all. Admission to care will usually be followed by a financial assessment of the parents with a view to an agreement for contributions which may well cause temporary hardship and inconvenience to the parents, and will not improve relationships between the social worker concerned and the family.

Admission to care under the 1948 Act is the opening of a door into the unknown, and may lead by a long, unforeseen process to long-term care or treatment, perhaps in a community home. Not only will this be costly, but it may well lead to a loss of identity and a life of unhappiness. There are children who have been in continuous care for many years, having been admitted ostensibly because of a mother's illness, without any thought at the time that care might be protracted almost indefinitely. The Children Act 1975 gives rise to other anxieties about the possible consequences of admission in the future notably in the operation of the "time limit" procedures (Circular LAC (76)(15), Appendix 2). Many seminars on the 1975 Act have found, in discussing its application to a particular child, that the crucial decision was the reception into care in the first instance. If, with hindsight, this was mistaken, it often turned out to be irreversible; its consequences dominated all consideration of the future of the child.

In the proposed "Charter of Rights",[2] B.A.S.W. has included Principle 3, which reads: "Before a child is admitted to care an assessment of his family and home environment should be undertaken which will include the preparation of the child and his family for the admission, and their participation in the plans that are made." There is every reason for applying this principle in every case, however transient the need may seem to be; in an emergency, when it occurs, the same principle ought to be followed after the emergency has been dealt with, either by admission to immediate care, or, as will be suggested below, by admission to accommodation of an appropriate kind.

In the "assessment of his family and home environment", the weaknesses will be apparent, but if the family is important for the child, the strengths must be sought. Before the Housing (Homeless Persons) Act of 1977 came into operation, Social Services Departments would not receive a child into care simply because his family was homeless; they preferred usually to accept the far greater cost of accommodating the family as a whole, and in this had the support of social workers and of D.H.S.S. Circular 4/74.

There should be a similar attitude to reception into care in other circumstances, especially in those where short-term care appears to be required, or perhaps has been specifically requested.

On the following pages is an algorithm setting out the enquiry which ought to be made in every case in order to satisfy requirements as to eligibility for admission. This enquiry need obviously only be short and direct in the small number of cases in which the child referred has no parent or guardian (or custodian) or has apparently been abandoned, or "left to its fate". This situation, or something akin to it, may arise in the case of a child in hospital if parental interest is not preserved; Circular LAC (78)(16) on the Maintenance of Family Links draws special attention to the need for preserving home contact and gives advice on the steps to be taken by hospital based social workers when a child appears to be in need of the intervention of the local authority.

But apart from such cases, the question that arises in the enquiry is whether or not the parent or other person having custody is prevented from providing accommodation and maintenance, and if so, for what reason. In considering this issue, in some cases, it may appear to a social worker that there are ways of making accommodation available either in the child's own home, or elsewhere, by using the resources of the Department and making them available to the parent for his or her use, so that the parent in turn can make them available to the child. Is it out of the question for an authority to set aside accommodation in a community home, or foster home, which can be made available to parents on these lines? They would then be able to place their own children there without in any way diminishing their parental status, and without formal reception into local authority care.

The alternative, commonly practiced, is for the important decision about reception into care to be confused with the availability or non-availability of accommodation. It is too readily assumed that if a local authority provides a child with accommodation and maintenance he is automatically in local authority care, though there are situations in which this is not the case (*e.g.* detention under a place of safety order, or accommodation under s. 9 of the Mental Health Act 1959 for a child not in care under the Children Act).

It may be said that the alternatives to care are unrealistic, or that they are not available. They would be available to a family able to afford to make its own private arrangements, and should be available to any family which has the will and strength to remain intact.[1] Many Social Services Departments would make money available for the kinds of service set out in the algorithm in Chart C,[3] if social workers stated the case more strongly, rather than making extensive use of short-term care, apparently without much question. The home help service is obviously one of the principal supporting services, but in its traditional form of a few hours per week, largely to help the elderly, it cannot provide anything like the kind of service needed if children are to be able to remain in their own homes instead of being received into care. Perhaps there is a need for seeking this kind of helper in the locality of the family concerned: are there not people willing to help in the home, without being home helps? There are also great possibilities in the recruitment of full-time salaried home helps willing to live temporarily in the family home, or at least to give full-time service at the time when it is needed. A belief in the value of family care, as opposed to short-term local authority care, should enable social workers to make a very convincing case for the diversion of resources including residential and other accommodation in the direction of this kind of support, as set out in Programme C in Appendix A.

It is difficult to see how it can be decided that local authority intervention is necessary in the interests of the welfare of the child without first having made these full enquiries. There is perhaps a need for a short period of reflection similar to that provided by a place of safety order. Such reflection would of course be required of a parent or other person having custody, who should at this stage be helped to understand the implications of local authority care. There might also be much to be said for the making of a formal decision to admit, which would be recorded. As it is, only the fairly small number of committals to care are the subject of a formal decision, made by a court. The far larger number of admissions under the Children Act are made without any record of the decision having been made deliberately, rather than, as it were, *de facto*.

Before decision, full investigation of the circumstances must be made; in some cases, it may be possible for the child's need to be assessed during his voluntary attendance at or residence in a children's home or other suitable place. If assessment facilities are developed locally, it should be possible for children to attend on a daily basis at an assessment centre near their own homes (see Chapter 6), so that the decision as to care can be deferred until a full enquiry has been completed. There will, however, always be some cases in which, after careful investigation, care in the full sense of the word must be provided under Section 1 of the Children Act 1948.

There are a number of channels of admission to local authority care (some rarely used) which may be summarised as set out on pp. 000ff.

VOLUNTARY ADMISSION TO CARE AFTER ENQUIRY BY THE AUTHORITY

1. CHILDREN ACT 1948, s . 1

This section details the qualifications for admission to care; it will be seen in sub-s. 1(c) that the intervention of the local authority must be considered necessary. This implies that full enquiry will be made into the circumstances of each case before any decision to receive into care is made. The criterion (subject to the qualifications set out below) is the welfare of the child, which may of course require that he should *not* be received into care.

The local authority concerned is the one in whose area the child is at the time when the need for care arises. This authority may have no prior

RECEPTION INTO CARE   CHILDREN ACT 1948, s.1

CHART B
RECEPTION INTO CARE   CHILDREN ACT 1948, s.1

*As this is not a penal statue, the words "other circumstances" in s.1 need not perhaps be construed too strictly, but this algorithm raises the question so that thought will be given to the reality of the circumstances and whether in fact they prevent a parent from providing for the child. Other considerations arise

knowledge of the child or any responsibility for him but, nevertheless, has the duty of receiving into care if necessary.

The child must be under 17 years of age. The age of 17 is attained at the first moment of the anniversary of the date of birth.[4]

Sub-section 1(b) sets out the various conditions which, if established, qualify a child for admission to care. These are:

A   that he has no parent or guardian ("guardian" means a person appointed by a deed or will or by order of court); *or*

B   that he has been and remains abandoned or lost ("abandoned" implies that the child has been left to his fate; it would not be considered that the child had been abandoned if he was left in a place where he was likely to be received into care); *or*

C   that the parents or guardian are *prevented* by some specific reason from providing for the child's proper accommodation, maintenance and upbringing. They may be prevented either "permanently" (*e.g.* under detention in mental hospital) or "for the time being". The reasons stated are mental or bodily disease or infirmity or other incapacity or "any other circumstances"; this last is so wide that it covers many circumstances, including short-term illness of parents, eviction, desertion, unsatisfactory home conditions, and the other reasons for admission to care set out in Chapter 6 (page 62).

Reflecting the spirit of the legislation, the section is flexible enough to meet cases where the parent is in agreement, and the child, if old enough, consents.

Admissions to care must be made within the framework of the Act and there are cases where care may be desirable but cannot legally be provided under this section. A typical case of this kind would be where an uncle and aunt of a child, who have brought him up for some years, apply for financial assistance which could, they think, be given by way of boarding-out allowances, but the parents of the child are perfectly able and prepared to provide for him themselves.

Mention has been made of "application" from parents for admission to care and although this is usually received it is not essential. Admission to care is not a "welfare right" of a parent; it is the right of a child when it is justified. A child may be received into care from the home of someone who is not the parent or may be received when the parent is sentenced to imprisonment without making provision for the child, even if she does not apply. It is usual, however, for children to be received at the request of a parent, or both parents, and where the request is made by one parent only, the other one is also seen if this is possible. Under this section the duty of the authority is limited to *receiving* the child—it cannot *take* him. Occasionally a young person may wish to be received into care for some reason. This can be regarded in the same way as the former provision (now repealed) for a child to take refuge in a place of safety, and should be accepted as such.

A further point is that any child may be admitted to care, including one mentally disordered.[5] (Such children are the concern of the Social Services

Department in any event, whether in care under the Children Act or not, and may be provided with accommodation without being "in care".)

Where an authority has received into its care under s. 1(4) a child who is ordinarily resident in the area of another authority the second authority may agree to take over the care of the child and, even if it does not do so, may agree to accept financial responsibility for the cost of maintenance incurred by the "care" authority. Where there is a dispute between the authorities concerned as to the child's ordinary residence this may be referred to the Secretary of State for determination and many cases have been decided in this way. The general principle appears to be that the child's residence is not necessarily that of his parents, but that if the parents have the intention of taking over the care of a young child at some future time their place of residence may also be his. An older child may, of course, have determined his own place of residence by leaving home voluntarily. Residence, however, is always at the time of admission and not at any time prior to that; but children who are living in a particular place by virtue of some order, or official arrangement, are not regarded as resident there for the purposes of this section. (This provision does not apply to adoption arrangements, *e.g.* placings by parents or adoption societies.)

2.   CHILDREN ACT 1948, S. 29(6)

Where a voluntary home is to be closed by the Secretary of State (after investigation) he may require the local authority in whose area the home is situated to receive into their care all, or any, of the children concerned. The local authority is obliged to comply with this requirement whether or not the conditions of s. 1 apply and notwithstanding the fact that any of the children may appear to be over the age of 17.

3.   CHILDREN ACT 1958, S. 7(4)

When a child is removed from a foster home to a place of safety by order of a juvenile court or magistrate the local authority may receive him into care whether or not the conditions of s. 1 apply and notwithstanding the fact that he may appear to be over the age of 17.

4.   ADOPTION ACT 1958, S. 43(3)

There is a similar requirement under this section with regard to protected children removed from unsuitable surroundings by order of a juvenile court or magistrate.

Note.—see Chapter 7, Protection.

COMMITTAL TO CARE BY ORDER
OF A COURT
(usually after enquiry by the local authority or the probation service)

1. CHILDREN AND YOUNG PERSONS ACTS 1933-69

The local authority, local education authority, constable or authorised person (N.S.P.C.C.) may institute *care* proceedings in respect of a child or young person if there is a reasonable belief that it is necessary for the authority of a court order to be obtained.[6]

Criminal proceedings may be instituted against a child who is of an age to be prosecuted as in the past. The "qualified informant" provisions of the Act are not in operation.[7]

Neither care nor criminal proceedings will be commenced, as we shall see, without consideration of many factors but if and when it is finally decided that such proceedings will be taken the person responsible for bringing the child or young person before the court must inform the local authority,[8] which is required to make investigations and provide the court with such information relating to the home surroundings, school record, health and character of the person in respect of whom the proceedings are brought as appear likely to assist the court.

Although the making of such investigations and reports have always primarily been the responsibility of the local authority, it has been the general practice for home surroundings reports to be made by the Probation Service under s. 35 of the Children and Young Persons Act 1933, where this was the wish of the court. Now, under s. 9(1) of the 1969 Act, the duty is laid entirely upon the local authority but s. 34(3) enables the Secretary of State to apply s. 9 in stages; the practice from 1973 is for the local authority to be responsible for all reports in respect of children under 13, while reports on children and young persons over that age may be made by either the local authority or by the probation service where this is at present the local arrangement. Gradually the age of 13 will be raised so that eventually investigations and reports will be made as a rule by the local authority. The court may in any case, however, require reports from other sources, in particular from a probation officer under para. 3(5) of Sched. 5 of the 1948 Criminal Justice Act.[9]

In the light of the reports it receives, the court has to decide which course of action to adopt, subject to the general rule that when dealing with a child or young person brought before them, juvenile courts must have regard to the welfare of the child and must where necessary take steps to remove him from undesirable surroundings and make proper provision for his education and training.[10]

One of the orders which may be made by the court is a care order.[11] Such an order may only be made when a court finds that

    (a) one of the seven primary conditions is met (see Chapter 7); and
    (b) the child is in need of care or control which he is unlikely to receive unless the court makes an order, *or*

A child or young person has been found guilty of an offence punishable in the case of an adult with imprisonment.[12]

A care order may be made either initially or in substitution for a supervision order; in the latter event a court must still consider whether the care order is necessary to ensure care or control.

The following are the main provisions of a care order, which differs in some respects from the previous fit person order:

A   A person may be committed to the care of a local authority only; it is the duty of that authority to receive him into care and to keep him in care notwithstanding any claim by his parent or guardian. The consent of the local authority to the order is not required. (Fit Person orders made before 1 January 1971 are now deemed to be care orders.)

B   The care order gives to the local authority the same powers and duties in respect of the person committed as his parent or guardian would have, had the order not been made. In addition the local authority may restrict the liberty of the committed person as it considers appropriate, subject to regulations made under s. 43. The local authority may not, however, bring up a committed person in any religious creed other than that in which he would have been brought up had an order not been made.

C   The authority to be named in a care order is that for the area in which the committed person resides or if that is not known the local authority in whose area the circumstances arise.

D   The care order ceases to have effect when the committed person attains the age of 18 unless he was 16 when the order was made, in which event it remains in force until the age of 19. An order expiring at the age of 18 may, however, be extended to the age of 19 in the case of a person accommodated in a community home or home provided by the Secretary of State if this is in the interest of either the person concerned or the public.[13]

E   The care order may be discharged by a court on the application of the local authority or the child concerned. A parent or guardian may not apply, except on behalf of the child or young person. When the order is made in care proceedings, but not in criminal proceedings, the court may debar the parent or guardian from using the general power to represent the child. (See Chapter 11.) On discharging a care order the court may make a supervision order valid for three years, or up to the age of 18.

F   A person in respect of whom a care order is made will be treated in the same way as a person in care under a voluntary arrangement and, as s. 13 of the Children Act 1948 (as amended) applies, may be allowed to be under the charge and control of a parent, guardian, relative or friend though the care order remains in force. (There are Guidelines of Procedure (October 1978) intended to discourage the indiscriminate use of this local authority power.)

2.   INTERIM CARE ORDER

An Interim Care Order is a care order and has the same effect but only for twenty-eight days, after which it lapses and a further Interim Order must be made if the circumstances justify it. Interim care orders may be made for the purpose of initial protection as described in Chapter 7 or at any time during care proceedings. There is a right of appeal to the High Court as described in Chapter 7.

3.   REMAND ORDER

At any time during criminal proceedings the court may make an order remanding a child or young person on bail *or* may commit him to the care of the local authority for the period of remand.[14] (See Chapter 7 for restrictions on the use of remand centres and prisons.)

4.   DETENTION IN CARE

Where a person aged 10-17 is arrested with or without a warrant and cannot be brought before a magistrates' court to be charged with an offence; the case must be enquired into by a senior police officer who may release him in certain circumstances or make arrangements for him to be taken into care by a local authority.[15]

(Detention in a place of safety, is detention under an order for the purpose of protection as defined in Chapter 7. All community homes are places of safety which may be used for the purpose of protection, but detention in them is only for that purpose and does not constitute "care".)

5.   MATRIMONIAL CAUSES ACT 1973, s. 43

The law requires divorce courts, when hearing applications for orders, to consider the welfare of any children of the family under the age of 16 or still receiving education or training. This includes children who have been *treated* as members of the family by both parties to the marriage, for instance, stepchildren and adopted children. Where it appears that the custody of a child under 17 should not be given to either of the parties or to any other individual an order may be made committing his care to the local authority within whose area he resides, under s. 43 of the Matrimonial Causes Act 1973. Sometimes if a child is already in care, the court will order that he should not be discharged from care without the consent of the local authority, or alternatively, without an order of the court. (Practice Direction 23 May 1955, suggests the following wording in such cases: "And it is further ordered that the (Petitioner) shall not take over the care of the said child from the (local authority) unless that authority is satisfied that to do so would be consistent with the welfare of the said child.")

6. MATRIMONIAL PROCEEDINGS (MAGISTRATES' COURTS) ACT, SS. 2 AND 4(2)

This Act contains a similar power in respect of applications for matrimonial orders, except that *no child who is already in the care of a local authority* may be committed, nor may any child who has attained the age of 16 years. (This Act is to be replaced by the Domestic Proceedings and Magistrates' Courts Act of 1978, when implemented.)

Note.—In both Acts, "child of the family" includes one who has been accepted and treated as one of the family though not being the child of both husband and wife. This is a complicated issue calling for legal advice. Committal to the care of the local authority under paras 5 and 6, is only open to the courts in *exceptional circumstances* and does not confer parental rights—it only confers care and control. The information on which the court acts in such cases will normally be a report which the court may require from either a probation officer or a local authority social worker. See Chapter 14.

The consent of the authority to committal is not required, but it must be given notice of the proposal to commit and any representations by the authority must be heard with regard to the making of the order itself and with regard to maintenance of the child.

In divorce court cases fourteen days' notice to the authority is required; in magistrates' court cases ten days.[16]

7. FAMILY LAW REFORM ACT 1969, S. 7(2) AND (3)

Under this Act, a court which has jurisdiction in wardship proceedings may, in exceptional circumstances, commit a child who is the subject of proceedings to the care of a local authority. A local authority unable to safeguard the welfare of a child by using other legislation may apply for him to be made a ward of Court, with the expectation that he may be committed to care under this Act.

8. GUARDIANSHIP ACT 1973, S. 2

This Act amends the Guardianship of Minors Act 1971 so that when a court is dealing with an application for custody under s. 9, it may now, in exceptional circumstances, commit the care of a minor to a local authority. This power may be exercised in respect of a minor who is either legitimate or illegitimate, and by the High Court, a county court or a magistrates' (domestic) court, whichever is dealing with the application under the Act of 1971.

9. CHILDREN ACT 1975, S. 17

In refusing to make an adoption order, a court may now, under this section, commit the child to the care of a local authority in exceptional circumstances.

10. CHILDREN ACT 1975, PART II (CUSTODIANSHIP)

When this Part of the Act is implemented, a court will be able to commit the care of a child to a local authority when it revokes a custodianship order, provided that after the revocation there would be no other person having the legal custody of the child (s. 36). And, as applications are governed by the Guardianship Act 1973, a court may make such a committal order when custodianship is being sought.

In cases arising under both 9 and 10 above, s. 4 of the Guardianship Act 1973 applies to a child so committed to local authority care.

GENERAL

To summarise, a court dealing with guardianship, matrimonial, wardship or adoption proceedings, in which minors are involved, has power to commit the care of a minor to a local authority in much the same way, subject to the limitations on the magistrates' courts with regard to age, and other matters. Such orders are not, however, "Care Orders" as defined in s. 24 of the Children and Young Persons Act 1969. This phrase is often used in connection with orders of committal to care under other legislation; it appears for instance in the child care statistics and in various official Circulars; its use can be a source of confusion to social workers in view of the considerable differences between orders made under the 1969 Act and those made under other legislation. The differences between children in care under the 1948 Act, Care Orders and others whose care is committed by the courts are set out in Chapter 11.

NOTES

1. "In defence of Parents", Holman, *New Society*, 1 May 1975.
2. "Children in Care—a Charter of Rights", B.A.S.W.
3. For further reading on the subject of reception into care, see *Casework before Admission into Care*, Jehu, and *Casework in the Child Care Service*, Noel Timms, London, Butterworths, 1962.
4. Family Law Reform Act 1969, s. 9.
5. Mental Health Act 1959, s. 9(3).
6. Children and Young Persons Act 1969, s. 1.
7. *Ibid.*, s. 5(9) and para. 75 of Guide to Part I.
8. *Ibid.*, s. 2(3) and s. 5(8).
9. *Ibid.*, s. 9(2).
10. C. and Y.P. Act 1933, s. 44.
11. Children and Young Persons Act 1969, s. 1(3).
12. *Ibid.*, s. 7(7).
13. *Ibid.*, s. 21.
14. *Ibid.*, s. 23(1) and (2).
15. *Ibid.*, s. 29(3).
16. Matrimonial Causes Rules and Matrimonial Proceedings (Magistrates' Courts) Act 1960. See also *Maintenance and Custody Orders in the Magistrates' Courts*, second edition, Brian Harris, Chichester, Barry Rose, 1974.

Chapter 10

THE POSITION OF PARENTS, STEP-PARENTS, GUARDIANS, RELATIVES AND CUSTODIANS

SUMMARY

COMMENT

There are certain inherent powers in the Family Division of the High Court independent of statutes but the lower courts are confined to making decisions in accordance with Acts of Parliament. Parents now have equal rights with regard to their children and may both, for instance, appoint guardians by will, or apply to a court for custody, access or order on matters affecting a child's welfare. The powers of the High Court as regards guardianship or otherwise are not affected by the Children Act 1975 (s. 104).

DEFINITIONS

As the phrases "parent", "guardian", "relative" and "custodian" appear fairly often in children's legislation, it would be as well to have these defined.

PARENT

Married couples who have children by their marriage are parents. The Children Act 1948 defines the mother of an illegitimate child as the parent, to the exclusion of the natural father. Definitions of "parent" as including adoptive parent, as in the Children Acts 1948 and 1958 are repealed by the Children Act 1975 as being unnecessary in view of the status of the adopted child set out in Schedule 1. ("Parent" is not defined in the Children and Young Persons Acts 1933-69 but is capable of a similar interpretation.)

The position with regard to the natural father of an illegitimate child is not, however, quite as simple as it appears because of the fact that a child may be legitimated by the subsequent marriage of his natural parents, even if they were not free to marry at the time of the child's birth. Similarly, a child of a void marriage (*e.g.* bigamy) may in certain circumstances be regarded as legitimate, the natural father becoming the lawful father.[1] Moreover, a natural father may apply under the Guardianship of Minors Act 1971 for the custody of his illegitimate child or for access. If he is given custody he acquires some of the powers of a lawful father for the purposes of the Guardianship Acts, and for adoption purposes becomes the guardian of the child.[2] The Family Law Reform Act of 1969 made changes in the relationship between an illegitimate child and his father, specially with regard to inheritance and registration of the child's birth. Section 93 of the Children Act 1975 (when in force) will further affect the question of registration.

STEP-PARENT

A very large number of children today have a step-father or step-mother following the remarriage of one parent after the loss of the other by death or divorce. Others, illegitimate children, have a step-father following the marriage of the mother to a man who is not the natural father.

The status of a step-parent has not been recognised in legislation prior to the Chidren Act 1975. Step-parents have no parental rights as such, but while they have the actual custody of a child they have the same duties towards him as if they had legal custody. They frequently feel that this is an unsatisfactory situation and may seek to acquire greater recognition of their position within the newly formed family unit. Without this, they have no legal standing if the child should appear before a court, or be received into the care of a local authority. For many years it has been usual for a step-parent to apply jointly with the natural parent for an adoption order, but one of the aims of the Children Act 1975 is to discourage such applications strongly by making it possible for a step-parent to acquire legal custody, which will to some extent meet the need for family recognition. In some cases, this can be done by using s. 42 of the Matrimonial Causes Act of 1973 under which the court may make an order granting custody to a step-parent who is married to a natural parent already awarded custody in a divorce case. For other step-parents, that is those who cannot use an already existing custody order, there may soon be the remedy of custodianship under Part II of the Children Act 1975.

CUSTODIAN

Step-parents may already in some circumstances become custodians—persons having legal custody of a child; the phrase "custodian" will be brought into operation when Part II of the 1975 Act is implemented, and will apply to a person in whom the legal custody of a child has been vested by an order of court. Such an order may be made on application by a relative, step-parent, or other person qualified by s. 33(3) to apply, or it may be made under s. 37 when the application is not for custodianship, but for an adoption order. Similarly it may be made under s. 37(3) when the application before the court is one for custody under the Guardianship of Minors Act, s. 9. The position of a custodian will be much the same as that of a legal guardian, and different from that of an adoptive parent. The order may contain a provision about access and the payment of maintenance by parents, and is revocable, on the application of the custodian, a parent or guardian of the child, or a local authority.

There will thus be possibilities of maintaining the link with the natural family; while a custodian will be in a position to give consent to marriage he will not be empowered to agree to adoption or to emigration, since these powers are reserved to parents or guardians.

GUARDIAN AND LEGAL GUARDIAN

A "guardian" is defined in the Children and Young Persons Act of 1933 as including any person who, in the opinion of the court, has for the time being the charge of, or control over, the child or young person.[3] The Department of Health and Social Security will regard as "guardian" anyone looking after an orphan child, or a child one of whose parents is dead and the other cannot be found.

There is a further definition of *legal* guardian in the Act of 1933, which means a person appointed according to law to be the child's guardian by deed or will or by order of a court. This latter definition is similar to the one included in the Children Act 1948, and in the Adoption Act 1958 as amended by the Children Act 1975, Schedule 1.[4] The powers of a legal guardian are of the same order as those of a parent and go far beyond merely having the charge or control of a child.

RELATIVE

A "relative" means a grandparent, brother, sister, uncle or aunt, whether full-blood or half-blood or by affinity. All references in previous Statutes to relatives by adoption are re-stated by the Children Act 1975, under the provisions of Schedule 1.

As regards illegitimate children, the father of the infant is regarded as a "relative" (though he may also be a guardian) as also are his relatives within the foregoing definition.[5]

Relatives have few rights but may be consulted in certain adoption cases.[6] Adoption by relatives, especially grandparents, has been widely practised but is now discouraged by the Children Act 1975. It is still permissible, but it is likely that custodianship, when available, will be considered preferable unless there are exceptional circumstances. (See Chapter 15.)

In legislation affecting the supervision of children there are certain commonsense exemptions where relatives are concerned.[7]

PARENTAL RIGHTS

Generally speaking, both lawful parents of a child, or any legal guardian of a child, are presumed to have the custody of the child, and do not lose custody simply by deserting the family or living separately from it.[8]

With regard to a child in the care of a local authority, therefore, the authority only has "actual possession or control" and this does not diminish the parents' rights *except* in the circumstances set out below. The status of a parent may be affected in one or more of the following ways:

1. CUSTODY ORDERS

These may be made by the Family Division of the High Court or, under the Guardianship of Minors Act, by the Family Division of the High Court, county court or court of summary jurisdiction. They may also be made by the Court in divorce cases or by the magistrates court in hearing matrimonial proceedings under the Matrimonial Proceedings (Magistrates' Courts) Act 1960 (to be replaced by The Domestic Proceedings and Magistrates' Courts Act 1978.)

In any of the foregoing cases custody may be given to one parent as against the other *or* may be given to a third party. (As mentioned above, a natural father may be granted custody in preference to the mother.)

When Part II of the Children Act 1975 is implemented, the High Court, a county court or a magistrates' court will be in a position to make custodianship orders which will confer the legal custody of a child on a person who is not a parent.

A court hearing an application for an adoption order but deciding to make an interim order may give the *custody* of the child to the prospective adopters for a period of not more than two years.[9]

The existence of any custody order as described above has an effect on the reception of children into care under the Children Act. Wherever the word "parent" or "guardian" appears in ss. 1-5 of the Act it is to be interpreted as referring to the person who has the custody.[10] It is, therefore, quite lawful for the child to be received into care from a parent or other person having custody without the consent of the parent or parents deprived of custody, but an important consideration in such cases is that the parent or parents deprived of custody may nevertheless have the right of access to the child and probably, therefore, a right to be informed of the action which is being taken. He, or she, cannot however claim the child from the local authority as of right. This has a particular bearing on discharges from care and will be considered later. Similarly, in juvenile court proceedings any parent or guardian may be required to attend, and this is held to include a person who has been deprived of custody by order of court.[11] When a custody order is made under the Guardianship of Minors Act 1971, the agreement of parents may be required for marriage and is required for adoption.[12]

2. CARE ORDERS (CHILDREN AND YOUNG PERSONS ACT 1969)

These may be either full care orders, interim orders or warrants remanding to the care of the local authority. Such orders commit the child or young person to the care of the local authority which then has the duty of receiving him into care and keeping him in care for the duration of the warrant or order notwithstanding any claim by his parent or guardian. The authority then has the same powers and duties as the parent or guardian would have, but for the order.

No care order permits the authority to bring the committed person up in any religious creed other than that in which he would have been brought up apart from the order. Nor does it empower the authority to consent to adoption or arrange emigration for the child without parental consent. The power to consent to marriage is uncertain, so that some custodial powers remain with the parents, while the care order conveys to the local authority the care and control of the child and possibly such powers as applying for a grant of administration, or changing the name of the child by deed poll. There is one additional power for the local authority. It may, subject to Regulations, restrict the liberty of the committed person to such an extent as it thinks appropriate. (This is referred to in Chapter 11.)

There are provisions for application for the discharge of interim orders and care orders.[13] There are also provisions for appeals against orders in criminal and care proceedings and for legal aid to be granted to a child by the court.[14] Applications for legal aid may be made to the clerk of the justices or the court Administrator, as the case may be, in advance of the hearing.

3. RESOLUTION

When a child is already in the care of a local authority under s. 1 of the Children Act 1948, the Council may pass a resolution assuming parental rights and duties in the following circumstances:[15]

A   that both parents are dead and the child has no guardian or custodian;

B   that *either* parent or guardian or custodian has abandoned the child. (If, after a child has been received into care, the whereabouts of any parent (or guardian or custodian) have remained unknown for twelve months, the child is deemed to have been abandoned);[16]

C   that he, or she, suffers from some permanent disability rendering him, or her, incapable of caring for the child;

D   that he, or she, suffers from a mental disorder (whether permanent or not) which renders him, or her, unfit to have the care of the child;[17]

E   that he or she is of such habits or mode of life as to be unfit to have the care of the child;

F   that he or she has so consistently failed without reasonable cause to discharge the obligations of a parent as to be unfit to have the care of the child;[18]

G   that a resolution on one of the foregoing grounds is in force with regard to one of the parents, who is or is likely to become a member of the household comprising the child and the other parent;[18]

H   that, irrespective of other grounds, the child has been in care throughout a period of three years, either entirely in the care of a local authority, or partly in such care and partly in the care of a voluntary organisation.[18]

In the case of A, a resolution would be in respect of both parents (if married) on the same ground, but otherwise it will be noted that a resolution may be passed in respect of *one* living parent or guardian or custodian and while it is in force that person loses his or her rights in respect of the child except those mentioned above under "care orders".

It is possible for a resolution to be passed with the agreement of the person concerned, but failing that, notice of it has to be served upon him and he is entitled to serve a notice in writing objecting to the resolution within a period of one month. In such cases the resolution will lapse unless the authority lays a complaint before a juvenile court within fourteen days. The court may order that the resolution shall not lapse by virtue of the notice served. Moreover, at any time while the resolution is in force application may be made to the authority for it to be rescinded or to a juvenile court for the resolution to be set aside.[19] There is now a right of appeal to the High Court from the decision of a juvenile court whether making or refusing to make a confirmation or termination order. This procedure is discussed further in Chapter 11.

Section 4B of the Children Act 1948, when in operation, will enable the juvenile court, or High Court, to make the child a party to the proceedings and to appoint a guardian *ad litem* to safeguard his interests.

4. ADOPTION AND OTHER ORDERS

An adoption order confers a new status on the child who is to be treated in law as if he were not the child of any person other than the adopter(s).[20]

5. MATRIMONIAL PROCEEDINGS ACTS

In either divorce or separation proceedings the court may in certain circumstances commit the care of the child, or children, to the local authority. It will be noted that it is the *care* and not the child which is committed and such orders do not confer parental rights on the local authority. The child must, however, continue in the care of the local authority notwithstanding any claim by a parent or other person. The court will not include any order as to access in such orders as this is a matter left to the discretion of the local authority concerned. A divorce court may declare a parent unfit to have custody of a child.[21]

6. WARDSHIP, ADOPTION, GUARDIANSHIP AND CUSTODIANSHIP PROCEEDINGS

In such proceedings, as in matrimonial proceedings, the court may in certain circumstances and with the same effect commit the care of a child to a local authority.[22]

7. GENERAL

It will be seen, therefore, that in dealing with children who have come into the care of the Council in any way it is most important that full information should be available as to the *method* of admission and the position with regard to parental rights and/or custody, especially as regards the natural father or other possible guardian or custodian.

Some children are admitted to care because of a deliberate decision by a court; in those cases the rights of parents are affected to a greater or lesser extent by the fact of admission, and in all such cases the parents lose the right to withdraw the child from care at will. By far the great majority of children are admitted, however, under Section 1 of the Children Act 1948 and this reception into care does not of itself affect the parent's legal status, or his right to withdraw the child from care. The position may change subsequently, by the passing of a parental rights resolution for instance, or by the requirement of 28 days' notice for the removal of a child who has been in local authority care for 6 consecutive months, or if the child should become a ward of court. Parental status may also be affected in the long term if a child in care should be placed with foster parents, since after 3 years they would be entitled to apply for custodianship (when available) and after 5 years for an adoption order, in both cases without parental consent or agreement.

But whether or not legal status of a parent is altered by the fact of a child's admission to care, there must inevitably be a change in the quality of day to day responsibility for the child. Once he enters the realm of "care", practical decisions will be made not by the parent but by the person providing daily care. There is a growing concern with the rights of children as individuals, and rightly so; but it is all too easy for the parents to lose their status and authority, if not their rights, unless active steps are taken to ensure that this does not happen, especially in those cases of children admitted for vaguely defined reasons, or without any clear plan for the future. This danger—loss of parental status by default—could often be minimised if, as suggested in a previous chapter, the admission to care under Section 1 could be deferred for full enquiry and explanation of the possible consequences; and even then made by a formal decision of the receiving authority.

Though it is no longer officially assumed that a parent whose child enters care is bad, and merits punitive treatment, it is still widely thought that the parent of a child in care ought to take the initiative in maintaining contact with him, and there is still a penalty for failing to do so. This attitude ignores the sense of loss and guilt which often accompanies admission to care; this is readily intensified by the virtual exclusion of the parent from the day to day care of the child, and by any failure of social workers to give the right priority to supporting parents in their need. The individual parent must feel helpless against the might of the local authority, and its staff, but there is some ground for believing that a group of parents of children in care could, given the opportunity, create a new dimension of "shared care" especially as regards children admitted under the 1948 Act. Experiments in group work with parents have been made, for instance in Nottingham, with encouraging results (*Social Work Today*, 2 October 1975).

PARENTAL DUTIES

GENERAL

The parents of children in the care of a local authority, even if deprived of some rights, continue to have duties. They must ensure that the authority, in whose care the child is, is kept informed of the parents' address; penalty for non-compliance is a fine of £10.[23] This was formerly only the case as regards children up to the age of 16 but the age limit has been raised to 18.[24] Parents are also liable to make contributions towards the maintenance of children, usually those under the age of 16.[25]

1. CHILDREN ACT 1948

Prior to the passing of this Act, the assessment of parents of children in care of Poor Law Authorities was governed by the Poor Law Act 1930, but the Act repealed these provisions and aligned the procedure as regards children in care under s. 1 of the Act with that already in operation under ss. 86, 87 and 88 of the Children and Young Persons Act 1933, in respect of children committed to care. The 1948 Act also introduced important changes in so far as the only persons liable *under these sections* to contribute towards the maintenance of a child were to be the father (excluding putative fathers of illegitimate children) and the mother (including mothers of illegitimate children). Payments by parents are due only so long as the child is *under the age of 16 years;* after that age he is liable to make contributions towards his own maintenance from his earnings, if any. Contributions under the 1948 Act are payable in respect of the following:

A Children in the care of a local authority under s. 1 of the Children Act 1948.

B Children committed to care under the 1969 Act, but not including children who are placed in their own home or those committed on interim care orders or remanded to care.[26]

ADOPTION

Contributions cease to accrue under (a) and (b) above where notice of intention to adopt a child is received by a local authority, but may be revived if the application to adopt is withdrawn or refused or if the application has not been made within twelve weeks from the date of notification.[27]

RECEIPT OF CONTRIBUTIONS

The "persons entitled to receive contributions" are the local authorities for the areas in which the parents reside. As the father and the mother are separately liable, more than one local authority may be involved if the parents are not living together.

AMOUNT OF CONTRIBUTIONS

Section 62 of the Act of 1969 amended the legislation relating to contributions under the Children Act 1948 and the C. and Y.P. Act 1969.

When a child is received into care or committed under a care order (except an interim order or a care warrant) and is under 16, the local authority must "propose" to the parents, known as the contributories, the amount of the contribution to be made. This amount may not exceed the weekly sum which the local authority would pay as a boarding out allowance, ignoring any "special" rate of allowance, for the child in question. In other words a parent is not liable for the running costs of a children's home or community home.

If the authority and the contributory cannot agree on the amount proposed within one month, or if they agree but the contributory defaults in one or more payments, the authority may apply for a contribution order. The court may not make an order for a sum greater than that proposed by the authority in the first instance. If an application is made to the court for a variation of a contribution order, the authority must propose an amount, and the variation ordered must not exceed that amount.

As stated above, contributions are not payable in respect of interim or remand orders, nor for any period when a committed child is living at home while a care order is in force.

TRANSFER OF PAYMENTS TO CARE AUTHORITY

Payments received by local authorities under agreements and under court orders in respect of children for whose maintenance other local authorities are responsible, are transferred to those local authorities half-yearly after the deduction of 10% administrative expenses.

AFFILIATION ORDERS

Where there is an affiliation order in force in respect of a child who falls in any of the classifications set out above, the local authority for the area in which the *putative father* is residing may apply to a magistrates' court in that area for the affiliation order to be varied for payment to that council. If the child in respect of whom the order is payable ceases to be in care and then at a later date returns, the local authority may apply for the order to be revived.[28] An affiliation order does not lapse on the death of the mother.

If there is no affiliation order in force when a child becomes in any way chargeable to a local authority then the local authority for the area in which the *mother* resides may try to make a voluntary agreement with the alleged father, or make application to a magistrates' court in the area for such an order to be made.[29] The application is dealt with as if it were being made by the mother herself but there is no need for her to appear unless the application is contested. In this event her evidence must be corroborated in a material particular, *e.g.* the blood test provision of the Family Law Reform Act 1969 (Part III). If the mother is dead or cannot be found to give evidence, no order can be made in a contested application.[30]

Money received under varied affiliation orders and affiliation orders made on the application of a local authority is paid over directly or through the Clerk of the Court to the local authority entitled to receive it, in the same way as the money paid under contribution orders.

RESTRICTIONS

An application by a local authority for an affiliation order must be made within three years of the date on which the child last came into the care of an authority.

ENFORCEMENT

In order to enforce payments due under affiliation orders application must be made to the magistrates' court for the area in which the *putative father* resides.

ATTACHMENT OF EARNINGS ORDERS

Orders made under s. 87 of the Children and Young Persons Act 1933, and s. 26 of the Children Act 1948, are defined as maintenance orders within the meaning of the Attachment of Earnings Act 1971. It is therefore possible for a local authority to apply for an attachment of earnings order in these cases. Money due under the orders is deducted from the contributor's earnings by his employer and forwarded to the Clerk of the Court for eventual transmission to the local authority. This is a very convenient method of obtaining money from unwilling contributors but if the contributor changes his employment, the order has to be re-directed to the new employer, if known.

CANCELLATION OF ARREARS

Courts have power to write off arrears of contributions due under court orders, usually in respect of sickness or unemployment. If a contributor is sent to prison in default, the arrears are not discharged by the imprisonment but may be remitted by the court subsequently. Arrears due under agreements may be enforced through the county courts as a debt, but alternatively may be written off by the local authority.

MOVEMENTS OF CONTRIBUTORS

The requirement that parents and putative fathers should keep the local authority informed of their whereabouts is intended primarily to enable the local authority to preserve the link between parents and their children. A secondary purpose is to assist local authorities to keep in touch with parents for purposes of parental contributions.[31]

When a parent moves away from the area of a local authority it is necessary for responsibility for the assessment and collection of contributions to be passed to the new area. The second authority will usually accept a voluntary agreement as the basis of contributions until such time as particulars of the contributor's means can be obtained and a new agreement completed. A similar procedure is followed in respect of contribution orders.

The second local authority will not usually accept responsibility for the collection of arrears which have accrued under voluntary agreements but will accept arrears due and enforceable under justices' orders.

The importance of prompt notification of changes in parents' addresses will, therefore, be appreciated. If a contributor moves sufficiently often from one local authority to another without giving notice, it is possible for him to evade payments and contact for a long period.

MISSING PARENTS

Attempts are made with varying success to trace parents whose addresses are not known. The Chief Officers of Police, the Salvation Army Bureau of Missing Persons, and in certain circumstances the Department of Health and Social Security are the chief avenues of enquiry. In addition, courts, but not local authorities, may obtain information from the Passport Office, the Ministry of Defence and the D.H.S.S., but only for the purpose of proceedings related to contribution orders.

RETROSPECTIVE CONTRIBUTION ORDERS

There is often unavoidable delay in obtaining contribution orders during which the contributor is able to evade payment. This is remedied to some extent by s. 30 of the Children and Young Persons Act 1963, which permits a court to make an arrears order with retrospective effect, provided the application for the order is made not less than three months after the end of the period of default. The period of default is defined as the period during which the person was liable to make contributions in respect of a child but no contribution order was in force. This provision for dealing with arrears covers the case of the contributor who defaults under agreement and an order is being sought against him.

2.   OTHER ACTS

MATRIMONIAL CAUSES ACT 1973
MATRIMONIAL PROCEEDINGS (MAGISTRATES' COURTS)
    ACT 1960 (DOMESTIC PROCEEDINGS AND MAGISTRATES'
    COURTS ACT 1978)
FAMILY LAW REFORM ACT 1969
GUARDIANSHIP ACT 1973, S. 2
CHILDREN ACT 1975, S. 17(3)

Provision is made under these Acts for court orders to be made requiring parents to contribute in respect of children whose care is committed to the local authority. The amounts of contribution are at the discretion of the court.

CHILDREN ACT 1975 (PART II)

Courts will be able to require the parents of a child to make payments to a custodian (not to the local authority) when a custodianship order is made.

CASE WORK APPLICATION

The view is widely held that the assessment and collection of parental contributions should be dealt with by administrative staff in the Social Services and or Treasurer's Departments of the local authority, in the same way as other financial matters. It is also considered by some local authorities that social workers will achieve a better relationship with parents if they are not responsible for this work.

There is, however, a need for liaison between the officers responsible for assessment and collections on one hand and social workers on the other. The obligation of the parents to contribute towards the maintenance of their children is an important factor in the relationship between the parents and the local authority.

The Social Services Department is responsible for dealing with families on other financial matters such as charges for home help services. In some instances a family will be receiving financial assistance under s. 1 of the 1963 Act at a time when money may already be due to the Authority in respect of one or more of the services provided.

The total financial position of the family can be considered by the department; authorities are in a position to integrate their procedures for assessment and collection (in respect of all services) in such a way as to support and reinforce their social workers in the best interests of the families concerned.

CHILD BENEFIT

The introduction of Child Benefit in place of Family Allowances (and sometimes tax relief for dependent children) seems to offer an opportunity of re-appraising policy on contributions in short stay cases under s. 1 of the 1948 Act; it would also seem to be relevant to consideration of a period of "accommodation" before formal admission to care in some such cases.

This Benefit is payable for the first 8 weeks of a period in care, whether or not the parent contributes towards the cost of maintenance. Thereafter it ceases to be payable during a period of care, except when the child lives at home for a period of at least one week during that period.

There is a procedure whereby a local authority informs the Child Benefit Centre of the movements of children in care.[32]

ACTUAL CONTRIBUTIONS FOR 1976-77

In considering the question of parental contributions generally, it is of interest to note that the cost of child care to local authorities for the year 1976-77 was £180m, excluding administration and field work; the average direct cost of maintaining a child in care was £42 per week, the total parental contributions amounted to £2,173,000, and the average weekly contribution by parents was less than 50p per child.[33]

It is obvious that the total amount contributed by parents is a very small part of the cost of the service, but it has to be remembered that in many cases a parent is assessed to pay a nil contribution, and that no payments are due in respect of children aged over 16 or of all those living at home while in care. There has for some years been disagreement about the value of assessing parents in those cases where the child is in care under the Acts of 1948 and 1969. In other cases, of course, the order is made by the court, after representations by the care authority, and not by the "proposal" procedure described above.

The obligation of parents to maintain their children dates at least from the Poor Law of 1601, and failure to do so is still an offence under s. 1 of the Children and Young Persons Act 1933, while the parent has the charge and control of the child. It is therefore argued that the obligation continues even though the child is in care; this view is expressed in the legal requirement that it is the duty of a parent to contribute, according to his or her means, while care continues, but only up to the age of 16.

In many cases there is no income apart from state benefits, so that if an initial assessment is made the money will in effect be laboriously transferred from the D.H.S.S. via the parent to the local authority, at considerable cost of time and effort. In other cases, there is income from employment, often with the addition of child benefit, and this is assessable according to whatever scale a local authority has adopted.

There are those who feel that parents find it hard to understand why they should be required to contribute towards the maintenance of their children while they are in care, since they do not make any payment when they are being maintained in hospital, or in a special school (apart from pocket money and clothing). If the duty to maintain in one set of circumstances has been eroded, why not in another? Advocates of this point of view also consider that the administrative costs of assessing and collecting parental contributions are so high as to make it unprofitable, and they also point out that the process in itself can create friction with a family, with detrimental effects upon the plans of the social worker involved. Social workers themselves very rarely find themselves called upon to deal with the contribution aspects of a case, and probably prefer to leave this to administrative staff, in rather the same way as Mr Spenlow in *David Copperfield* left all the unpleasant work to his partner Mr Jorkins. Whatever the merits of these two opposing views, the position broadly is that the willing contributors pay, while others do not, there being very limited powers of enforcement by the courts even if an order is obtained.

That there is a "duty" to contribute is not in doubt, but it is for each local authority to decide whether to enforce the duty, and, if so, by what means and to what extent. Automatic assessment in every s. 1 admission is not effective as a deterrent, if that is seen as its purpose. It is more likely that deterrence will be achieved by helping parents to understand the possible consequences of admission before giving their agreement to it; that should be a part of the preliminary investigation and discussion.

NOTES

1. Legitimacy Act, ss. 1 and 2.
2. Guardianship of Minors Act 1971, s. 14.
3. Children and Young Persons Acts 1933, s. 107(1).
4. *Ibid.*, Children Act 1948, s. 59(1), Adoption Act 1958, s. 57 as amended.
5. Children Act 1948, s. 59(1), Adoption Act 1958, s. 57, Children Act 1958, s. 36, Nurseries and Child-Minders Regulation Act 1948, s. 13, all as amended.
6. Adoption (C.C.) Rules 1976.
7. Nurseries and Child-Minders Regulation Act 1948, Children Act 1958, as amended, Adoption Act 1958.
8. C. and Y.P. Act 1933, s. 17 for example.
9. Adoption Act 1958, s. 8.
10. Children Act 1948, s. 6.
11. C. and Y.P. Act 1933, s. 34.
12. Guardianship Act 1973.
13. C. and Y.P. Act 1969, s. 21(2).
14. *Ibid.*, Schedule 1 and Home Office Circular 299/1970.
15. Children Act 1948, s. 2.
16. *Ibid.*
17. *Ibid.*
18. *Ibid.*
19. Children Act 1948, s. 4.
20. Children Act 1975, Schedule 1, Part II.
21. Matrimonial Causes Act 1973, s. 42(3).
22. Family Law Reform Act 1969; Guardianship Act 1973; Children Act 1975.
23. Children Act 1948, s. 10; C. and Y.P. Act 1969, s. 24(8); Matrimonial Causes Act 1973, s. 43; Matrimonial Proceedings (Magistrates Courts) Act 1960, s. 3; Family Law Reform Act 1969, s. 7; Guardianship Act 1973, s. 4(6) which also applies to a child committed under the Children Act 1975, s. 17.
24. C. and Y.P. Act 1969, s. 24(8).
25. Children Act 1948, ss. 23 and 24.
26. C. and Y.P. Act 1969, s. 62.
27. Adoption Act 1958, s. 36.
28. C. and Y.P. Act 1933, s. 88.
29. Children Act 1948, s. 26.
30. Affiliation Proceedings (Amendment) Act 1972.
31. Home Office Circulars 204 and 206/1963.
32. Child Benefit (D.H.S.S.).
33. *Children in Care 1977.*

Chapter 11

TREATMENT OF CHILDREN IN CARE

SUMMARY

This subject, which was at one time the most important component of "child care" is dealt with in Part II of the Children Act 1948, as amended by the Children and Young Persons Act 1969 and the Children Act 1975. Sections 11-22 apply to all children in care, but there are some modifications affecting some of those committed to care by the courts, and it is therefore important in all cases to ensure that the authority for admission is clearly and readily apparent. This can be achieved by some simple system such as the use of different coloured files according to the category of care.

"Treatment" in this context has no therapeutic meaning; it merely means that there are various ways in which children in care may be dealt with; general guidance is to be found in s. 12(1) which contains the "welfare principle" introduced by the Children Act 1975 with its concern for the child's welfare "throughout his childhood", and the consideration of his "wishes and feelings" in arriving at any decision about him. It should not be thought that there is anything new in this principle; it has always been implicit in child care practice, but is here given formal recognition. It is obviously right to consult young people on matters affecting them as individuals, such as where they shall live while in care, but, as the Association of Directors of Social Services has had to point out, the rights of children should not be used by other people as a device to secure political or administrative ends.

The wishes and feelings of a child can only be considered if they are known and expressed; s. 12 therefore requires the local authority to "ascertain" what they are, as far as practicable; this implies that there will be some one person who will know the child well enough to be able to enter into his inner hopes and thoughts. The Curtis Report of 1946 envisaged a child care organisation in which each child in care would have one person to whom he could look for continuous care and concern. In the simpler ethos of those days, it was expected that this one person would receive the child into care, keep in touch with him wherever he might be, advise and befriend him, and see him safely out of care at the age of 18, or—if he could return to his family—whenever that was possible.

In the event, continuity of this calibre was rarely achieved because of staff changes, the pressures of added responsibilities and practical difficulties arising from the geographical scatter of accommodation. In more recent years social workers have been increasingly involved in preventive work, though still without halting the admission to care of large numbers of children, often for purely temporary accommodation. They have also been much involved in dealing with children, mostly young, who are living at home but still at risk of ill treatment or neglect by their parents.

These activities have absorbed so much social work time and skill that too little attention has been paid to those children of all ages who have entered the state of Care and are likely to remain in it indefinitely. The plight of some of these children, all aged under 11, was examined in *Children who Wait* which stimulated a great deal of concern and activity. Some older young people have spoken for themselves in *Who Cares?* and in other groups which local authorities have promoted in an attempt to find out what being in care means to the children themselves.

There is now a growing recognition that children have rights of their own; this will receive further emphasis in the International Year of the Child. So far as children in care are concerned, B.A.S.W. has drawn up a Charter stating that every child in care has a right to:

1. individual respect and consideration, even though his rights and needs will be closely associated with those of others;
2. be looked after by skilled adults who have been specially selected and who have a commitment to the understanding and meeting of his individual needs;
3. A full assessment of his family and home before he is admitted to care; and to preparation for admission and participation in the plans made at that stage;
4. live in an environment which is conducive to his emotional, physical, social and intellectual development;

5. individual attention which shows recognition of, and respect for, his unique identity;
6. information concerning his circumstances and participation in the planning of his future;
7. administrative standards and procedures within his caring agency which will protect him and promote his interests;
8. the protection of the law (including Section 2 of the Children Act 1948).

This Charter establishes the child as a "client" in his own right; point 3—an addition to the original draft—stresses the fundamental importance of proper preliminary enquiry under s. 1 of the Children Act 1948 which was discussed in Chapter 9. Once in care under that section the child is subject to the hazards of separation from home and family, and to the possible operation of the time limit provisions which may change the whole course of his life.

The other points in the charter would best be met in a continuous relationship between the child and one social worker; but as this has largely proved to be impossible for various reasons efforts are being made to meet the need for continuity in other ways. One of these is the appointment of a "key worker" (either a field or residential social worker) who is recognised as the focal point for future planning. Another is the emergence of teams of social workers concerned only with children in long-term care, and with no other duties. But whatever the arrangements made for continuity the essential element is the capacity of those concerned to communicate with the child himself, to know him as a person, and to stand by him during his time in care. Words are not enough to help a child to understand what is happening in his life which seems to be controlled and directed by others. There must be understanding of his thoughts and perhaps gestures, or his play. To attain the proper level the social worker must be prepared to work with, rather than for, the child, and to see the world through his eyes. This is a demanding task but one which cannot be avoided if the child is to find any meaning in his experience of care. Some idea of the depth and breadth of this aspect of social work is to be seen in the training material called "Planning for Children in Long-term Care", and in "Working with Children who are Joining New Families".[1] Its importance was also emphasised in papers given at the B.A.S.W. Child and Family Care Conference in 1977, under the arresting title "Face to Face with Children".

However, the rights of children in care, though important are not paramount; they do not take precedence over any need to protect members of the public; s. 12(1A) therefore empowers a local authority, if necessary, to act in a manner which may not be consistent with the welfare principle set out in s. 12(1).

Under s. 12(2) which is of general application, a local authority is also required to make use of facilities and services which are available for children who are in the care of their own parents; this is necessary to avoid discrimination between children who are living in their own homes and children who are in care. This involves the use of such facilities as special schools or hostels for handicapped children (provided by the Education Department), youth employment service, hospitals, mental hospitals and any other form of treatment or service available to children living with their own families. Education Committees have certain welfare powers and in order to avoid conflict with these, there are regulations which lay down how they are to be applied to children in care; thus children in care do not receive free school meals, free milk or clothing provided by the Education Committee, as the authority is regarded as a parent having sufficient resources to pay for these services. On the other hand, a child in care who is placed in a special school or similar educational establishment is maintained there by the Education Committee, except as regards clothing and pocket money, which are provided by the local authority acting as parent.

Section 12 taken as a whole regards a local authority as a surrogate parent to all the children in its care; but in practice the quality of this "parenthood" will vary according to the method of admission to care. All court orders committing children to care entitle the authority to retain possession of the child, regardless of any claim by a parent or guardian (or custodian). Orders made under the 1969 Act go further in that they confer upon the authority the same powers and duties as a parent or guardian; and further still empower the authority to restrict a child's liberty to an appropriate extent.

All children committed to care by court orders are in a very real sense in the care of the authority, rather than in the care of parents. On the other hand, children admitted to care by the decision of the local authority itself may remain the responsibility of the parents who do not, by the fact of admission, forfeit any of their natural rights, powers, or duties. There is thus an inherent difference between children entering care in these two ways; the difference is basically that of the status of the parents. When their status is not restricted by an order of court, the local authority has an underlying duty to secure that the care of the child is taken over from the authority by a parent, guardian, relative or friend (with safeguards regarding religious upbringing) provided that this transfer of care is consistent with the welfare of the child. In such cases there should therefore be a positive effort towards restoring children to families or friends; advice guidance and assistance to this end must be made available under s. 1 of the Act of 1963.

In the case of children coming into care as a result of court orders there is no similar duty to make positive efforts to restore them to their families, though s. 1 of the 1963 Act may still be invoked when such a restoration would promote the welfare of the child concerned. A court order thus infringes the status of parents and gives effective control of the situation to the authority. An authority wishing to obtain the same kind of control over a child who has been admitted to care voluntarily can take administrative action to achieve it, subject to a number of safeguards.

PARENTAL RIGHTS RESOLUTIONS

Whenever it is felt that positive efforts should *not* be made to return a child in voluntary care to his parents, or whenever an immediate request for his return would be unwelcome, there may well be a case for consideration of a resolution under s. 2 of the 1948 Act, by which the rights of either or both parents might be assumed by the authority.

There is a wide variation between authorities in the use of this provision, and there is reason to suppose that many of those children who have been in care for considerable periods of time should have the protection that a resolution would afford. In the well-known study *Children who Wait*,[2] it is argued that most of the children in care with an uncertain future have family backgrounds which would justify the use of s. 2. The existing grounds are already very wide, but are not perhaps always understood in some authorities as they are in others.

Reluctance to take the necessary action may be due to an opinion that the passing of a resolution is punitive towards parents who are themselves in need of help; or it may be felt that a resolution will bar the way to rehabilitation; or, simply, that the decision is a hard one to take and tends to be deferred from one crisis to the next. Possibly the resolution is viewed in the wrong way altogether, and is looked upon as a dramatic intervention against a child's parents rather than as a means of ensuring the creation of a plan of what will be best for both child and parents in the longer term. The effect of a resolution is to give to the local authority the care and control of the child in a way very similar to that of a care order, so that it can plan the future either towards rehabilitation into the family, or away from it, without the constant threat of parental intervention at the wrong time or for the wrong reason; for instance because of some concurrent action in connection with financial assessment or enforcement of 'arrears. There is no need for a resolution to remain in force for a long period if a shorter time is sufficient for the purpose; and even while it is in force, the child may be placed with his parents and live with them in a normal way, though still remaining in care. But its very existence, for either a short or long period, gives protection to a child, and makes objective planning of the future possible. None the less, the use of s. 2 powers is not to be undertaken lightly; it is an administrative action by the local authority, but is subject at every stage to the scrutiny of the courts, and the parents are eligible for legal aid. A helpful Practice guide on the subject of s. 2 Resolutions has been published by the Association of British Adoption and Fostering Agencies. It examines the principles and illustrates their application to children in several different, but typical, situations.

When the passing of a resolution is contemplated, there are a number of steps to be taken, the following being the suggested order.

1. Find out when and by whom a resolution will be passed. The powers vest in the local authority but are almost certainly delegated to the Social Services Committee, which may have redelegated them to a sub-committee or to some specially constituted panel of officers and

members. Any such delegations must be duly recorded in the minutes of the authority and may later have to be proved in evidence.

If the powers have *not* been delegated by the Social Services Committee only that Committee can pass a resolution, and there may therefore be delay until the next meeting. To overcome this difficulty, some authorities have instituted special panels which may be convened at short notice and possess delegated powers to deal with certain urgent matters, such as this.

2. Consider the grounds on which a resolution may be passed (see Chapter 10) and decide which is to be used, that is to say which can be proved in the event of an objection.

3. Except in the case of (a) and (b), discuss with the parent concerned the needs of the child, the present parental circumstances, the need for unhurried planning of the child's future, and the long-term objectives, with a view to securing the agreement of the parent to the passing of a resolution on the appropriate ground. If agreement is obtained it must be in writing and contain an acknowledgement of a full explanation of the nature and purpose of a resolution, the parental rights which it would convey and those it would leave with the parent, and the possibility of its being rescinded or revoked at a later date. There are other matters such as continuing liability to maintain the child, but these are usually contained in a specially designed form of agreement for this purpose. The obtaining of parental agreement offers the best opportunity of planning long-term care of a child, with a parent who is fully aware of the views of the social worker and who can, at the same time, be offered help in arriving at the right decision for the child in all the known circumstances.

4. If, however, agreement is not obtained, the evidence for a resolution must be assembled, *e.g.* proof of death in (a), proof of abandonment in (b), medical evidence in (c) and (d) and social worker evidence in (e), (f), (g) and (h).

5. Produce a report for the Committee or other body empowered to pass a resolution, stating the full names of the parent or parents concerned, date of reception of the child into care, the stated reason, the present circumstances and relevant previous history, especially of periods in care.

6. After the resolution has been passed and recorded, no further action is necessary in cases in which there is no parent or guardian, or in which a parent has given written consent as in 3 above. In all other cases, a notification of the passing of the resolution and the grounds for it must be personally given or sent to the parent concerned by recorded delivery at the last known address. The notification must inform the parent of the right to object, in writing, to the authority within one month of the receipt of the notification, and of the action which will be taken if a notice of objection is in fact received. (It is usual for there to be a form of notification in these cases, but normally it will be accompanied by a less formal letter of explanation. The contents of this letter will vary according to the attitude of the parent when the possibility of agreement was being discussed.)[3]

7. If no notice of objection in writing is received within one month of the delivery of the notification, the resolution stands.

8. If a written notice of objection is received, immediate action must be taken by the authority to lay a complaint before a juvenile court (not before the clerk or a single justice). The complaint may be made in person or in writing, but if it is not validly made to a juvenile court within fourteen days of the receipt of the objection, the resolution will lapse and become null and void.

On hearing the complaint, the juvenile court will, if satisfied with the substance of it, fix a date for the hearing of the case and will issue summonses to the parent or parents concerned, but not to the child. It is then that the evidence in support of the resolution will have to be given on behalf of the authority, which will almost certainly be represented by a member of its legal staff. It is necessary to prove not only that the grounds for the passing of the Resolution existed, but also that those, or other, grounds still exist at the time of the court hearing, *and* that it is in the interest of the child for the Resolution to continue.

The juvenile court at this hearing may either uphold the resolution by ordering that it shall not lapse, or refuse to make such an order. Either the parent or the local authority has the right of appeal to the High Court against the decision of the juvenile court. At any subsequent time, a parent may apply to the authority for the resolution to be rescinded by another resolution, or may apply to a juvenile court which may, after hearing the evidence, set it aside. There is provision in the new s. 4B for the juvenile court or the High Court to make the child a party to the proceedings and to appoint a guardian *ad litem* to safeguard his interests, but this is not yet in force.

The emphasis of the Act, however, is clearly on co-operation with parents with a view to returning children to their care eventually and this underlines the need for the position of parents to be continually borne in mind even in those cases in which the authority has parental rights, unless a decision has been made that the child's future does not lie with the parents.

The assumption of parental rights by a local authority or the committal of a child to care, which were discussed in the previous chapter, do not generally authorise the authority to act directly contrary to the parents' wishes where these are reasonable, and there are certain matters in which the parents' rights are preserved. These are as follows:

RELIGIOUS PERSUASION

Each Act dealing with children and young persons in care contains provisions with regard to religious upbringing, though only in a negative way. A care order or Resolution does not authorise a local authority to cause the person concerned to be brought up in any religion except that in which he may have been brought up but for the order or Resolution.[4]

So far as children in care under the Children Act are concerned, the authority would normally expect to arrange for a child to follow his own religious persuasion. This is normally the religion of the parents, particularly the father, but this is to be considered in conjunction with the welfare of the child himself. If, for instance, a child has been brought up, before coming into care, in a faith other than that of his parents it is considered that there should be no disturbance of the situation. It would also be possible for a child of mature judgement to decide to change his own religious persuasion, even if this was not in accordance with the wishes of his parents. In any event, however, parents who were available would be consulted on all matters of this kind.

MEDICAL TREATMENT

It is usual for parents to be asked to authorise the Social Services' Committee to give consent for any immunisation, operative or medical treatment which may be necessary while the child is in care. Some parents may have conscientious objections to a particular form of immunisation or treatment and even where the authority has parental rights these are not generally used to overrule the parents' wishes. Moreover, any authority having a child in care would make it the normal practice to inform the parent of any serious accident, illness or operative treatment which may be required and would normally endeavour to obtain parental agreement before giving the necessary authority. "Blood" cases are dealt with in Chapter 8. Under the Family Law Reform Act 1969 (s. 8), a minor over the age of 16 may himself consent to any surgical, medical or dental treatment and if he gives consent, that of his parent or guardian is not required.

EMIGRATION

Although the local authority is permitted, with the consent of the Secretary of State, to arrange for the emigration of any child in care (except those committed in matrimonial, wardship, guardianship, adoption or custodianship proceedings), the Act requires that the parents or guardian shall be consulted; in this context "parents or guardian" includes those who have been deprived of their parental rights.[5] For procedure see Chapter 12.

ADOPTION

Although the authority may have obtained the rights or powers of the parent, or parents, concerned, it is not empowered to give agreement to the adoption of a child in care.[6] As we shall see, the only agreements required are those of the parents of a child and if these cannot be obtained the court can either dispense with them on certain grounds or decline to make the order. The powers of the local authority cannot be used to overrule the wishes of the parents in this matter.

MARRIAGE

The powers of a local authority under a resolution are thought to include the power to give consent to the marriage of a child but, here again, it would be the normal practice for this consent to be obtained from a parent, if possible, before the authority exercises its powers.

GENERAL CONSIDERATIONS

Children and young people enter care at all ages up to 17; some, under present arrangements, remain for only a very short time, while others may stay in care for many years, sometimes up to the age of 19. Some may be expected to return to their families, but others need, and are entitled to receive, a form of care which will be constant and secure; which will equip them to take up the responsibility of adulthood at the age of 18.

All those in care, if even for a short time, are in a sense the wards of the local authority for so long as care lasts but so far as possible their parents should be consulted about important decisions; even when the authority has parental rights, or powers, it must exercise them carefully and with due consideration for the future of the child and his relationships with his natural family. At the same time, it must be remembered that decisions have to be made in order to avoid the drift into unplanned indefinite periods of care, which have recently been shown to be not uncommon. If decisions are not made consciously they will be made in default by circumstances; one of the most important of these is the passage of time.

Not only is the time factor important to a child, in that it will affect his power to appreciate relationships with those nearest to him; it is vital to the planning of any period of care; its effects must be carefully explained to parents not only at the outset, but before each landmark is reached. This is particularly important in the case of a child in care under the Children Act 1948, since for him there are successive stages at which parental status and freedom may be impaired. But for all children there are stages at which those in foster care may be virtually lost to their natural parents by either custodianship, or adoption. The full range of the time limit provisions, restricting the removal of children from care, is set out in Appendix 2 to LAC (76)(15), together with the decisions and position assessments which must be made at the appropriate time.

The A.B.A.F.A. publication *Practice Guide to the Children Act 1975* or *The Saga of the Smiles Family* examines and uses the principles of the Act in relation to fictional children. It has been widely used for training purposes.

REVIEWS

Though every child in care should have one social worker who is primarily responsible for the planning of his life in care, the periodical review should be the principal instrument for decision making. To quote the Seebohm report, para. 190:

"The progress of children committed to the care of local authorities must therefore be regularly and statutorily reviewed to establish whether it is necessary or desirable for them to remain in the particular kinds of care in which the authorities have chosen to place them. Parents and children must have the right to express their wishes at these times, taking account of the fact that some parents and most children will be unable or unwilling to challenge effectively the decisions which are taken."

This principle is partly recognised in s. 11 of the 1948 Act which requires the authority to review at least every six months the case of every child in its care.

It should be noted that when a local authority is carrying out a six-monthly review of the case of a child in care *under a care order*, it is required to consider specifically whether or not it should apply for the order to be discharged by the court. The initiative rests with the local authority.

There is no such specific requirement with regard to children not subject to care orders under the 1969 Act but this will presumably be adjusted, for children in care under the Children Act 1948, by the Regulations to be made by the Secretary of State. Other children, committed to care in matrimonial and other civil proceedings, can only be discharged from care by an order of the original court to which the authority can always make an application when it appears from a review that this step is justified.

Pending the issue of Regulations, the conduct of reviews is determined by each authority. Too often it seems that the pattern of the Boarding-out Regulations Review is applied, so that there is more concern about the child's immediate "welfare" than about the possibility of his restoration to his family. The reality of this issue is often obscured because reviews are carried out on an individual, rather than a family, basis. If two or more children of a family are in care and living apart from each other, probably in different kinds of "accommodation" and with different social workers, it is difficult to form any reliable overall view of their position or future as a family. Concentration on the immediate situation of each child as a separate person may be justified sometimes, but it has often lead to a loss of contact between siblings and to a failure to make decisions about the family as a whole. Reviews which are family oriented (following the general Seebohm principle) are time consuming and need careful organisation; but they offer a real prospect of incisive decisions, which should be the outcome of any review.

The expected Regulations will cover such matters as the frequency of reviews, the persons who should carry them out, the people who should be present, or whose views should be obtained, the content of the review, and the records to be kept. It is to be hoped that they will give clear guidance on the extent to which children and their natural parents should be involved as a matter of right.

The Review is, or should be, the focal point in the provision of substitute care for a child. It presents a regular opportunity of re-examining the reason for admission, the long-term intention of the family and the care authority, and the steps being taken to achieve that goal—which will usually be either restoration to family, or separation from it. It will therefore need to pay special attention to the physical placement of the child, since that may have a profound effect upon the plan for a child, and may even pre-empt it or abort it altogether.

METHODS OF ACCOMMODATION

A local authority having a child in its care under any of the relevant statutes has general responsibilities towards him and should exercise a form of parental care and concern through a particular social worker. At the most elementary level the child must be provided with accommodation and maintenance while in care; this may be done in several ways, most of which are laid down in the Children Act 1948, s. 13, but making a choice between them, either initially or at a later stage, is far from easy. As the Charter of Rights, mentioned earlier, shows, there are so many conflicting factors to consider that the use of any particular kind of accommodation ought always to conform with the long-term intention, so far as this can be reasonably determined at the outset. In other words placing should follow some rational assessment, not only of the child's needs, but of his likely future.

ADOPTION

Adoption is one possibility which can be considered for some children; it was advocated in the original Circular on the Children Act in 1948, when local authorities had no power to act as adoption agencies and would have had to seek the services of one of the voluntary societies. Later, authorities received adoption powers in the Act of 1958, but seem to have used them little, except in a small way for children boarded-out in the first instance. The Children Act 1975 will in due course introduce the new "freeing for adoption" procedure, thus bringing adoption into the main stream of child care as a means of providing for some children a permanent placing into a substitute family undertaking full responsibility. There is however no reason why adoption should not be seen as the right placing for some children without waiting for the new procedure; it is already possible if parental agreement has been given, or if there are proper grounds for dispensing with it.

BOARDING-OUT

This is still the statutory term for the process now widely known as "fostering" or "foster care"; these terms are themselves "generic" and are used to describe a number of very different arrangements. But they always refer to a situation in which a child has been placed by the authority in a household not his own with the intention that he will, for the time being, live there as a member of the family of the foster parent, or parents, as the case may be.

Foster parents range from the old-fashioned warm welcoming mother figure prepared to look after any child presented to her, to the more sophisticated foster parents living in a house provided and furnished by the organisation, and caring for a specified number of children in what is really a Home, but is called a foster home. This and many other experimental forms of foster care have been used during the last century. Diversity of method seems to be essential, as foster care is an important part of the service, though fortunately it no longer is the automatic first choice for any and every child and young person in care.

Recent years have seen the growth of schemes for recruiting and training foster parents, including "special" or "professional" foster parents for children presenting particular difficulties, or for older children who have tended in the past to remain in residential care. Some authorities have promoted special projects for the latter group, sometimes operating outside the main stream of foster care, while others differentiate between "special" and other foster parents by the treatment they accord them. Still other authorities consider that all foster parents have the same need for training, participation, and mutual support as partners in child care, but on financial matters deal with each in accordance with the task they are being asked to undertake.

Foster parents, or many of them, feel the need for support and in many areas have formed themselves, with local authority encouragement, into groups. There is now a National Foster Care Association with its own staff and publication devoted to the promotion of foster parent skill and interest. The Association considers that the Boarding-out Regulations of 1955 need revising, and has prepared a draft of "Foster Care Regulations" which might replace them. For the present however, the 1955 Regulations made under the 1948 Act govern all forms of boarding-out by local authorities and voluntary child care organisations. Though 24 years old, they contain many valuable provisions and are intended primarily as a safeguard for the child. There are indications in research that from the point of view of the child the Regulations are still somewhat in advance of day to day practice.

So far as social workers are concerned, the most important features of the Regulations are as follows:

A   *"Boarding-out"*.—Means placing a child to live with foster parents as a member of their family (but does not include the placing of a child for adoption, which is done under the Adoption Agencies Regulations).[7]

B   *Foster parents.*—A child may only be boarded-out with:

   i   husband and wife jointly;

   ii   a woman only;

   iii   a man who is a grandfather, uncle or elder brother of the child;

   iv   a man who was acting jointly with his wife as a foster parent but whose wife has died or left the home.[8]

C   *Conditions.*—Before a child is boarded-out a social worker must have visited the foster home and have reported, in writing, on the material conditions, stating that the home is likely to meet the needs of a *particular child.*[9] The officer must either know the child concerned or be fully informed about him. The officer must also make a written report on the reputation and religious persuasion of the foster parents and their suitability in age, character, temperament and health for the care of a particular child, and must further report whether any member of the foster parents' household suffers from any physical or mental illness or has been convicted of any offences which would make the placing of the child undesirable (see Appendix C for suggested all-purpose investigation).

(NOTE: In practice, the latter enquiries as to health and criminal record are made officially in writing, as there are certain difficulties about obtaining sufficient information.)

Before a child is placed in a foster home which has been approved he must have been medically examined during the previous three months and a written report as to his state of health[10] must be available.

D   *Medical care.*—Arrangements must be made for medical examination of the child within one month of boarding-out if under the age of 2 years. Thereafter six-monthly while under the age of 2 and annually[11] if over that age. (This requirement is resented by many young people, especially after they reach school leaving age. It may be possible in suitable cases, for the authority to overcome opposition by deciding that the young person should be discharged from "care", and be offered after care.)

Arrangements must also be made for the child to receive medical and dental attention as required.[12]

E   *Undertaking.*—The foster parents are required to sign a form of undertaking,[13] which may be modified if the child is over compulsory school age.[14]

F   *Visitation.*—In addition to a visit within one month of the placing, the officer is required to visit a child under 5 years of age every six weeks for the first two years and thereafter once every three months. A child over 5 years of age at the time of the placing must be visited every two months for the first two years; thereafter every three months.[15]

With regard to children over compulsory school age, the regulations do not, in fact, require visits to be paid but state that the officer must *see the child* within three months of attaining school-leaving age and thereafter every three months.[16] (This provision can be very useful in certain cases if there should be any difficulties about visiting the foster home, though normally visits are paid as in the case of young children.)

In addition to the periodical visits or interviews laid down above, an officer must visit the foster home or see the child within one month of any change of address and *immediately* if any complaint is received about or from the child himself.

The officer must make a written report on the child's welfare, health, conduct and progress after each visit and after each interview with the child.[17] (*It should be noted that the frequency of visits laid down in the regulations is to be regarded as a minimum.*) If the authority is of opinion that the boarding-out of a child with particular foster parents is no longer in his interest[18] it is required to remove him from the foster home; in emergency, an officer has the power to remove a child forthwith, though normally this would be done after consultation with a more senior officer.[19]

G *Reviews.*—The case of each child should be *reviewed* before placing with foster parents, within three months of the placing and thereafter not less than every six months, and such reviews are to be made by persons not acting as visitors.[20] (These reviews may also serve as the reviews required for all children in care, whether boarded-out or not. The review after three months is vital; though it is only mandatory for a child who has been boarded-out, it should be applied in every case, and is recommended in the "time limit" table in Appendix 2 of LAC(76) (15).)

H *Short-stay boarding-out.*—Short-stay boarding-out is still extensively used in the cases of children who come into care for a short period, for instance, during mother's confinement, operation, etc. The principles of the regulations apply but there are certain modifications if the period of stay is expected to be less than eight weeks; these are as follows:[21]

i   the report on the foster home must be made in writing by the officer indicating that this placing is likely to be suitable for a particular child;[22]

ii the foster parents need not complete a form of undertaking but they must be informed of the child's religious persuasion and their obligations as foster parents;[23]

iii visits must be made within two weeks of the placing and thereafter not less than every four weeks;

iv in the case of children over compulsory school age a visit must be made within one month;

v   in all cases a visit must be paid on receipt of any complaint about or from the child.[24]

If the short-stay boarding-out lasts for eight weeks and is then expected to exceed a further four weeks, the boarding-out must be treated as long-stay and will come under the full scope of the regulations.[25]

I *Child already in foster home—Reception into care.*—It sometimes happens that a child is received into care while living in what amounts to a foster home. Such cases include those where an uncle or aunt, or other person, is caring for the child without financial assistance and applies for the child's reception into care so that an allowance may be paid. In such instances, the regulations provide that the child shall *not* be removed from the home in order that the necessary enquiries can be made.[26] (There seems to be some scope for examining such cases more carefully, and for considering whether the intervention of the authority is necessary in the interests of the child, under s. 1 of the Children Act. If a child has been cared for by the relative, perhaps for many years, and the only problem is caused by a lack of finance, there are ways of providing help without recourse to "care", and all the consequences of the Boarding-out Regulations, which may not be at all necessary in the interests of the child.)

J *Children boarded-out by other authorities or voluntary societies.*—The regulations apply to such children and a local authority officer may be required to visit them on behalf of the authority or society concerned.[27]

There is no nationally agreed scale, each local authority having its own, with various additions for special expenditure or responsibility, and now often including an element of payment in respect of the service provided. The use of different scales for "short stay", "long stay" "special" and "professional" foster parents is not without its difficulties.

Though boarding-out allowances are usually paid to foster parents they are not governed by regulations and in rare cases foster parents do not wish to receive them. The payment or non-payment of the allowance does not, however, affect the foster parents' position and responsibility, which are based on the form of undertaking (see para. E, ante).[28]

L *Application.*—By definition the regulations do not apply to children in care who are:

i   in lodgings and not living as a member of the family;
ii in residential employment;
iii staying with a family for a holiday not exceeding three weeks;
iv living in a hostel, for example, one provided by the Y.M.C.A. or Y.W.C.A.

Such children and young people obviously require supervision while they remain in care but this is not exercised under the Boarding-out Regulations.[29]

M *Contact with parents.*—Bearing in mind what has been said previously about the position of parents, it will be obvious that in many cases they have a right to see their child who is boarded-out. This creates a rather difficult situation in which it is necessary for the foster parents, the child and the parents to be treated with every possible consideration. Some foster parents, particularly those taking children for short periods, are willing for parents to visit but in other cases it may be necessary for meetings between parents and children to be arranged at some neutral point, such as a children's home. The truly professional foster parent will wish to have direct contact with the parent.

Parents should, in general, be informed that the local authority may decide that a child should in his own interests be placed in a foster home and they should be helped to avoid the wrong impression which they have sometimes formed from reports appearing in the press.

Many parents feel that boarding-out and adoption are indistinguishable and, because of their own failure to provide for their children, are inclined to be hostile towards boarding-out; but with understanding on all sides it is frequently possible to use this method of care for the benefit of all concerned, always provided that the local authority pays full regard to its duties towards the parents of the child in care.

Clearly these attitudes to care should be examined before placing occurs; in this the regulations can be seen to serve the interests of the child.

First they differentiate between short- and long-term foster care (para. H above). Obviously, if a placing is known to be for three or four weeks, the long-term considerations will not arise in such an acute form. All the parties will know what the position is and the short-stay foster parent will probably accept parental visits (especially if she knows the parents and has been recruited on that basis). There is therefore a need for a decision by the social worker as to whether or not this is a short-stay case, not expected to remain in care for more than twelve weeks at the most. If it is said that this is sometimes an impossible decision at the outset, para. G above provides for a review within three months, and this gives the opportunity to review the whole circumstances before deciding that the conversion to long term is inevitable. The question then is whether the existing foster mother is prepared to maintain her attitude for a longer period, or whether in fact she can continue at all. If not, then other arrangements must be made, and if they involve foster care, that must be provided on a long-term understanding. Long-term fostering should be based on a conscious decision that it will meet the needs of the child, rather than simply allowing it to develop from a short-stay situation. In both short- and long-term placements, the regulations require a report including a statement that the placing is considered suitable for *a particular child* (para. C and H (i)) and this is obviously more important for the long-term placement.

There is evidence that in this respect, practice, even in the former Children's Departments, left much to be desired.[30] In considering whether a placing is suitable for a particular child his relationship with his own family is obviously a very important factor which must be taken in account. Rosamund Thorpe in her study looked at the situation of a number of long-term foster children and suggests that their well-being is enhanced by (a) a clear understanding of the placing in the foster home, (b) continued identification with the actual parents, and (c) real contact with the parents.

George's study concerns the relationship of social workers and foster parents (in the days when there were child care officers and children's departments). He suggests that the social workers mainly looked upon foster parents as "colleagues", but half the foster parents saw the social workers as "friends", and some of the others as "colleagues". In neither group did many see the social worker as "supervisor", and neither thought it at all necessary to inform a child's parents about any incident, such as stealing, even if the social worker had been informed, which was not by any means always.

While there are foster parents who think of their role as professional, in this study most of them considered themselves as parents in effect, and were naturally not keen that real parents should visit. Visits by the social worker served to remind them of what they did not want to know—that the child was not a part of the family. George suggests that this is the essence of the "lay" foster parent, and that it is the "professional" who should be able to improve the child's relationship with his own family in spite of difficulties. But there was little commitment to this, even by the social workers concerned.

So here again there is a stimulus to find a foster parent (perhaps a relative or friend) who knows the child and the circumstances of the family and is willing to give the help required. If this is not possible, a foster home will be chosen from those which have already had general approval by the department. But in choosing the foster home for the "particular child", several points have to be considered:

1. Is it intended that the child will eventually return to his family? If so, after how many years? (This is the basic hard question referred to in an earlier chapter.)
2. If so, do his parents understand what fostering means?
3. Does the child understand the position?
4. Are the chosen foster parents willing to meet the parents before the placing? And the child?
5. Will they accept a refusal of the placing by the parents?
6. If the child is placed, will they allow the parents to visit, welcome them, and even inform the social worker if visits are not made?
7. Do they recognise the importance of keeping parents informed directly about any events, good and bad, in the life of the foster child?

If they cannot accept a code of this kind, can they implement the policy to which the social worker is committed by decision 1 above? George thinks not.

After a child is placed he must be visited at stated intervals (as a minimum) and in emergency (paras F and H). What is the purpose of the visit? Is it for a social chat with the foster parents? According to the regulations, it is to visit the child and to write a report on a number of matters, including progress. The word implies forward movement towards some goal—in this case possibly the child's return to his parents. What has happened in the way of parental contact, or visits to or from brothers and sisters of the family? Are there any significant events which ought to be related to parents? How is the child himself dealing with the possibly long drawn out difficulties which are keeping him away from home? Questions of this kind give pointers to the work which still has to be done to reach the goal. Always there is the fundamental question as to whether this placing is in the interests of the child: should he be removed from it if it obstructs the long-term plan, and if so, to where? This is one of the matters to be dealt with at the review (para. G) every six months, when the social worker must have the advice of someone not dealing with the case, for instance a team leader. The review should be first of the file, to see that all the requirements of the regulations have been carried out, and then of the situation bearing in mind the original decision. When more than one child of a family is in care, there is much to be said for arranging the reviews to coincide with the six-monthly review of all children in care, boarded out or not. It is has been found profitable for parents and children to attend these reviews and for foster parents to be present, or if they cannot, to prepare a brief report on the position as they see it.

Foster parents who can fulfil the demanding task described can claim to be acting professionally, and will welcome support and training for the vital work of helping to carry out the planned restoration of a child to his family.

Those long-term foster parents who look upon themselves as "parents" and who cannot subscribe to the idea of restoration will be affected by the Children Act 1975. When Part II comes into operation, possibly in late 1979, they will be able to apply for a custodianship order after caring for the child for periods totalling 12 months, providing that they have parental consent. After periods totalling 3 years they will be able to apply without parental consent. There is some doubt as to how far these provisions will be used by local authority foster parents, since an order would take the child out of local authority care, and would make the foster parent responsible not only for his custody but also for his maintenance. An order for maintenance may be made against a parent, and a local authority may make a contribution towards the cost of the child's maintenance, but there is no present certainty that these measures would be used or that they would be effective.

Such foster parents may even now decide to notify the authority of their intention to adopt, and after 5 years' care of the child may do so without the agreement of the parent or the local authority, safe in the knowledge that the child cannot be removed without the authority of a court.

The subject of foster care, and the use of it, is almost inexhaustible and new literature continues to appear. The D.H.S.S. *Foster Care: A Guide to Practice* contains a great deal of careful and detailed analysis but gives no overall recommendations, since practice—as pointed out in previous chapters—is heavily influenced by departmental structure. However the Guide merits close study and contains charts which should be of great help in promoting the desired partnership between foster parents and agency. As the Guide points out, however, no local authority can assume that there exists a supply of foster parents, or potential foster parents, who can be called upon to meet the growing demands for the placing of children, and especially young people in some form of family care. As pressure mounts for the placing of older children, and those with special problems, authorities are engaging in recruiting campaigns and using all kinds of devices for encouraging would be foster parents to offer their services. This is not a new phenomenon, and there is some evidence to suggest that more effort is needed in retaining the interest of some former actual foster parents who have been "lost", even at the expense of efforts to obtain new ones.

There are however new factors, which make it necessary to try to break new ground and to look beyond the one time traditional type of foster parents. One factor is the changing age structure of children coming into care, and the growing numbers committed by the courts in either care or criminal proceedings. Another is the decline in the number of married women aged 35 to 54 who are not gainfully employed outside their homes. There are others which are referred to in published work, such as Dr Parker's *Foster Care in Context.* Efforts to recruit more foster parents, or to make better use of those already known, now call for a more accepting attitude, for a re-appraisal of former requirements (age, for instance, or full-time employment of potential foster parents) and for fresh insights to be used in the process of "selection", or "approval". One voluntary society seems to have found that life experiences which would at one time have been thought detrimental in a foster parent may in fact have given added strength and wisdom which can be used to the benefit of a child placed in foster care.

RESIDENTIAL CARE

Under the heading "resources" in Chapter 2 are set out the various types of residential establishment which are now community homes under the Regional plan. The local authority should be able to accommodate in any appropriate community home any child or young person in its care but in practice this only relates to an authority's own community homes (see under "Community homes with education on the premises", *post.*)

All community homes which were formerly directly provided by *a local authority* (including any assessment centres, remand homes or approved schools publicly owned) are subject to the control of the authority which is known as the "responsible body", and may or may not appoint "managers". Broadly speaking the responsible body, or the managers if there are any, are responsible for the administrative arrangements, but the day-to-day care and discipline of each child or young person is under the direct control of the person appointed to be in charge, in consultation with the Social Services Department which has the child in care.[31]

Although field social workers may not be concerned in the actual conduct of these homes, which include nurseries, they have many opportunities of co-operating with the staff in them, and it is therefore important that they should have some understanding of the principles and methods involved.

These principles are as suggested in para. 427 of the Curtis Report, which reads as follows:

"If the substitute home is to give the child what he gets from a good normal home it must supply:

I Affection and personal interest; understanding of his defects; care for his future; respect for his personality and regard for his self-esteem.

II Stability; the feeling that he can expect to remain with those who will continue to care for him till he goes out into the world on his own feet.

III Opportunity of making the best of his ability and aptitudes, whatever they may be, as such opportunity is made available to the child in the normal home.

IV A share in the common life of a small group of people in a homely environment".[32]

Though ideas on the purpose of residential care may have changed, and it is now thought of primarily as a form of treatment for children who cannot for some reason live in their own homes, these principles still need to be borne in mind. But in most cases there is no question of a child being cared for until "he goes out into the world on his own feet". Residential care should be preparing him in most cases for his return to his own family and should be involved in contact with families to this end. Alternatively it may be a preparation for some other form of care, such as adoption or fostering. Or it may be the most suitable and helpful method of providing care for a child "throughout his childhood", in which case it must be able to oversee the transition from care to independence.

LOCAL AUTHORITY COMMUNITY HOMES

Advice on the daily running of homes was contained in a Home Office Memorandum on the Conduct of Children's Homes of 1951, which no longer applies to community homes, but some of its ideas are mentioned here, together with a reference to the relevant new Regulation. It is doubtful whether all homes have yet reached the standard expected in 1951.

A *Type and Size of Children's Homes*

Before 1948 many children's homes were annexes to workhouses or were very large institutions, sometimes accommodating hundreds of children. Since then there has been a move towards the provision of much smaller homes, including what were known as "family group homes" accommodating between eight and twelve children. Some authorities provided homes of this kind on housing estates so that the children lived in a normal housing environment. The type of home provided, however, is a matter for each local authority and there is usually a combination of very small homes, larger homes accommodating up to about twenty-five children, and in places where they exist, cottage homes, which are in effect a group of family homes placed together and under the supervision of a superintendent and matron. There is as yet little specialist provision of homes to deal with children with special difficulties, for instance, those who are mentally or physically handicapped, but some progress is being made under the Regional Plans.

Each home, whatever its size, is to be conducted in such a way as to secure the well-being of the children in it, both physically and emotionally.[33] Local authorities have made great efforts ·to create a reasonable, not luxurious, standard of comfort within the homes, by providing brighter decorations, furnishings and facilities for hobbies and handicrafts, but the more important factors affecting the child's happiness depend as they always did on the attitude of the residential staff. Residential work is now therefore firmly regarded as a part of social work, and a single pattern of training for both field and residential social workers is being implemented as recommended by the Central Council for Training and Education in Social Work.[34]

B   *Daily Life in the Home*
The larger home particularly has to be run by a daily routine which avoids institutionalism. This does involve, however, regular mealtimes, bedtimes and activities, from all of which children tend to acquire a sense of security. Much can be done by the staff in the normal course of everyday life, especially at mealtimes, to give them ideas about citizenship and about the world and events outside the home.

Apart from the routine arrangements, it is necessary for children to have every opportunity for recreation, both indoor and outdoor, and in this connection organisations, such as Scouts and Guides, are used for those children who are interested in them. Many children, however, prefer to follow their own interests within the home and it is important that facilities should be available, and also that money should be available for outside outings and visits.

The children in such homes attend normal schools and thus spend a large part of their life in the company of other children who are living at home with their parents.

The regulations provide that a child must have the opportunity of following his own religious persuasion.[35]

C   *Personal Possessions*
It is important that children should have their own personal clothes, shoes and toys. They should also be responsible for their own pocket money, given to them on a scale according to age, and in the case of older children it is desirable that they should have some say in the expenditure of the allowance which is provided for clothing or that they should be allowed to spend it personally.

D   *General Care*
The Regulations provide that a medical officer may be appointed for each home and that the children, while they remain there, must be provided with medical, psychiatric and dental care.[36]

There is now no regulation concerning punishment. Control of homes is to be on the basis of good relationships between staff and children, but the responsible body has power to introduce further measures for control at its discretion. It may in this way make rules for the administration of those additional measures, if any.[37] (One such "measure" is the use of corporal punishment which provokes considerable debate. It was permitted under the 1951 Regulations and is not prohibited under those of 1972. Some authorities have banned it, while others have authorised staff to use it within firm guidelines. The social worker associations wish to see all physical punishment banned by Regulations, but some individual members still feel that it should be retained, and even that children in residential care may feel that punishment is more fair and just than other less immediate forms of "therapy".)

The most important matter for residential staff, in which field officers are involved, is the question of contact with relatives and friends. It is the general intention that a child's link with his own family should be preserved wherever it is possible and this may often involve visits to parents in order to encourage them to keep in contact with the children. The new regulations provide that there must be facilities in the home for visits by parents, relatives and friends of the children.[38] Where there are no parents or relatives or contact is undesirable, it is possible for children to form friendships with older people who will invite them out occasionally, and in this way such bodies as the Round Table, W.R.V.S., etc. may often prove to be helpful.

E   *Administration*

The regulations prescribe that records must be maintained in each community home, and they also provide for visitation by either members of the staff or members of committee, so that a report on each home may be made, in writing, once a month.[39] There is a regulation concerning precautions to be taken against fire and accident.[40]

F   *Ages of Children*

There are no definite ages laid down but it is usual for local authority community homes to accommodate children from about the age of 3 up to 16 years of age or older. Nurseries are, for the purpose of the regulations, community homes and although they normally have children from 0-5 years, some of them accommodate older children; conversely, not all children under the age of 5 need to be in a nursery. Nor is it necessary for a child to leave a home at school-leaving age; it has been the general practice to try to arrange for children either to be boarded-out before they leave school or to remain at the home after starting work until such time as a suitable placing can be made for them or they can return to their parents.

G   *Contact with Field Officers*

As will be seen there is every reason for field officers to work in co-operation with residential staff. This is especially so in the maintaining of contact between a child and his parents. It should be possible for this to be shared by both field and residential social workers, visits being paid by either according to the circumstances, and the impressions of the situation being shared without reservation. It must be remembered, however, that the people responsible for running the home are the residential staff, and if this is borne in mind a good deal of unnecessary friction can be avoided. On the other hand, the whole period of care, whether in foster homes or homes, must be seen as a continuous process, the two forms of care being complementary to each other.

H   *Observation and Assessment*

In addition to other facilities for assessment which may be carried out in a variety of ways, the residential accommodation provided by a local authority must include some accommodation, with the necessary facilities for observation and assessment. This requirement is now met under the Regional Plan which designates some community homes to carry out the function. Although such a home is subject to the regulations, it is run in rather a different way, with more generous staffing, because of the particular demands of the work, and usually includes a school with teachers experienced in remedial work with backward children. The main object of the assessment is, however, to observe children; to collect from social workers and others information about them and their family backgrounds. After a period of observation, lasting for some weeks, the staff report on each child, normally to a Case Conference which meets periodically, and by that time it is usually established that a particular form of care is necessary for each child. This may, of course take the form of boarding-out, return to parents or transfer to a community home or, occasionally, to a voluntary society home which is not a community home.

RESIDENTIAL CARE—COMMUNITY HOMES WITH
EDUCATION ON THE PREMISES

The former approved schools provided by bodies *other than local authorities* are now included in regional plans, and are community homes, subject to the regulations, though they are usually referred to as having "education on the premises", to distinguish them from the more numerous small homes from which children normally go out to near-by schools. They are called either controlled community homes or assisted community homes, depending on the number of managers appointed by a named local authority, and whether or not its nominees are in a majority. Here again, the managers are only concerned with administration, control of care and discipline being vested in the person appointed to be in charge. The regulations otherwise apply in just the same way as to any other community home.

Although courts have no power to commit a child or young person to any particular place, but only to the care of the local authority, there is a marked tendency for local authorities to place in these homes those young persons who have been committed following an offence, and they are thus carrying out broadly the same function as they did when they were approved schools. This type of community home expects admission to be arranged as a result of a recommendation from the more sophisticated kind of assessment centre or unit, so that in fact the present practice differs little from the old, the route being court—assessment in special unit—recommendation—consideration—acceptance or rejection. In addition, there is quite rightly a growing expectation that young persons will have some choice of placing in order to avoid the idea of a sentence to some kind of penal establishment. For these reasons, local authorities do not in fact have ready access without question to all the facilities set up under the regional plan, as seemed to be the original intention. There is some danger that for this reason a social worker may take steps to apply for a care order not because it is essential, but because it makes admission to a C.H.E. a more likely proposition.

The big difference between the old system and the new is that, once admitted, the young person is clearly in the care of the local authority to which he was committed, and not in any way under the control of the managers of the community home. The person in charge of the home is responsible for the day-to-day care, but the long-term planning in the case is the province of the authority. This includes such matters as home leave, parental contact, suspension of privileges, dealing with absconding, review of progress, and the form of care to be used after discharge from the home.

As a consequence of this, there is great concern about numbers of young person who are recommended for placement in a community home with education on the premises, but who for one reason or another are not accepted. As they are still in care and the local authority has clear responsibilities towards them, they are sometimes placed in their own homes, though this is not considered appropriate, or they may be placed in a smaller community home, even one of the very small family group homes, which may well be inadequately staffed, and in any event has no really effective way of providing "control".

RESIDENTIAL CARE—SECURE ACCOMMODATION

With the approval of the Secretary of State, a "responsible body" may provide secure accommodation within a community home, usually in a home with education on the premises. The regulations carefully prescribe the conditions for its use by the person in charge, and the time limits which apply. When a community home has no secure accommodation of its own, application may be made for a young person to be admitted to secure accommodation elsewhere; there are various safeguards against the wrong use of this type of treatment which is intended primarily for a small hard core of persistent offenders or absconders, and the latter group may contain children in care, but not subject to care orders under the 1969 Act. It is essential for a local authority to know that a child in its care is in secure accommodation so that it can monitor the observance of time limits laid down in the Regulations. The Ombudsman has already had occasion to comment on one case of maladministration in this respect.

Community homes provided by a local authority, or controlled community homes, but not assisted community homes may also be required by the Secretary of State to detain a young offender convicted on indictment of a grave crime. Such a person would not in this way enter the care of a local authority, and the expenses of his maintenance would be recoverable from the Secretary of State.

RESIDENTIAL CARE—HOMES PROVIDED UNDER s. 64

This section empowers the Secretary of State to provide, equip and maintain homes for children in the care of local authorities who need facilities and services which are considered to be unlikely to be available in community homes. A local authority may apply for the admission of a child in its care on terms to be determined by the Secretary of State. A very detailed history is required.

Such homes are available for the accommodation of young persons convicted of grave crimes and sentenced to detention during Her Majesty's pleasure, or sentenced to detention for a specified period. Such a sentence is not to imprisonment, but is intended to provide suitable education and training. Sentencing to detention however need not always be the decision of the court, as there will be power to make a care order if this appears appropriate. Section 64 will however provide the local authority with an alternative method of accommodation in such cases, or other cases, if this seems necessary.

RESIDENTIAL CARE—VOLUNTARY HOMES, ETC.

Many voluntary homes, including some which were formerly voluntary approved schools, came into the regional plan for community homes, either as controlled, or as assisted homes. They are under no obligation to do so however, and notwithstanding the community home system, may continue as voluntary homes under the Children Act 1948.

Voluntary homes are those provided by such societies as the Church of England Children's Society, the National Children's Home, Dr. Barnado's, the Catholic Rescue Society, etc. Except for those which are community homes, they are subject to the 1951 Regulations and it is always open to an authority to decide to place a child in a voluntary home for some particular reason. This may be in order to facilitate visits by parents or to provide some special form of education or training available at a particular voluntary home.

Where a child in the care of a local authority is placed in a voluntary home payment is made by the authority for his maintenance and it is the authority, and not the voluntary society, which is responsible for visiting him and for all decisions affecting his welfare and future treatment.[41]

In addition to community homes, authorities may of course accommodate children in care in other establishments within the control of the Director of Social Services, such as hostels for the mentally sub-normal, or in other accommodation such as schools for handicapped pupils, or in hospitals, or in any other accommodation which seems appropriate to the child's needs. There are, for instance, many privately run children's homes which accept children in the care of local authorities and look to them for payment of the cost of maintenance. Not being either community homes, or registered voluntary homes, these private establishments escape all controls, except that they are subject to inspection by the Secretary of State; and that any local authority placing a child in them is responsible for his supervision. It may, if the private home is at some distance from the child's own home area, ask the appropriate local authority to undertake supervision of the child, but there is no guarantee that this will be agreed.

Before placing a child in such a home an authority should obtain an opinion from the relevant authority which is likely to have information about the general standards of care and the suitability of the home for children with particular needs.

Private homes, though not subject to any Regulations, provide an additional form of care, and it has been found that most of them will respond to offers of advice and support from social workers, until such time as they are brought into the ambit of existing Regulations.

Older children in care may be placed in residential employment or in bed and breakfast accommodation, or in lodgings, or may provide for themselves, for instance by joining one of the Services. Some of these young people who have left school while still in care are expressing their need for independence and when they have been able to make their own arrangements the question arises as to how far being "in care" is a reality. But there is much cause for concern about others who, after leaving school, or community home, do not wish to stay in any form of local authority accommodation and either have no effective family, or do not wish to return to it. Some of them lose contact with their care authority altogether and cut themselves off from any help they ought to have in growing towards full independence by the age of 18. There would seem to be a great need for some kind of unstaffed accommodation in which such young people could live on a group basis so that social workers could at least offer support and supervision during the critical last year or two of official care.

OTHER ACCOMMODATION—IN OWN HOME

Section 13 contains an important provision by which any child in care may be allowed to be in the charge and control of a parent, guardian relative or friend. This provision is intended to enable a department to make a deliberate decision to allow a child to live with his parents or other persons for a fixed period or indefinitely, while still remaining in care. It is widely used and seems to account for about one sixth of all children in care at 31.3.77. It applies to children in care under s. 1 of the Children Act 1948 when no s. 2 Resolution has been passed and parents still retain their rights. The mere fact that such a child is placed at home does not bring care to an end, unless that is the clear intention. If it is not, this must be clearly understood by the child and parents, and be recorded in the file; the continuity of a period of care will have to be fully proved if at any future time the authority wishes to invoke s. 1(3A) (notice of removal from care after six months) or s. 2(1)(d) (parental rights resolution after three years' continuous care).

The provision applies also to children subject to care orders or s. 2 Resolutions, and to those remanded to care. It may also be used in the case of a child subject to an interim care order; but if the child has applied to the High Court for release and has been refused, the provision may not be used without the consent of the High Court which may in any event give directions to the local authority.

ACCOMMODATION GENERALLY—LIMITATIONS ON THE
EXERCISE OF POWERS BY A LOCAL AUTHORITY

In addition to the above limitation in respect of an interim care order,
there are those arising in any other case in which the High Court has been
concerned. As mentioned earlier, that Court acting in wardship, divorce,
guardianship or adoption proceedings may commit the care of a child to a
local authority; the child is then to be treated as being in the care of the
local authority, but the sections of the 1969 Act relating to care orders do
not apply to him. Moreover, the authority must exercise its powers with
regard to accommodation and welfare in accordance with any directions
which may have been given by the Court. Even if no such directions have
been given, it would be prudent to ask for directions before taking any
important decision, such as using the power to place a child in care in his
own home.

There is now a further caveat which, though not a legal limitation,
should be carefully considered. It concerns children remanded to care or
committed to care by a juvenile court. The *Guidelines on Procedure* of
October 1978 make it clear that when making such orders the magistrates
expect and presume that the child will not be placed in his own home,
unless there are very special circumstances which should be made known
to the court. Children subject to such orders should not in any event be
placed in their own homes solely because there is no local accommodation
available.

The Guidelines have been accepted by the local authority associations
and though some social workers may not agree with them, they are
valuable in stressing the need for full co-operation between courts and
social services departments. This need was originally set out in the Guide
to Part I of the Children and Young Persons Act 1969, and is essential to a
proper understanding and administration of the Act.

COMMITTAL TO BORSTAL

When a person aged 15 or over is subject to a care order (1969 Act) *and*
is detained in a community home, the authority may bring him before a
court, with the consent of the Secretary of State, in order to apply for his
removal to a borstal institution. This step is only to be taken as a last
resort, and the court has to be satisfied that his presence in a community
home is detrimental to the other persons accommodated there with him,
because of his "behaviour".

If the court makes an order for removal under this section, the care
order ceases to have effect.

Before making such an order, for a male young person only, the court
may make an order for detention in a remand centre, but not a prison, for
a period of up to twenty-one days, which may be extended from time to
time but not so as to exceed eight weeks in all. If there is no remand centre
available, the court may only adjourn the case, and care will continue. The
period of detention in a borstal institution if ordered may not run beyond

the date on which the original care order would have expired, *i.e.,* at the age of 18, or 19, according to the person's age at the time when the care order was made.

There is provision for appeal against a removal order, and for legal aid to be provided.

THE APPLICATION OF "CARE"

The provision of accommodation and maintenance (physical care), though important, is only a part of the local authority's duty; in behaving towards the children in care as a good parent would, it has a duty to ensure the mental, emotional and spiritual well-being of each child. An authority, however, is a corporate body, a legal "person", so that its functions as a parent must be carried out by *people*—that is, by its social workers in residential establishments or "in the field". They are called upon to care for children of all ages, at all stages of physical and emotional development, with varying needs to be met and differing expectations to be satisfied.

The quality of care for each child will be expressed largely through the people actually in contact with him so that the type of care selected is of the highest importance. But all forms of accommodation should ideally be seen as a continuum, rather than as a series of quite separate methods of care-taking which can be hastily changed at a time of crisis.

Research findings indicate that many children are "inappropriately placed" and that their wishes and feelings do not receive enough consideration. If the welfare principle is to have any real meaning there must be better and more decisive planning of each period of care; some authorities, as mentioned earlier, have assigned social workers to this task and some progress is being made in identifying those children, specially those in long-term care, whose placing urgently needs review.

Though some studies have demonstrated that some children in residential care ought to be placed for fostering or adoption, children's homes have a vital part to play in the provision of substitute care, and are for some children the most helpful and constructive means of ensuring it, a first choice rather than a last resort. "What shall we do with the children?" is a question continually in the minds of staff concerned in planning. It is also the title of a booklet which, while it contains no easy answers, reports on a small project involving over 500 children and the field and residential staff responsible for their care. This study gives due weight to staff discussions about the proper placement for the children, but also takes full account of the expressed attitudes of the children themselves. It concludes with some pertinent comments on the need for a genuine partnership between field and residential workers built on mutual respect for the skill and knowledge of each party.

TREATMENT OF CHILDREN AND YOUNG PERSONS IN NEED
OF CONTROL

It may seem objectionable to differentiate between the treatment of
children in need of care and those in need of control, but there is a
distinction in the phrase "care *or* control" in s. 1 of the 1969 Act. This
would perhaps be even more relevant than now if s. 5 were in operation
and care proceedings were much more widely used in dealing with young
offenders.

The White Paper *Children in Trouble* on which the Act of 1969 is
based suggested in para. 6 that delinquent behaviour may frequently be
"not more than an incident in the pattern of a child's normal development.
But sometimes it is ... a symptom of a deviant damaged or abnormal
personality". Later, the same paragraph speaks of a variety of facilities for
"long-term care, treatment and control, including some which are highly
specialised". Again in para. 20, it states that "effectiveness (of the
measures taken) means helping children ... in some cases it also means
firm control of anti-social behaviour", and again mentions the need for a
variety of facilities. Yet again, para. 49 states that "firm and consistent
discipline is a normal and necessary part of a child's upbringing. Children
may require control as well as help ... and society may have to provide
this control for its own protection and for the sake of the child, where the
parents are unable to do so". These passages from the White Paper have
perhaps received less attention than those which advance the more
generalised aims of dealing with young persons who commit offences by
the same methods as are applied to those who are in need of care.

But the Act itself seems to recognise that there are differences, and in
the first instance states that "care" includes protection and guidance and
"control" includes discipline (s. 70(1)). Section 5, if and when it becomes
operative, provides that in certain circumstances prosecution for an offence
will be authorised, notwithstanding care considerations. Section 22(5) and
23(2) and (3) envisage a situation when, even before a final order has been
made, a young person is "of so unruly a character that he cannot be safely
committed to the care of a local authority" and may, unless a female, be
sent to a remand centre if one is available.

Section 24 empowers a local authority acting under a care order to
restrict the liberty of the person committed to its care, and s. 27(2)
authorises the authority to exercise its general powers in a way which may
not be consistent with its general duty, if this is necessary for the
protection of the public. Section 27(3) enables the Secretary of State to
direct a local authority with regard to the exercise of its powers if he
considers this necessary for the protection of the public. Finally, s. 31 deals
with the procedure for bringing about the removal of a person aged 15
from a community home to borstal, but only with the consent of the
Secretary of State and an order of a juvenile court.

These sections of the Act imply that there are some young people for
whom "control" including discipline is almost the overriding consideration, even though the principles of care should of course also apply

to them. The great majority of such young people will have been committed to care following conviction for an offence, and will probably be known as persistent delinquents since if the Act has been applied as intended they will already have failed to respond to voluntary measures or to a supervision order, with or without "intermediate treatment". They form a comparatively small proportion of all children in care, but a much higher proportion of those in long-term care. They will almost invariably be placed at some stage in a community home (with education on the premises) in very much the same way as their predecessors were sent to the former approved schools. They present a powerful challenge to the "responsible body" which may also be required to detain in a community home young offenders convicted on indictment of certain grave crimes, though not being in the care of a local authority.

This is the difficulty which gives rise to the demand for secure accommodation,[42] and to other problems associated with the use of community homes within the regional plan. It may possibly spring from serious misconceptions of the very nature of delinquency (meaning persistent and repeated law-breaking) and of the young persons concerned. Although deviant, are they necessarily damaged or abnormal personalities, as suggested in the White Paper? Or are they delinquent because offending has become habitual, and after a time provides an acceptable status? These questions are discussed in "Delinquency: the problem for treatment"[43] which merits close study.

There has also been a suggestion (at a conference organised by the Institute for the Study and Treatment of Delinquency) that there may be a case for the addition of a security provision to a care order. This would have the purpose of providing for boys aged 13 and over intensive therapy within perimeter security. Remission of detention would be possible.[44] More recently there has been some pressure for the introduction of secure care orders, but a private members' Bill intended to make these available to juvenile courts, was defeated.

From another angle, the closure of all juvenile institutions in Massachusetts in 1972 offers an interesting commentary. It is reported that the boys in the juvenile institutions were placed either in foster homes or small residential units within their own local community, where treatment on the lines of "intermediate treatment" was applied. The essential element was that no child was sent away, but was placed within his own locality. It was then found that for the whole State, there was a need for *one* small secure unit for those young people who were disturbed, dangerous or a social threat.

This approach has inspired experiments in this country to place "delinquents" in local foster care, but there is continuing concern about the whole problem, and especially about the rise in the number of young offenders sent to penal establishments and the decline in the number supervised in the community. All the social work organisations whose members are involved in work with delinquents have combined to form a new group "New Approaches to Juvenile Crime". The group concedes that there is a small number of young people who pose a serious threat to society, and that they should be locked in secure accommodation. This conclusion follows that of the Massachusetts authorities.[45] But the group also follows others in stressing that there is little or no evidence to suggest that more committal to community homes will have any effect on the rate of crime. Apart from the small minority who should be in secure forms of care, the best hope for young offenders lies in supervision in the community supplemented by local forms of care, including foster care, and by useful and purposeful activities provided by local authorities.

Advance along these lines will call for more effort on the part of social workers to use all other options before recommending the making of care orders, and for the diversion of resources from residential care—especially the highly expensive secure accommodation—into community development.

NOTES

1. Both published by A.B.A.F.A.
2. *Children Who Wait,* A.B.A.F.A. 1973.
3. For a suggested form of notification, see J.P. Vol. 136, p. 75.
4. Children Act 1948, s. 3(7), C. and Y.P. Act 1969, s. 24(3).
5. *Ibid.,* ss. 17 and 9.
6. Adoption Act 1958, s. 4(3), and Children Act 1948, s. 2(11).
7. Boarding-Out Regulation 1.
8. *Ibid.,* 2.
9. *Ibid.,* 17.
10. *Ibid.,* 6.
11. *Ibid.,* 7.
12. *Ibid.,* 8.
13. *Ibid.,* 20.
14. *Ibid.,* 23.
15. *Ibid.,* 21.
16. *Ibid.,* 23.
17. *Ibid.,* 9.
18. *Ibid.,* 4.
19. *Ibid.,* 5(1).
20. *Ibid.,* 22.
21. *Ibid.,* 24.
22. *Ibid.,* 25.
23. *Ibid.,* 27.
24. *Ibid.,* 28.
25. *Ibid.,* 30.
26. *Ibid.,* 1(4).
27. *Ibid.,* 13 and 14.
28. Children Act 1948, s. 13(1), as amended.
29. Boarding-Out Regulation 1(1).
30. Studies by R. Thorpe and V. George, "Mum and Mrs So and So", S.W.T. 7 February 1974, and "Foster care workers" 2 December 1971.
31. Community Homes Regulations 1972, Regulation 3.
32. Report of the Committee on the Care of Children 1946.
33. Community Homes Regulations 1972, Regulation 3.
34. *Residential Work is Part of Social Work,* C.C.E.T.S.W. No. 3.
35. Regulation 8.
36. Regulation 5.
37. Regulation 10.
38. Regulation 9.

39. Regulation 3.
40. Regulation 7.
41. Children Act 1948, s. 54(4).
42. Community Homes, Regulations 11–14.
43. Rod Ryall, *Social Work Today,* 16 May 1974.
44. J.P. 1973, p. 138.
45. Social Work Today, 15 February 1977 and *Care and Treatment in a Planned Environment,* D.H.S.S.; see also "Community Care", 2 August 1979.

Chapter 12

SPECIAL PROVISIONS RELATING TO CHILDREN IN CARE

SUMMARY

As children may come into care at any time from early infancy to the age of 17 (exceptionally 18) and may remain in care until the age of 19, the time spent in care in some cases will be considerable. During this period the authority is responsible for the child's upbringing which should as far as possible resemble the upbringing by parents of a child not in care. There are however some situations which arise directly from the fact that the child is in local authority care; special provision for some of these situations is made in the Children Act and other legislation.

It should be remembered that Part II of the Act applies to all children in care irrespective of the method of admission. But in committing the care of children to a local authority the High Court or divorce court may give directions to the authority as to the exercise of care in accordance with the legislation dealt with in Chapter 9.

SERVICES AVAILABLE TO CHILDREN

ADOPTION

A local authority has power to make, and participate in, arrangements for the adoption of children and, as we shall see in a later chapter, this includes the power to place for adoption children who are not in care.[1]

With regard to children *in care* who are boarded-out with foster parents the question of adoption by the foster parents sometimes arises. This is particularly so in the case of young babies whose mothers decide that they will be unable to provide for them, and in the occasional cases of abandoned or orphaned children who have been received into care or committed to care. There is, however, no age limit for adoption so long as the child is under 18 and has never been married; it therefore happens that children who have been boarded-out with foster parents even for a number of years may be the subjects of adoption applications. Present interest in the needs of some "hard to place" children is also increasing the number of older children who are boarded out with a view to adoption. Foster parents and the local authority in such cases have to comply with the Adoption Act 1958, and the Adoption Agencies Regulations, which will be dealt with in a later chapter. There are, however, certain provisions of the Adoption Act relating to children who are already in care.

The prospective adopters do not have to obtain the consent of the local authority to notify their intention to adopt and they may, therefore, decide on this course without the authority's agreement or permission, though this is rarely the case. On receipt of the notification of intention to adopt, the child remains subject to the Boarding-out Regulations,[2] except that the authority cannot demand the return of the child under the terms of the Foster Parents' Undertaking and must instead demand his return by notice under the Adoption Act.[3] If, at the time, the application has already been lodged with the court the notice cannot even be given unless the court consents. Subject to this, however, the foster parents *may* be required to return the child to the authority within a period of seven days. (This will not apply if the foster parents have cared for the child for 5 years, and are protected by Section 34A.)

No contributions are payable by the parents for a period of at least twelve weeks following the notification.[4] It is usual though not essential, for boarding-out allowances to be stopped when notification of intention to adopt is received, so that the foster parents become fully responsible for the child's maintenance. It is not essential that a child who is to be placed for adoption should first be boarded-out; there is no reason why a child in residential care should not be directly placed with prospective adopters under the Adoption Agencies Regulations.

When an adoption order in respect of a child in care is refused by the court or the application is withdrawn, the child need not be returned to the local authority unless his return is demanded by them. Section 17 of the Children Act 1975 may however be used if the court refuses an adoption order and the child is not in care under a care order, or if supervision is necessary.

Adoption is more fully discussed in Chapter 15.

APPOINTMENT OF GUARDIAN

When a child in care has no parent and no properly-appointed guardian, or other *person* having parental rights, the High Court, a county court or juvenile court may on application appoint any person as legal guardian.[5] This is a useful provision when it is desired to provide a child with a guardian, for instance one of his own relatives who may be acting as his foster parent.

Where a child has no parent or guardian but a *local authority* has parental rights under the Children Act, the court may still appoint a guardian but the resolution in such cases is terminated.[6]

APPOINTMENT OF CUSTODIAN (WHEN POSSIBLE)

It does not seem to be intended that a local authority should intentionally place a child for the purpose of obtaining a custodian for him; nor is custodianship available only to children already in care. It may be however that after a child has been placed with a foster parent or a relative an application for custodianship will follow at some future date. The possibility of this should therefore be borne in mind both at the time of placing, and at subsequent reviews of the position of the child.

EDUCATION

Among the facilities and services available to children is the full range of the local authority's educational system, including special schools, technical schools, grammar schools and grants for university or other higher education. So far as higher education is concerned, the child in care is normally regarded by the Education Authority as eligible for full grant aid. The Social Services Committee has power to assist persons over 17 who were formerly in care.[7]

It sometimes happens that foster parents wish to arrange for their foster child to attend a private school but this is normally regarded as a matter of personal preference for which, if they wish, they may be expected to meet the costs involved.

EMPLOYMENT

The advice of the Youth Employment Service or Careers Advisory Service is available to children in care and a member of the social work staff normally attends interviews. When a child is handicapped, for instance by mental sub-normality, he may be eligible for treatment as a disabled person and for admission to an Industrial Rehabilitation Unit. It is always open to the authority to arrange for special training not provided by the Youth Employment Service or the Ministry, for instance at a voluntary establishment such as a voluntary home. In the matter of employment it is, of course, important that any child in care should be placed in work or training suitable to his abilities and ambitions.

APPRENTICESHIP

In the past local authorities have, in some cases, been required to enter into apprenticeship agreements, acting as parents of the boy or girl concerned. This was not very satisfactory as the period of care ends at 18 and after that the authority had no lawful responsibility or power. It is now provided that where an authority enters into a guarantee under a Deed of Apprenticeship or Articles these shall be valid until they expire, irrespective of the fact that the child may no longer be in care.[8]

EMIGRATION

A local authority may arrange the emigration of some children in care subject, however, to the consent of the Secretary of State.[9] This consent will not be given unless the Secretary of State is satisfied that emigration would benefit the child, that suitable arrangements have been made for his reception in the country to which he is going and that his parents or guardian have been consulted, or cannot be consulted.

The Secretary of State may consent to emigration even if the child is too young to express an opinion, provided that the emigration is to be in company with a parent, guardian or relative or for the purpose of joining a parent, guardian, relative or friend.

It will be remembered that in this sub-section "parents" or "guardian" include all actual parents or guardians.[10]

The Secretary of State has sometimes refused consent for emigration because of the prohibition contained in s. 52 of the Adoption Act 1958, against sending a British subject under 18 out of the country with a view to adoption in law or in fact. This difficulty was overcome in the Act of 1963 so that the Secretary of State may now give consent to emigration in any case where it would benefit the child and the other conditions of the Children Act have been fulfilled.[11] There is a procedure to be followed before any definite arrangements are made, and it is unlikely that consent will be given retrospectively in any case. The procedure is laid down in Circular LAC 16 of 1975.

Although children whose care has been committed to local authorities under Acts other than the Children and Young Persons Act 1969 are to be treated generally in the same way as other children in care, there is a specific exception in that the authority may *not* arrange for their emigration.[12]

TREATMENT IN MENTAL HOSPITAL

When a child in care is mentally disordered and is compulsorily admitted to hospital he does not cease to be in the care of the local authority. If the child is in care under a care order the authority is deemed to be his nearest relative—except for husband or wife. If the authority has assumed parental rights by resolution it is deemed to be the nearest relative, except for husband or wife, or a parent whose parental rights have not been assumed by the authority.[13] The authority is to be regarded as the nearest relative for the purpose of making application for the child's admission to hospital in view of the Social Services Committee's powers under Parts II to VI of the Mental Health Act 1959.

On the admission of a mentally disordered child in care to any hospital, if the authority has parental rights it must arrange for him to be visited and must take such other steps in relation to him as would be expected to be taken by his parents.[14]

CRIMINAL PROCEEDINGS

Children in care, like other children, may commit offences. Normally the police will consult the authority as to whether proceedings should be taken and in some cases it is decided that a caution should be administered or that the authority should make different arrangements for care. The police may decide, however, to take proceedings, in which case the local authority and probation officer will be notified in the usual way.[15] Although probation officers normally undertake home surroundings enquires it is the usual practice for them to leave this to the local authority which has the child in care and which is in a better position to make a report to the court. It may sometimes be desirable for the probation officer to make a completely independent report. There is great need for liaison with the probation service in such cases.

A child in care is liable to the same treatment by the juvenile court as any other child and may, therefore, be given an absolute or conditional discharge, be fined, remanded, sent to an attendance centre or detention centre (if a boy aged 14 or more), be placed under supervision, be committed to care, or if over 15 be sent to Borstal under certain circumstances. If he is in care under a previous care order, however, there is no point in the making of a second such order.

COMPENSATION

There are, however, cases in which a young person may have committed serious offences, with which he may be charged. If he is found guilty, the question of a fine or compensation may arise. Under s. 55 of the Children and Young Persons Act 1933, the court may order that the payments should be made by the parent (if he has conduced to the commission of the offence by neglect or otherwise); if the young person is in the care of a local authority by virtue of a care order, or if a s. 2 resolution is in force in respect of him, then the local authority has parental powers or rights and *duties*, and may be regarded as liable to make payments in the same way as a parent. Alternatively the local authority may be liable as the "guardian" which includes a person having charge or control of the child.

There have been several cases on this point. Some authorities have already had payment orders made against them for quite large sums (£400 is the limit in criminal proceedings in magistrate's court but the claim is often made in the civil courts), but the question of "neglect of duty" is a wide one, in view of certain features which do not apply to a local authority in quite the same way as to a parent. The position was fully set out in the judgement given by Lord Widgery, C.J., in *Somerset County Council* v. *Kingscott* 1975.[16]

This does not appear to mean however that there may not be cases in which the local authority would be liable and indeed an order was made against the Essex County Council in 1979. But the issue is complicated, and it has been laid down that in cases of this kind, it is not enough for a social worker to attend the court. It is essential that the local authority should be legally represented, as an order for payment of fine or compensation is a legal, rather than a social, matter.

SUPERVISION ORDER

When a supervision order is made naming a probation officer, it is necessary for there to be some working arrangement between the authority and the probation officer whereby he can exercise supervision without unnecessary duplication of visiting.

(It may be mentioned here that if a child is already subject to a probation or supervision order when admitted to care, the order remains in force but, in view of the changed circumstances, the court may be recommended by the probation officer to discharge it.)[17]

ILLNESS, ACCIDENT AND DEATH

When a child in care dies the local authority may arrange for his burial or cremation, provided that cremation is not contrary to the child's religious persuasion.[18] The authority may in such cases claim a death grant and may recover from the parent of a child under 16 the balance of expenses incurred. The authority must be notified of the death of any child living in one of its homes and of the circumstances. It is usual for the authority to notify the Secretary of State of the death of other children in care, for instance boarded-out, though this was not required by the regulations but the Home Office Circular 28/1964. Parents and guardians must also be informed if a child in a community home has an accident, or a serious illness, or dies. This practice, though not obligatory, is also followed as regards children in care and accommodated elsewhere, for instance, in a foster home.

CONTACT WITH PARENTS

Much has been said about the need for preserving the link between a child and his parents; the authority has power to meet the expenses of parents in travelling to see their children or in attending the funeral of a child in care. This power may also be used with regard to other persons, for instance relatives, but is always subject to the proviso that assistance should only be given when the visit would be otherwise impossible without causing undue hardship.[19]

There is no specific power to pay the expenses of a child visiting parents, relatives or friends but these can now be provided under the general powers contained in the 1963 Act, if the visit will promote his welfare by diminishing the need for him to remain in care.[20]

MARRIAGE

It sometimes happens that a child in care, usually a girl, wishes to marry while under the age of 18. The law relating to the marriage of minors is contained in the Marriage Act of 1949. The main points are:

A   That a marriage solemnized between two persons either of whom is under 16 is void.

B   An infant aged between 16 and 18 requires consent in order to marry. The consents required are set out in the second schedule to the Act, which is set out **opposite.**

C   When the minor is subject to a custodianship order, the consent of the custodian is required.

D   Where a local authority has parental rights by a Resolution its consent should be obtained additionally, but we have already seen in an earlier chapter that the consent of the authority should normally only be given after consultation with any parent who is available to give consent. When a local authority has the same powers and duties as a parent by virtue of a care order, it is not clear whether parents have been "deprived of custody" or whether the consent of the local authority is required.

E   If any required parental consent cannot be obtained because of the parent's absence, inaccessability or disability the Registrar General may dispense with consents altogether or, alternatively, an application may be made to a court for consent, which then has the same effect as the consent of a parent.

Finally, it should be noted that if the child in care is a Ward of a High Court the consent of the High Court must also be obtained.

The fact that a boy or girl in care marries does not appear to invalidate any care order or resolution assuming parental rights though it is difficult to see what parental rights, powers or duties remain after marriage.

PARENTHOOD

Young people in care sometimes become parents and in this event the child concerned has to be dealt with as a separate individual; if for instance, the question of need for his admission to care has to be

"I. WHERE THE MINOR IS LEGITIMATE

Circumstances	Person or Persons whose consent is required
1. Where both parents are living:	
A if parents are living together;	Both parents.
B if parents are divorced or separated by order of any court or by agreement;	The parent to whom the custody of the minor is committed by order of the court or by the agreement, or, if the custody of the minor is so committed to one parent during part of the year and to the other parent during the rest of the year, both parents.
C if one parent has been deserted by the other;	The parent who has been deserted.
D if both parents have been deprived of custody of minor by order of any court.	The person to whose custody the minor is committed by order of the court.
2. Where one parent is dead:	
A if there is no other guardian;	The surviving parent.
B if a guardian has been appointed by the deceased parent.	The surviving parent and the guardian if acting jointly, or the surviving parent or the guardian if the parent or guardian is the sole guardian of the minor.
3. Where both parents are dead.	The guardians or guardian appointed by the deceased parents or by the court under section four of The Guardianship of Minors Act 1971, s. 3 or 5.

II. WHERE THE MINOR IS ILLEGITIMATE

Circumstances	Person whose consent is required
If the mother of the minor is alive.	The mother, or if she has by order of any court been deprived of the custody of the minor, the person to whom the custody of the minor has been committed by order of the court.
If the mother of the minor is dead.	The guardian appointed by the mother."

considered separately, the young person in care already is regarded for all purposes as the parent.

BEHAVIOUR DIFFICULTIES

We have already dealt with the question of children in care who commit offences and may appear before the juvenile court. There are, however, a number of behaviour difficulties which may not result in criminal acts but which require serious consideration by the local authority.

Children in residential care particularly may show the effects of their deprivation by aggression or by such symptoms as pilfering, lying, dirty habits, inability to form relationships, wandering or absconding. As we have seen, it is essential that the staff of children's homes should be able to understand these difficulties and to relate them to the child's previous history.

With regard to children in foster homes or lodgings; there may be similar problems but here it is the duty of the social worker to interpret the behaviour problem to the foster parents and to endeavour to obtain their understanding and co-operation. If this cannot be done there is likely to be a breakdown of the placing and when this seems to be inevitable it may be necessary for the child to be removed under the Boarding-out Regulations.[21]

A similar difficulty may arise in the case of children who are in care but living with their parents by permission of the local authority.

Any behaviour problems manifested by children in residential care or elsewhere require investigation and serious consideration of the suitability of the placing. If the difficulties are serious and persistent they call for a review of the child's whole history and for reconsideration of his relationship with his family and home. In situations of this kind it is usually helpful to refer the problem for psychiatric assessment and to follow any recommendations which may be made. To deal with the immediate problem, however, it will often be necessary to move the child from his foster home or children's home for a period of observation and assessment, which may be provided by the authority in the most suitable way, either residentially or on a daily basis.[22] The authority will of course be able to apply for admission to any accommodation permitted under the Act which is considered suitable as a result of the assessment (see Chapter 6).

The final sanction is for an application to be made by the local authority to a juvenile court for a care order if this is essential for ensuring control. Such an application could also be made by the police (in cases of an offence), the local education authority (in cases of non-attendance at school) or the N.S.P.C.C. in other cases, but there would first be consultation with the care authority, and the care or control test would have to be satisfied, except of course in the case of a prosecution for an offence.

If however a care order is already in force, and the local authority cannot otherwise provide for the accommodation of the child concerned, it could consider applying to the Secretary of State for the child's admission to a special centre under s. 64, or for permission to bring him before a court with a view to his removal to borstal, if he is already in a community home. (See Chapter 11.)

INDEPENDENT VISITORS

Unfortunately there are still some children in care who either have no parents or guardian or have little contact with them. In such cases the local authority will usually endeavour to ensure that the child has the benefit of a foster home, or that if he is in residential care he has contact with both children and adults in the world outside. Contact with other children will be provided in most cases at school and in leisure activities; contact with adults will often be provided by relatives, or by relatives of the residential staff, or by "unofficial aunts and uncles" who are encouraged to take a continuing interest in a particular child.

The Act envisages however a situation in which a child over the age of 5, *who is the subject of a care order,* is accommodated in a community home or other establishment such as a school or hospital where he may spend practically all his time and have little contact with anyone outside.

Section 24 of the Act requires a local authority to appoint a visitor for such a person if:

A   The child has not been allowed to leave the home or other establishment during the previous 3 months for the purpose of attending school or work.

B   The authority considers that contact between the child and his parents or guardian is so infrequent as to call for this step to be taken. The appointment of a visitor will be called for if the child has not lived with, visited or been visited by either parent or guardian for a period of 12 months.

The visitor appointed must be independent of the local authority, must be a voluntary worker, whose expenses may be claimed from the local authority, and has the duty of visiting, advising and befriending the child concerned, in the same way as would be expected of his parents.

In addition, the visitor has the legal right to apply to the court on behalf of the child for the care order to be discharged.

ABSENTEES

CHILDREN IN CARE BUT IN CHARGE OF PARENTS

Under s. 13(2), of the Children Act 1948, as amended, as we have seen, a local authority may allow a child in care to be in the charge and control of a parent, guardian, relative or friend, either for a fixed period or indefinitely.

A position may arise in which the authority considers that the child should be returned at the end of the fixed period, or, if there was no fixed period, at once. In this event the authority must serve a notice in writing requiring the person who has the charge of the child to return him at a specified time. Anyone harbouring or concealing the child after that time, or preventing him from returning as required is liable on summary conviction to a fine of up to £100 or imprisonment for two months or both.

There is a greater penalty (£400 or 3 months) for any person taking such child out of the care of the authority, assisting him or inducing him to run away, or harbouring or concealing him after he has run away.[23]

So far as children in the care of a local authority under a care order are concerned, if they are for the time being in charge of a parent, guardian, relative or friend, they may be required by the authority to return to live at premises specified by the authority, and if they fail to do so would be dealt with as "absentees".

OTHER ABSENTEES

Section 32 of the 1969 Act is a general section dealing with absentees from any place where they are required to live for the time being, and applies to persons subject to care orders, interim orders, remand warrants or to arrangements made by the police and the local authority under s. 29(3) in respect of a person who has been arrested but not released. The section also relates to children in places of safety whether detained in a community home or elsewhere.

If it is believed that a specified person is able to produce an absentee, a magistrates' court may issue a summons requiring this to be done. Failure to comply with the requirement is an offence carrying a penalty of a fine of £100.[24]

Any person knowingly compelling, persuading, inciting or assisting a child to become or remain an absentee will be guilty of an offence carrying a penalty of a fine of £400 or up to six months' imprisonment, or both.

As absentees may well abscond from England and Wales into other parts of the United Kingdom, there are provisions for their recovery. These are referred to in paras 242-246 of the "Guide".[25]

TRANSFERS WITHIN THE UNITED KINGDOM

By s. 25 of the Children and Young Persons Act 1969 arrangements may be made for a person subject to a Care Order (made in England or Wales) to be transferred to Northern Ireland if his parents or guardian go to live there. There are reciprocal arrangements in respect of persons subject to similar Orders made in Northern Ireland.

Transfers to and from Scotland are provided for in the Social Work (Scotland) Act 1968—see Home Office Circular 78/71.

Section 26 deals with persons subject to "relevant orders" made in the Isle of Man or the Channel Islands, and admitted to accommodation (*e.g.* a community home) in England or Wales. Such a person may be deemed to be subject to an order committing him to the care of the local authority in whose area he is accommodated for the time being. Such cases are not subject to the statutory review under s. 27(4).

NOTES

1. Adoption Act 1958, s. 1.
2. *Ibid.*, s. 36(2).
3. *Ibid.*, s. 35.
4. *Ibid.*, s. 36(2).
5. Guardianship of Minors Act 1971, s. 5 (such a guardian is not only the guardian of the person, but also of the estate, *i.e.* property).
6. *Ibid.*
7. Children Act, s. 20, Children and Young Person's Act 1963, s. 46, and Table, Chapter 13.
8. Children and Young Persons Act 1963, s. 47.
9. Children Act 1948, s. 17.
10. *Ibid.*, s. 9.
11. Children and Young Persons Act 1963, s. 55.
12. Matrimonial Causes Act 1973, s. 43; Matrimonial Proceedings (Magistrates' Courts) Act 1960, s. 3(2); Family Reform Act 1969, s. 7; Guardianship Act 1973, s. 4 (governing also orders made in custodianship and adoption proceedings).
13. Mental Health Act 1959, ss. 10 and 50.
14. *Ibid.*, s. 10.
15. Children and Young Persons Act 1969, ss. 9 and 34(3).
16. [1975] All E.R. 326. See also "Compensation Orders", R. Jones, *Social Work Today,* 16 January 1979.
17. Children Act, s. 6(1).
18. Children Act 1948, s. 18, Community Homes Regulations 1972, Regulation 6.
19. Children Act 1948, s. 22.
20. Children and Young Persons Act 1963, s. 1.
21. Boarding-Out Regulations, Regulation 4.
22. See Chapter 6.
23. Children and Young Persons Act 1963, s. 49 and Children Act 1948, ss. 3(8) and 1(3A).
24. Children and Young Persons Act 1969, s. 32 and Children Act 1975, s. 68.
25. Guide to Part I of the Children and Young Persons Act 1969.

Chapter 13

PROVISIONS FOR DISCHARGE AND AFTER CARE

SUMMARY

DISCHARGE

As there are various ways of coming into care so there are various ways of being discharged from it. These are as follows:

1. ATTAINMENT OF THE AGE OF EIGHTEEN

At this age care under s. 1 of the Children Act 1948, expires, as does care under any enactment except the Children and Young Persons Act 1969.[1]

Resolutions in respect of children in care under s. 1 also cease to have effect.

Care orders made under the Children and Young Persons Act 1969, expire at the age of 18, unless previously discharged or extended to the age of 19 by a court. (A care order made after the age of 16 is in force until the 19th birthday unless previously discharged.)[2]

2. CARE ASSUMED BY PARENT, GUARDIAN, RELATIVE OR FRIEND

So far as a parent or guardian is concerned, there is a general *right* to take over the care of a child who is in care under s. 1 and in respect of whom no resolution has been passed,[3] provided that the parent seeking to take over the care of the child has not been deprived of custody by a court. This is not an absolute right, however. The authority cannot keep the child in care, but has no absolute duty to return a child from foster parents to the care of a parent (*Krishnan* v. *London Borough of Sutton*, [1969] 3 All E.R. 1367). In some cases arising from such circumstances an application has been made for the child to be made a ward of court but this is a step which should only be taken on legal advice in view of decisions already made by the Court of Appeal in *Re(T), an infant*, [1970] 2 All E.R. 865 and in other cases where the Family Division of the High Court has been asked to use its wardship powers for the protection of children. Though the court will not usually interfere with the exercise of statutory powers by a local authority, it might in an exceptional situation make the child a ward of court as an extra protection for a child already in care. It has been held that a child in care may be made and remain a ward of court. In cases of complexity, it is open to the local authority to seek the guidance of the High Court and this practice is growing. The new sub-s. 3A of s. 1 of the Children Act 1948 is intended to limit the apparent right of a parent under sub-s. 3; it provides that if a child has been in s. 1 care for six months the local authority must consent to his leaving care, or that the parent must have given 28 days' notice of removal. The intention was that during those 28 days the authority could arrange a planned discharge from care, or could consider whether there were grounds for the passing of a s. 2 Resolution. This was made clear in the model leaflets for parents which should form the basis of information given at the time of admission under s. 1 and which may well need to be supplemented by verbal explanation (see Appendix F).

There have been a number of conflicting cases on this issue, since it was not clear as to when and how the parent expresses the "desire to take over the care of the child".[4] There is no requirement that this should be done in writing and it may be thought that a verbal message—or even a private thought or wish—is enough. But if a unilateral decision by a parent constituted a desire to take over the care of the child and thus brought a period of care to an end, it would follow that no Resolution could be passed within the 28 day period because the child would no longer be in care under s. 1.

This situation has now been clarified by the House of Lords judgement in *London Borough of Lewisham* v. *Lewisham Juvenile Court Justices* (1978), Times, November 1, overturning *Johns* v. *Jones* and the full report of this should be read by all social workers. From a practice point of view the full and proper explanation to parents of "care" and its possible consequences is obviously of the highest importance.

So far as relatives or friends are concerned, they have no *right* to demand the discharge of a child from care unless, of course, they happen to be duly appointed guardians.

It will be remembered that the authority has a duty to secure that the care of the child is taken over by a parent, guardian, relative or friend if this is consistent with the child's welfare. In this section the word "child" refers to anyone under the age of 18 and there may be cases, of older children particularly, who refuse or do not wish to be discharged from care. In such cases there will probably have been a long period of separation or estrangement affecting both the child and his parents and the situation must be dealt with having regard to their understanding of the position, and their genuine wishes. It is to be hoped that situations of this kind will arise less frequently in future, as local authorities look more closely at the possibility of assuming parental rights where this is justified and at the same time examine the desirability of involving both parents and children in the six-monthly review.

3.   RESCISSION OF A RESOLUTION

A resolution of a local authority assuming parental rights in respect of a child in its care may be rescinded by the authority if this action appears to be for the benefit of the child.[5]

Or, a parent or guardian in respect of whom a resolution has been passed may make a complaint to a juvenile court at any time while the resolution is in force, asking that the resolution be determined, and the court after considering the facts may determine the resolution. On the rescission or determination of a resolution, but not otherwise, the child will cease to be in the care of the authority. Legal aid is available in such applications, and there is a right of appeal to the High Court in those cases heard by a juvenile court.

Older young people in care may wish to be discharged from care without returning to a parent or guardian. The authority may discharge if this is in the interest of the welfare of the child—an all embracing term. But if there is a s. 2 Resolution in force, proper steps should be taken to terminate it. (See the D.H.S.S. report on the case of Menheniott, March 1979.)

4.   DISCHARGE OF A CARE ORDER

A person subject to a care order, or the local authority concerned may apply to any juvenile court in the authority's area, or in the area of the child's residence for the discharge of the order. Legal aid is available. A parent or guardian does not have a right to apply for discharge, but may do so on behalf of the child or young person unless prevented by an order of the court from doing so. Under s. 32A of the Children and Young Persons Act 1969 the court will ultimately be able to make such an order whenever it appears in care proceedings that there is or may be a conflict between the interests of the child and those of his parents. But at present this power applies only to applications for the discharge of orders, when there is no opposition. It should therefore apply when either a child or young person, or the local authority, applies for an order to be discharged, and the application is *not opposed* by the other party. The only exception is that the court need not make the order of "separation" of interest if it is satisfied that it is not necessary in the interests of the child to do so. This decision can hardly be made unless the clerk of the court has, in the first place, some information apart from the names of the parties and the nature of the application.

Having made the separation order however, the clerk must decide whether or not to appoint a guardian *ad litem* for the child. If it seems that the child is of an age to represent himself or to instruct a solicitor, for instance, a guardian *ad litem* may not be necessary.

The whole procedure is set out in a D.H.S.S. circular of March 1977 (Separate Representation in Care and Related Proceedings) which appears to suggest that in appropriate cases, a guardian *ad litem* will be appointed as a general rule, but in practice it seems that so far little use has been made of this provision, which was intended to safeguard the child against both the parents and the care authority.

Needless to say a guardian appointed must be quite independent of the local authority concerned in the case; experienced social workers not currently employed may be appointed, but in the main either probation officers or practising social workers from a neighbouring authority seem likely to undertake the greater part of this important work of representing children at a crucial stage in their lives.

If satisfied as to Section 21(2A) the "care or control test", the court may discharge the care order and may, not must, make a supervision order, provided that the person concerned has not attained the age of 18.

If the order is not discharged, no further application may be made without the consent of the court during a period of three months.

If the order is an interim order, and is discharged, a supervision order may not be made. If it is not discharged no further application may be made without the consent of the juvenile court, but an appeal may be made to the High Court.[6]

5. ADOPTION

As an adoption order vests the parental rights in the adopters, the child concerned is obviously discharged from the care of the authority and a resolution or care order in respect of him ceases to have effect.

6. EMIGRATION

Emigration does not automatically terminate care, as if the child emigrates with the foster parents he is still in care and the Boarding-Out Regulations still have to be observed by arranging for supervision through an agency such as International Social Services (or in H.M. Forces Families, S.S.A.F.A.). There are cases, however, in which a child may emigrate with a parent, guardian or relative or for the purpose of joining a parent, guardian, relative or friend and in such cases the child would be discharged from care, as under s. 1(3).

7. DEATH

8. DISCHARGE

Discharge of a committal order made under Acts other than the Children and Young Persons 1969 terminates care. The application may be made to the court either by the local authority, by any person having the legal custody of the child, or by any person who is applying at the same time for the custody of the child.

9. LAPSE

With minor exceptions, there is no provision for care simply to lapse, except by reason of age. It should usually be brought to an end by some positive act such as a court order, or by a decision by the authority to discharge, as under s. 1 of the Children Act 1948.

10. REMOVAL TO A BORSTAL INSTITUTION

When this is ordered by a court in respect of a person aged 15 who is subject to a care order, and accommodated in a community home, the care order is discharged (see Chapter 10). In any other case of a child in care, committed to Borstal the care order does not lapse and if it is superfluous it should be revoked by the juvenile court on application. Committal to a detention centre does not discharge a care order, and application must be made if it is thought that the order should cease. If there is a s. 2 resolution, care will continue, as will parental rights, unless the resolution is rescinded, or set aside.

COMMENT

The steadily increasing number of children in care at the end of each statistical year seems to indicate a need for more attention to be paid to the question of discharge. The increase in numbers takes place against a background of a falling under 18 population and a decline in admissions; it can only be due therefore to some degree of failure to bring about discharges by one or other of the methods set out above. Though discharge from s. 1 care to that of parents accounts for many children who have been in short-term care, a high proportion of children who have been in care for more than 5 years first came into care under that section; it is surprising to find that one child in every 6 of the total in care is actually in the charge of a parent or guardian and that local authority care—in the full meaning of the word—can be little more than supervision, with the addition of the authority's right to recall the child under the care order or resolution which exists in the majority of such cases.

The present trend towards more long-term care is most likely to be arrested by improved decision making, notably at reviews; these should always be based on some real understanding of the nature of the "care" status, and on a firm commitment to bring care, under whatever authority, to an end when it is no longer necessary. It is known from research findings that children, especially older children, may not know that they ought to be consulted more than they are at present. Unless this position is improved there will be new demands for each child in care to have an advocate to represent him at reviews—as is already being suggested by "The Voice of the Child in Care" and other interested bodies.

AFTER CARE

It will be clear that there are cases of children who are discharged from the care of the authority but who require supervision, advice and possibly assistance after their discharge. There are various provisions in the Acts to meet this situation:

A   When a child is in care under Section 1 of the Children Act 1948, and is discharged from care when over compulsory school age, the authority has a duty to continue to advise and befriend him unless they are satisfied that his welfare does not require it.[7] If at the time of discharge he goes to live in the area of another authority that authority must be informed, but the decision as to whether to exercise supervision is for the authority in whose area the child resides and not for the authority which has discharged the child from care. There are no requirements or regulations as regards the extent of the supervision, except that it may continue until the age of 18, and there is no power under this section to give financial assistance. The Children Act contains no provision for the after-care of children who are discharged while of compulsory school age, or below school age, but supervision may now be exercised, with the consent of the parents, under the general powers of the 1963 Act, s. 1.

B   When children are in care under a care order this remains in force, as we have seen, until the age of 18 or 19 unless before that time it is discharged by a juvenile court.[8] In such cases a supervision order *may* be made for a period of not more than three years. It is important to note, however, that no supervision order in care proceedings is now to have effect over the age of 18. Supervision orders are dealt with in Chapter 14.

After a care order has been discharged the local authority has no duty to exercise after-care supervision unless named in the supervision order or to give financial assistance, except to meet the cost of any facilities which may be provided under the order.[8]

C   In certain circumstances the authority has power to give financial assistance by supplementing the earnings of young people under the age of 21 who have been in care at any time since ceasing to be of compulsory school age, and are aged 17 years or more. Moreover, the financial assistance may be continued after the age of 21 for the purpose of enabling a boy or girl to complete a course of education or training already entered upon.[9]

The giving of financial assistance is not to be confused with care and is quite independent of any duty to advise, supervise or befriend. Such financial assistance may now be available to both the more successful young people, such as apprentices or students in training college or universities, and to the less successful who after the age of 17 pass out of care into borstal, prison, mental hospitals, etc., but in such cases financial aid is only to be given in exceptional circumstances.

The Children and Young Persons Act 1963 considerably amended and expanded the powers and duties of a local authority with regard to children formerly in care. The Act of 1969 in effect makes the local authority the sole substitute parent for all the purposes of the Act. In this way it provides a continuing responsibility for care up to the age of 18, or in some cases 19, thus making the former "approved school after-care" unnecessary.

The Table on page 000 sets out the functions of local authorities in regard to persons formerly in care whether under care orders or otherwise.

It will be noted that these functions may be exercised by any local authority, not only by the authority in whose care the person has been.

NOTES

1. Children Act 1948, ss. 1 and 4(1); Matrimonial Causes Act 1973, s. 43; Matrimonial Proceedings (Magistrates' Courts) Act 1960, s. 3(4); Family Law Reform Act 1969, s. 7; Guardianship Act 1973, s. 4(1).
2. Children and Young Persons Act 1969, ss. 20 and 21.
3. Children Act 1948, s. 1(3) and s. 6.
4. See "The case for retaining a child in voluntary care", Richard White, in *Family Law,* 1976.
5. Children Act 1948, s. 4.
6. Children and Young Persons Act 1969, ss. 21 and 22(4).
7. Children Act 1948, s. 34.
8. Children and Young Persons Act 1969, ss. 21 and 18(4).
9. Children Act 1948, s. 20, Children and Young Persons Act 1963, ss. 46 and 58.

FUNCTIONS OF LOCAL AUTHORITIES IN REGARD TO PERSONS FORMERLY IN CARE

Qualifying conditions	Relevant enactment	Function exercisable by	Nature of power or duty to befriend, etc.	Nature of power to give financial assistance	Function exercisable while person concerned is
That the person concerned ceased to be in care when over compulsory school age	Children Act 1948, s. 34	Local authority in whose area the person is	Duty to advise and befriend him unless his welfare does not require it	—	Under the age of 18
	Children Act 1948, s. 20(1)	Any local authority	—	Power to make contributions to cost of accommodation and maintenance near place where employed, seeking employment or receiving education or training	
That the person concerned ceased to be in care when aged 17 or on attaining the age of 18	Children Act 1948, s. 20(2)			Power to make grants towards expenses of receiving suitable education or training	Aged 17 and under 21
	Children and Young Persons Act 1963, s. 58	Any local authority	Power to cause him to be visited, advised and befriended, at his own request	Power in exceptional circumstances to cause him to be given financial assistance	

Notes:

1. This table is only a guide to the statutory provisions and does not reproduce their exact wording.
2. The same person may fulfil more than one of the conditions mentioned in the first column of the table.
3. Section 34 of the Children Act 1948, applies only to children who have been in care under s. 1 of that Act. The other enactments mentioned in the second column of the table apply also to persons who have been in care under orders or matrimonial orders or orders under the Family Law Reform Act 1969.
4. The powers conferred by sub-ss. (1) and (2) of s. 20 of the Children Act 1948, are exercisable in regard to a person aged 21 or over in the circumstances mentioned in sub-s. (3).
5. Where a local authority has acted as guarantor under a deed of apprenticeship or articles of clerkship entered into by a child in their care, they may assume the same obligation under any supplemental deed or articles even if he is no longer in their care. (Children and Young Persons Act 1963, s. 47.)

Chapter 14

OTHER SERVICES

SUMMARY

SUPERVISION IN MATRIMONIAL, WARDSHIP, GUARDIANSHIP AND ADOPTION CASES

Another type of supervision is that exercised under the authority of court orders.

There are some cases in which children are already being supervised under orders made in divorce or matrimonial proceedings; to these may be added those wards of court who may be placed under supervision under the Family Law Reform Act 1969 and those supervised under the Guardianship Act 1973 and s. 17 of the Children Act 1975. In all such cases, the court has had power to make an order relating to a child, but has considered that there are exceptional circumstances which make it desirable that he should be under the supervision of an independent person. A supervision order has therefore been made nominating either a probation officer, or a local authority to undertake the supervision of the child; the court making the order retains the power to vary or discharge it. Such orders will continue to be made, probably more frequently, in the future. They are not to be confused with the supervision orders which can be made under the Children and Young Persons Act 1969, in either care or criminal proceedings instituted under its provisions. The main differences are set out in question and answer form in the following pp. 201-212..

SUPERVISION ORDERS UNDER THE 1969 ACT

Such supervision orders succeed the former type of supervision order which was made by juvenile courts in care, protection or control proceedings under the 1963 Act, or following the revocation of a Fit Person Order; they also succeed the former probation order in respect of a person under the age of 17, and may therefore be made by a juvenile court, or by a crown court.

These supervision orders were dealt with extensively in the Guide to Part I of the Act, in paras 108-150. Some of these paragraphs are referred to by number in the notes which follow but have been modified by the Criminal Law Act 1977.

Supervision orders follow either criminal or care proceedings before a court, in the same way as care orders. When made in criminal proceedings, a supervision order is a sentence, unlike a probation order (para. 81). It does not contain a minimum period of supervision, but there is a maximum period of three years, which means that in some cases supervision may continue until the person supervised is well over the age of 18. After that age, only an adult court has power to vary or discharge the order, and may impose punishments (fine, attendance centre order) whether allowing the supervision order to continue in operation, or not. The court may order fine or imprisonment if it decides to discharge the order (142/143).

A juvenile court has power to deal with applications for variation or discharge of a supervision order while its subject is under the age of 18, and unlike the adult court may make an interim care order while considering what action to take upon the application before it. Where the person supervised is over 17, but not yet 18, the juvenile court may elect to use the powers of the adult court referred to in the last paragraph.

It may be thought that supervision orders made in criminal proceedings have much in common with the probation orders they replaced, but they may not include a condition of residence in a probation home or hostel and this has been regretted in some quarters.

In *criminal proceedings* a social report will be available to the court after it has decided the question of guilt. The report will have been compiled either by a probation officer or on behalf of a local authority and will indicate which of the various forms of treatment might be thought appropriate. (See para. 77 of the Guide.) If of all the alternatives the court chooses to make a supervision order, it may be thought that this most closely approximates to a probation order, although there are differences between the two.

In *care proceedings*, a supervision order may be made for a maximum period of three years, but is of no effect after the subject of it attains the age of 18. In these proceedings, of course, the order can only be made if the care or control test is satisfied, and it must therefore be assumed that in all cases (including those in which the offence condition is alleged) there has been a referral to the Social Services Department. Following this, either voluntary supervision, voluntary admission to care, or other suitable facilities would have been considered and offered to the individual concerned and his family; either they have not been accepted, or they have not been successful in providing the necessary care or control, and it has been thought essential for the person to be brought before a court so that a suitable order can be made.

It follows that the question of consent to the supervision order, in general, does not arise. Had there been co-operation there would have been no need to apply to the court.

As we have seen, before making an order, the court will itself have to apply the care or control test, and when it has decided that an order is necessary will consider reports provided by the probation officer, or the local authority, or perhaps both. Such reports in care cases will often be based on the information and insight gained during a period of voluntary supervision, or the attempt to provide it, and will indicate why an application is being made to the court, and what needs to be done to provide the individual concerned with

    (a) the care, or

    (b) the control, which he needs.

The court itself will then need to choose between the various orders which it may make under s. 1(3) and in particular perhaps between a care order, which may be used to remove a child from his home on a long-term basis, and a supervision order, which may not. There are of course other possible orders as set out in Chapter 8.

There may seem to be little difference between a care order if under it a child is allowed to live at home (s. 13 of the Children Act 1948, as amended) and a supervision order, except that the care order is effective

SUPERVISION UNDER ORDERS OF COURT (ENGLAND)

CONTENTS

These notes relate only to supervision carried out under court orders.

They do *not* cover supervision under statute, such as the Adoption Act 1958, the Children Act 1958, or the Boarding-Out of Children Regulations.

Nor do they refer to:
(1) Duties to advise and befriend under s. 34 of the Children Act 1948 or other statutes.

(2) The provision of advice, guidance and assistance under the Children and Young Persons Act 1963.

(3) The supervision exercised in respect of children in the care of other local authorities.

QUESTION	CHILDREN AND YOUNG PERSONS		ORDERS FOR SUPERVISION IN:			
	Criminal Proceedings†	Care Proceedings	Matrimonial Proceedings†	Divorce Proceedings	Wardship Proceedings	Guardianship Proceedings*
Statute	C. and Y.P. Act 1969, s. 7(7). Also under s. 21(2) following discharge of a care order provided that, from January 1976, the "care or control" test is satisfied.	C. and Y.P. Act 1969, s. 1(3)	Matrimonial Proceedings (Magistrates' Courts) Act 1960. Supervision may be ordered as part of matrimonial order under s. 2(1) and s. 4	Matrimonial Causes Act 1973, s. 44	Family Law Reform Act 1969, s. 7(4)	Guardianship of Minors Act 1971, extended by the Guardianship Act 1973 [1]
Court	Juvenile court or crown court	Juvenile court	Magistrates' Court (Domestic Proceedings)	Family Division of High Court or County Court with Divorce jurisdiction (Matrimonial Causes Act 1967)	Family Division of High Court	High Court, County Court, Magistrates' Court (Domestic Proceedings) [2]
Rules	Magistrates' Courts (Children and Young Persons) Rules 1970		Magistrates Courts (Matrimonial Proceedings) Rules 1960			Magistrates' Courts (Guardianship of Minors) Rules 1974 [3]
Age at which orders may be made	Under 17 at the date when proceedings are commenced; s. 15 provides that no person aged 16 who is or has been married may be made subject to care proceedings (C. and Y.P. Act 1963 (s. 29 as amended))		Under 16 (s. 2(1) (d))	Under 18	Under 18	Under 18 [4]
Are enquiries made prior to the order?	Yes.—Under C. and Y.P. Act 1969, s. 9, by local authority, but the home surroundings part of enquiry may be made by the probation service under arrangements under s. 34(3) for children of a specified age which may not be higher than 14. It is now 13 (1974) Rule 10	Rule 20	Court may call for a report from the probation officer or from local authority. S. 4 (2). The ten days' notice is not required (r. 1)	A court may request a probation officer to make enquiries and a report with a view to helping in the making of a decision. Rule 31 of the Probation Rules requires probation officers to make such reports on request. There is a memorandum regarding consultation with local authorities in divorce proceedings		[5]

* Section 3 of the Guardianship Act 1973 deals with supervision orders made under that Act and applies also to orders made on the refusal of an Adoption Order (Children Act, s. 17). It will also apply to supervision orders made when a custodianship order is revoked (Children Act 1975, s. 36).

† See fn. 29, infra for important additions made under the Criminal Law Act 1977 which affect supervision orders made in criminal proceedings only.

In what circumstances may the order be made?	Person has been found guilty of an offence s. 7(7). Note that unless the offence is homicide proceedings may be care proceedings, using condition (f)	Court has found that one of the conditions (a) to (f) in s. 1 is satisfied, *and* that necessary care or control is not likely to be provided unless an order is made. The order made must be for the welfare of the child or young person (C. and Y.P. Act 1933, s. 44). Note that "care" includes protection and guidance, and "control" includes discipline (C. and Y.P. Act 1969, s. 70(1))	In an application by one spouse for a matrimonial order, a child of the family has been committed to the custody of a parent, or other person, and there are exceptional circumstances making independent supervision desirable S. 2(1) (f)—See s. 16 for meaning of "child of the family"	The court has jurisdiction to make an order for custody of a child and there are exceptional circumstances making independent supervision desirable, the child having been committed to the care of a person. (Not custody)	The minor is a ward of court (not already committed by the Family Law Reform Act to the care of a local authority) and there are exceptional circumstances making independent supervision desirable	The court has made an order under the Guardianship of Minors Act 1971 (s. 9) giving the custody of a minor (under 18) to a person, but there are exceptional circumstances making independent supervision desirable. (Such an order may be made if the child is illegitimate (s. 2(6)) [6]
		A supervision order may also be made by the court which discharges a care order (but not an interim care order) s. 21(2). See Note 1, *ante.* In making a supervision order the court must be satisfied that the person concerned will reside in the area of a local authority (s. 18(1))				
Can other orders be made at the same time?	No, except that in making a supervision order, the court *may* discharge any previous existing care or supervision order (s. 7(7)) (s. 1 (4)) But there is power to make a separate order for compensation in criminal or care (offence condition) proceedings. (Criminal Justice Act 1972 and C. and Y.P. Act, ss. 3 and 6(3))		No, apart from the principal order referred to above. That is to say, a supervision order cannot be made at the same time as a committal to the care of a local authority (s. 2(4) (c)) s. 44(3)) (s. 7(3)) [7]			Orders for payment or in respect of financial arrangements may be made separately as appropriate
Can an order for supervision be made if the child is in care?	Yes, if charged with and found guilty of an offence in respect of which a supervision order can be made. The court may at the same time discharge any existing care order, supervision order or parental recognisance s. 7(7)	Yes, if the "care or control" test is satisfied. In s. 1(2) (a) the present tense "is" may be taken as applying to the situation as it would normally be; a child may in this event be brought before a court under s. 1(1) even though in care under the Act of 1948	No—s. 2(4) (b) The present Act will be superseded by the Domestic Proceedings and Magistrates' Courts Act 1978 which will bring magisterial powers more closely into line with those of the Divorce Court.	Yes, unless in care as a result of an order of the court committing the child to the care of a local authority under these Acts [8]		

	CHILDREN AND YOUNG PERSONS		ORDERS FOR SUPERVISION IN:			
QUESTION	*Criminal Proceedings*	*Care Proceedings*	*Matrimonial Proceedings*	*Divorce Proceedings*	*Wardship Proceedings*	*Guardianship Proceedings*
Who is to be responsible for supervision?	A probation officer appointed for the petty sessions area named in the order—if (a) the supervised person is above a certain age—now (1975) 13, and (b) the supervised person is under that age, but the probation officer is already exercising duties in relation to another member of the household, *and* the local authority has requested him to undertake supervision under the order *or* The local authority for the area in which the supervised person resides,* or a different authority if it agrees to be named, (ss. 11, 13. A "child" in s. 13(2) is as defined in s. 34(1) (a)—at present not over 13)	No	A probation officer for the petty sessions area in which the supervised person will reside,* or a specified local authority (s. 2(1) (f) as amended by Local Government Act 1972)	A welfare officer—that is to say a probation officer selected under arrangements made by the Secretary of State, or a local authority selected by the court s. 44(2)		If an order under this Act is made in a magistrates' court, a probation officer for the Petty Sessions area in which the supervised person will reside,* or the local authority for that area 9
Is the consent of the supervised person required as in probation orders?	No, in criminal proceedings it is a sentence, and may therefore be the subject of an appeal. *But* if the person is over 14, his consent is required to the insertion of a requirement to undergo treatment under the Mental Health Act 1959 s. 12(4). Though consent is not in general required, Rules 11 and 21 of the Magistrates' Courts (C. and Y.P. Act) Rules 1970 provide for the court to allow representations to be made unless the court considers this either undesirable or impracticable on account of age and understanding	No	No, but when the court contemplates making the order, the parties to the case (parents) must be served with a notice setting out the powers which the court may invoke. See r. 3 of Magistrates Courts (Matrimonial Proceedings) Rules 1960	No	No	No
			Supervision under these Acts makes no demands upon the children who are to be supervised			10

* Resides means "habitually resides" (s. 7) (1). This is of special importance when a supervision order is made in respect of a child or young person already subject to supervision by another local authority—residence is not necessarily at the place where he lives for the time being.

	11	12	13	14
What is the purpose of the order?	Not stated, but by implication it creates opportunity for the supervisor to establish a personal relationship with the supervised person. (Guide, para. 120). The supervisor may then bring to bear influences which while not punitive will discourage further offences	Similarly, by implication to create a personal relationship which will provide care (including protection and guidance) or control (including discipline) which is unlikely to be provided without the order	Not stated, but it is to provide independent supervision for a minor who has been involved in domestic civil proceedings. It should be remembered that the order can only have been made in exceptional circumstances	
What are the duties of the supervisor?	To advise, assist and befriend the supervised person (s. 14). This provides the basis for the personal relationship referred to in 11 above. The relationship is primarily with the person to be supervised rather than with any other persons. (Probation officers in exercising their supervisory duties are subject to the Probation Rules 1965, which specify the records to be kept, explanation of the order, frequency of visiting and other contact, enquiry as to progress at school, use of voluntary and other facilities and reports to the case committee and the court. These may serve as a guide to local authority social workers undertaking supervision under orders pending the issue of Regulations)		The Probation Rules 1965 may be applied to any person under supervision, so far as is suitable to the circumstances of the case. Application is therefore discretionary, but the Rules of course apply only to probation officers.	
Is the supervisor named in the order?	No. The order names the area of the local authority (see 9 above), and the petty sessions area in which the supervised person will reside. * S. 18(1)		No. (See under "Who is to be responsible for supervision?" above)	
What provision may the order contain?	Any which will help the supervisor to assist, advise and befriend, including any prescribed under the Justices of the Peace Act 1949, s. 15. These are optional but may require the supervised person to inform the supervisor of any change of address or employment, and/or to keep in touch with the supervisor as instructed. Magistrates' Courts (Children and Young Persons) Rules 1970, r. 28(2). It appears from s. 12(2) that if *these* provisions are included in the order by the court, the supervisor is not free to decide whether or not they should be complied with * See note, *ante* on "resides"		None relating to supervision itself, but the whole order may contain other provisions relating to custody, access, maintenance and other such matters	

CHILDREN AND YOUNG PERSONS   ORDERS FOR SUPERVISION IN:

QUESTION	Criminal Proceedings	Care Proceedings	Matrimonial Proceedings	Divorce Proceedings	Wardship Proceedings	Guardianship Proceedings
What other requirements may the order contain?	These are to be found in s. 12 1. A requirement to live with a specified *person*, who is agreeable to this, such as a relative. There is no power to make a requirement for unlimited residence at a specified *place*. This residence requirement may be overridden by the others, set out below: 2. A requirement to comply with directions of the supervisor to take part in "intermediate treatment" (either residential or non residential) for a period or periods not exceeding 90 days during the existence of the supervision order. No requirement under (2) may be included unless it is available under the regional plan approved by the Secretary of State. The supervisor may or may not give any directions under (2), but if he does, may give them orally or in writing (if orally, it is suggested that a note should be kept for record purposes). Costs under 2 are to be met by the local authority (s. 18(4)). Costs under 1 (residence with a named person) may be met by the Probation Committee under r. 40, if a probation officer is the supervisor. If the court is satisfied by medical evidence that a person needs mental treatment, but not under a hospital order, the supervision order may contain a requirement that he shall undergo such treatment as is appropriate without time limit—but not beyond the 18th birthday. Such a requirement may only be made if the court is satisfied also that the treatment can be provided. If the person to be supervised is over the age of 14, his consent to this requirement is necessary, s. 12 (4), (5) See note* on p. 211	—See previous page—	—As above—		

What is the duration of the order?	Not more than three years, and the period may extend beyond the 18th birthday. S. 17(a) It is desirable that there should be a standard explanation of a supervision order for the information of the supervised person.	Not more than three years – not valid after the 18th birthday S. 17(b)	Up to the age of 16 S. 3(9)	Up to the age of 18	If the parents are living together when the order is made, the court may direct that the order shall not be operative while they continue to live together, *or* the court may order that the supervision order shall cease to have effect if they are still living together three months after it was made, S. 3(2). Otherwise expires at age 16. (Mag. Ct.) or 18 (Higher Cts.) 16
Can an order be cancelled before it would otherwise expire?	Yes by a juvenile court only, if the supervised person is under 18. But if the supervised person is aged 17 but not yet 18, the juvenile court may discharge the order, or may decide to use the powers available to a magistrates court in dealing with the persons aged 18, s. 15(2). The above applies also when the supervision order was originally made on the discharge of a care order made in care or criminal proceedings. S. 15(2). If the supervised person is aged 18, discharge of the order can only be dealt with by a magistrates' court, s. 15 (3, 4)	If the Order was made in care proceedings, cancellations will be dealt with by a juvenile court which may, on cancelling the supervision order make a care order, s. 15(1). But in discharging a supervision order whether or not making a care order, the court must apply the care or control test, s.16(6). If the application is unopposed, s. 32A(2) applies (separate representation of child)	Yes, under ss. 8 and 10 (d,f)	Yes; it is rare for orders to be made after the age of 16 in the High Court, and therefore many orders can be considered for cancellation before or, at, that age.	In the Magistrates' courts, orders expire at 16, but may be cancelled before then

17

CHILDREN AND YOUNG PERSONS   ORDERS FOR SUPERVISION IN:

QUESTION	Criminal Proceedings	Care Proceedings	Matrimonial Proceedings	Divorce Proceedings	Wardship Proceedings	Guardianship Proceedings
Who may apply for cancellation?	The supervisor or the supervised person s. 15(1) (3), or his parent or guardian if he is under 18, s. 70(2). If the supervised person is over 18 and has failed to comply with any requirements in the order, the application may only be made by the supervisor, s. 15(4)		The parties to the marriage, any parent, the supervisor, any person having or seeking the custody of the child (The child under supervision under these Acts is not served with a copy of the order, and has no right of direct application for its discharge)	Either party to the marriage, a parent, or other person who has custody, an appointed and functioning guardian, the supervisor or a parent seeking custody	Either party to the marriage, a parent, or other person who has custody, any guardian appointed and functioning guardian, the supervisor or a parent seeking custody	Either parent, or other person who has custody, any guardian appointed and functioning and the supervisor, s. 3(3) 18
Can the order be varied while it is in force?	*General Note:* The courts having jurisdiction to vary or discharge supervision orders under the 1969 Act are the juvenile or magistrates' courts acting for the petty sessions area which is named in the supervision order at the time of the application. Subject to 17 and 18 above the juvenile court has jurisdiction to deal with an application which is pending when the supervised person attains the age of either 17 or 18 as the case may be	In dealing with persons under the age of 18, the juvenile court may: (a) amend the duration of supervision within the limits set out in 16 above; (b) name another local authority or petty sessions area and probation officer for supervision purposes; (c) cancel any requirement contained in the order; (d) insert or substitute provisions in the order. (Except that a new requirement of residence at a specified *place* may not be inserted later than twelve months from the date of the order. Nor may a new requirement to undergo treatment for mental disorder be inserted later than three months from the date of the order, and consent is required if the supervised person is over 14.	Yes, by adding or altering provisions as to custody	Yes, in the High Court, in any way thought necessary in the interests of the child		In magistrates' courts, s. 3(3) of the Guardianship Act 1973 applies

19

...requirement to undergo mental treatment may only be inserted or varied on receipt of a report from a medical practitioner)

Apart from minor variations, the court may only insert, cancel or vary requirements in a supervision order or make a care order in place of it, if it is satisfied that as a result of the variation, the "care or control" test will be satisfied, ss. 15 and 16(6)

An adult (magistrates' court) or a juvenile court which has decided to use the powers of an adult court in dealing with a supervised person aged 17 but under 18 may:

(a) amend the duration of the order;

(b) vary the local authority and petty sessions area for supervision purposes

(c) cancel any of the requirements in the order—but may not insert or vary any requirement. The "care or control" test does not apply. Usually, proceedings in respect of persons aged 17 and 18 will arise from a failure to comply with requirements, and the application will be made by the supervisor. In such cases, the court may impose a fine up to £20 or make an attendance order and may, or may not, vary or discharge the order. If the order is discharged, the court may deal with the case in the same way as a breach of probation would be dealt with in the magistrates court. (See note at 17 above)

Only the juvenile court may vary an order made in care proceedings. In care proceedings only a supervision order may include, or be varied to include, a requirement that the supervised person shall be medically examined. As this is not a "minor" variation under s. 16(5) the supervised person must be before the court when the requirement is made. Procedure in detail is set out in Circular LAC (78)12 of July 1978.

See above

| | CHILDREN AND YOUNG PERSONS | | ORDERS FOR SUPERVISION IN: | | | |
QUESTION	Criminal Proceedings	Care Proceedings	Matrimonial Proceedings	Divorce Proceedings	Wardship Proceedings	Guardianship Proceedings
Who may apply for variation?	The supervisor or the supervised person, s. 15(1)(3); or his parent or guardian, if he is under 18, s. 70(2). If the supervised person is over 18 and has failed to comply with any requirements in the order, the application may only be made by the supervisor, s. 15(4)		The parties to the marriage, any parent, the supervisor, any person having or seeking the custody of the child (The child under supervision under these Acts is not served with a copy of the order, and has no right of direct application for its variation)	Either party to the marriage, a parent, or other person who has custody, an appointed and functioning guardian, the supervisor or a parent seeking custody		Either parent, or other person who has custody, any guardian appointed and functioning and the supervisor, s. 3(3) 20
Can a supervision order be made in the absence of the child or young person concerned?	No	Yes, if he is under 5 and the parents or guardian are in the court, or have been given adequate notice of the proceedings, s. 2(9). No, if he is over the age of 5	Yes	Yes	Yes	Yes 21a
Can a supervision order be discharged or varied in the absence of the child or young person concerned?	Yes, if the application is for discharge, cancelling or reducing the duration of any requirement or provision in the order, or for a change of supervisor or supervising area, s. 16(5). But see s. 32A if application is unopposed. For other variation, the person must be present, s. 16(1)		Yes	Yes	Yes	Yes 21b
How can attendance at court, when required, be secured?	For a variation, the normal practice is for notice to be served, Rule 14 but a justice may issue a summons or warrant, s. 16(2). S. 16 also deals with procedure after arrest in pursuance of such a warrant.					22
Can any number of applications be made for the discharge of a supervision order?	Yes, but when such an application is dismissed no fresh application can be made within three months, unless the court consents, s. 16(9)		There is no similar provision for orders under these Acts			23
Can a child or young person subject to a supervision order be admitted to care under the Children Act 1948, s. 1?	Yes	Yes	Yes, but note that if so received into care, the only parent for the purposes of ss. 1–5 (admission, discharge and assumption of parental rights) is the person who has been awarded custody by the court (Children Act 1948, s. 6)			24

Can the local authority pass a resolution in respect of him under s. 2?	Yes, s. 6	Yes, s. 6	Yes, subject to above—s. 6
			25 In the High Court cases this might well be one of the situations in which the supervisor might seek the direction of the court. This should be done whenever there is any serious cause for concern regarding the welfare of the child
When is a supervision order cancelled automatically?	If a supervised person under the age of 18 appears before a juvenile court under s. 15(1), and the court makes a full care order, the existing supervision order is thereby discharged, s. 15(1). If a supervised person is aged 17 and the order was not made in care proceedings nor on the discharge of a care order, the juvenile court may decide to use the powers by an adult court acting in the case of a person aged 18, s. 15(2). If punishment is imposed under s. 15(4) (b) in respect of a person aged 17 or 18 the supervision order is discharged, (see Q. 19 above)	Apart from C. and Y.P. Act 1969, s. 15(2) and 15(4) (b) no supervision order is automatically cancelled. There may thus be a supervision order in force for a person who has been sent to a detention centre or to a borstal under different legislation; supervision will also be provided under that other legislation and the original supervision order may be superfluous. (Application for a discharge should be made under s. 15(1))	Supervision orders under these Acts will not be cancelled automatically except by the expiration of the period of supervision according to age. Application for cancellation must be made to the appropriate court 26
Appeals (in the first instance)	To crown court on questions of law or fact, or—on point of law only—to Divisional Court of Appeal. The child, not the parent, is the appellant		From magistrates' courts, appeals lie to the Court of Appeal, Civil Division, which also hears appeals from county courts and the High Court, Family Division. In these cases the child is not the appellant 27
Legal aid	The child may make application for legal aid under the Legal Aid Act 1974		Application may be made for legal aid, but not by the child himself 28
Statute	Criminal Law Act 1977 * This Act leaves intact existing provisions with regard to supervision orders made in criminal proceedings, or on the discharge of a supervision order		Some of the difficulties and anomalies arising in the exercise of the various orders for supervision which are not made by a juvenile court, are examined in an article in *Social Work Today* of 4 September 1975. See "Supervision Orders in matrimonial and guardianship cases" by Edward Griew and Alastair Bissett-Johnson of Leicester University

29

QUESTION	Criminal Proceedings	Care Proceedings	Matrimonial Proceedings	Divorce Proceedings	Wardship Proceedings	Guardianship Proceedings
Statute	originally made in such proceedings, but introduces new sanctions which may now be used by juvenile courts in dealing with persons charged with an offence. The sanctions do not apply to orders made in care proceedings. The court may now impose conditions requiring the supervised person to be of good behaviour, to attend school (if of school age) and may add any requirement it thinks necessary to prevent further offences, subject to the consent of the young person or his parents. Failure to comply with any conditions in the order will enable the supervisor to apply to the court which may order a fine of up to £50 or may make an attendance centre order. The additional requirements may be imposed directly by the court which will expect the juvenile to comply with them, and to be answerable to the court for any "breach" of them rather in the same way as under the former probation order.					

until the age of 18 (or 19) while the supervision order is valid only for three years. There are however other differences to be borne in mind. The care order entrusts the care and control of the child to the local authority which has freedom to exercise its legal powers for the whole period of care, whereas the supervision order may contain requirements inserted by the court.

One of these is that the person to be supervised shall live with a person named in the order, with that person's consent. This could clearly be a valuable provision when it is considered that a child or young person would benefit from living, for instance, with a relative or friend rather than with his own parents for a time, but that it is not necessary to make a care order conferring parental rights on the authority. It must be assumed however, in care cases, that the local authority or other person taking the proceedings would have considered this possibility before bringing the case to court, but had met opposition from either the child or his parents. This provision is rarely used.

It will be noted that there is no power to make a requirement that a supervised person shall live at a particular place, as under a probation order. If this is thought necessary it can be better achieved by the making of a care order (119).

The second requirement that a court may make is one relating to mental treatment—unlimited as to time within the span of the order except that it may not extend beyond the 18th birthday, and may be varied from time to time, subject always to the care or control test, which in this instance applies to the variation of orders made in criminal proceedings (117, 138-140). This requirement may be imposed on anyone under 14, but after that age his consent must be obtained (117-139). This will be valuable when there is an apparent need for mental treatment, but not such as to warrant the making of a hospital order. The requirement can only be made however if the court is satisfied that there are available facilities for treatment by a doctor, or as an outpatient or inpatient of a hospital and the treatment period is to be specified in the order. A court might find this a useful provision when dealing with a young person addicted to drugs, but again in care cases the requirement would not be necessary had there been co-operation on a voluntary basis before the proceedings were instituted.

The third requirement is that the supervised person shall comply with any directions given to him by his supervisor to take part in "Intermediate Treatment" activities for not more than 90 days. The local authority will be required to meet the expenditure (s. 18(4)) whether one of its own social workers or a probation officer is the supervisor.

Here again, in non-criminal cases any of these arrangements could have been made on a voluntary basis during the period before the proceedings were instituted, and it must be assumed that the co-operation of the juvenile or his parents was not forthcoming. In orders arising from criminal proceedings in which a requirement is imposed the effect may be seen to have something in common with the detention centre or attendance centre order which it is designed ultimately to replace but so far the comparison has not been much in evidence.

It is to be noted that the supervision order itself does not direct the supervised person to *do* any of the things specified in the requirement. It simply gives the power to the supervisor to direct him to comply to the extent thought fit within the limits imposed in the order; whether the supervisor actually uses this power is a question for him to decide as indicated in Appendix C *to Children in Trouble.* But this discretion of the supervisor is removed if in *criminal proceedings* the court uses the powers contained in the new sub-s. 12(3A) and (3B).

Orders made in care proceedings only may require the child to be medically examined. Details of procedure are set out in LAC (78) 12.

Supervision orders made in either criminal or care proceedings, have the effect of

A naming the area of the local authority and the petty sessional division in which the supervised person is to reside (109);

B laying upon the supervisor the duty to advise, assist and befriend (114);

C containing any provisions to be prescribed by Rules for assisting the supervisor in that duty. A requirement may be made for instance requiring the supervised person to visit his supervisor;

D containing, where appropriate, a requirement that the supervised person shall live with a named individual (not at a particular place) or shall submit to mental treatment;

E containing any of the requirements inserted into the order to assist the supervisor or (in criminal proceedings), to prevent further offences. Before such requirements (loosely called intermediate treatment) are included in an order, the facilities for carrying them out must be contained in a regional plan and known to the court, except for those given general approval by the Secretary of State.

There is a body of opinion which considers that regional plans should have been directed towards these facilities in the first place, rather than to the establishment of a system of residential care and secure accommodation in community homes. The requirement for up to ninety-days treatment (not necessarily all in one period) might for instance have prevented a number of admissions for much longer periods in community homes with education on the premises.

With a few exceptions, there are no specially provided places for the meeting of this requirement, and even when such a place exists, there seems to be some confusion as to the real purpose of the requirement, though it is agreed that both the staff and the boys concerned may find the experience enjoyable. A study of the experience of boys in eighteen approved schools, as they then were, suggests, among other things, that the "community homes" might make available short-term experience and projects, even for weekends, and that they might act as bases from which boys could undertake community service work under supervision.[1] There would seem to be no reason why more local homes should not be used in a similar way for short placements, but something more than mere residence would be needed, and might not be readily provided.

The lack of the facilities for the ninety-day residence provision may well be one reason for the increase in the courts' use of the detention centre order; if this is to be diminished there must be viable alternatives in the regional plan.

There has been a great deal of interested discussion of "intermediate treatment" which at present consists largely of non-residental arrangements. In the D.H.S.S. Development Group Report of 1973 some of the projects then in existence are described;[2] they consist of a camp, a day centre, holiday camps, various activity groups, and a children's club. The impression is that these were all arranged for groups of children and young persons known to the respective authorities (including some who had appeared before a juvenile court) and attendance was of course voluntary. There seems to be no mention of anyone attending in accordance with a requirement in a supervision order that he should "take part in specified activities", or "present himself to a specified person at specified times". Similarly in the Report on the Feltham-Hanworth Intermediate Treatment Group", it appears that a number of adolescents in the group have been before the court, some being under statutory supervision and some being in care under orders but living at home. In assessing the effect of the group, the report points out that its involvement with the boys is for two hours weekly, and implies that there is a need for more help from other agencies such as the Youth Service. It is not suggested in this report that a greater impact might be made by short residential placements within the *local community*—but perhaps there were insuperable problems. A later account of methods used is contained in *I.T. in Action* a pamphlet issued to be used with a film of the same title. This refers to a number of earlier publications and restates the two objectives to be served. One of these is the provision of a wide range of preventive services under the Children and Young Persons Act 1963, s. 1., mentioned earlier under "Prevention" and "Admission to Care". The other objective is to make supervision orders made by juvenile courts more effective. Some of the schemes described in the film include periods of residence at centres established for the purpose and staffed partly by volunteers.

There is as yet little mention of anything in the nature of community service being developed as a part of supervision even on a voluntary basis. There is, however, one county which would use the "supervision" requirement in order to see that offenders made good damage they had caused. There is at present great interest in the development of community service for a group of offenders above the "juvenile" level; it seems surprising that Social Service Departments, which have so many needs for service within their own day and residential establishments, have not more often found useful work for young people subject to supervision orders.

"Intermediate treatment" is a phrase applied to a great deal of activity which is really preventive work and very valuable as such, but it seems to have little to do with supervision under the terms of an order of a court.

There is increasing investment in it, but so far it is not known to what extent it is being successful in its second stated objective. When requirements are inserted into an order, they are meant to assist the supervisor, who should keep them under review and not hesitate to ask for changes if necessary. In dealing with adolescent offenders, it seems that few social worker supervisors have seen the relevance of requirements to the essence of the supervision order, which is a relationship between the supervisor and an individual, rather than a group. This reluctance to use the supervision order as a means of "control" may be responsible for the changes brought about by the Criminal Law Act 1977. The inherent difficulties of social work in supervision activities are examined at some length in the B.A.S.W. Guide to the 1969 Act; the Guide also sets out some implications for practice.

The supervisor under supervision orders is to be a probation officer, or a local authority, normally that for the area of residence (110).

If the person to be supervised is under 13 years of age the local authority will be named, unless it asks that a probation officer should be named because he is concerned or has been concerned in exercising supervision under some statutory authority in respect of an adult or juvenile member of the household (111-112).

If the person to be supervised is 13 years old or more, either the probation officer or the local authority may be named, and courts will presumably make their decision in accordance with the circumstances of each case and the local conditions prevailing at the time.

The dividing line at the age of 13 is for the time being and may be raised when thought appropriate under s. 34. In the meantime local authorities are supervising some young people in the age group 13-17, and may feel the need to seek the advice and counsel of the probation service for some time to come. In particular they may need to draw upon the accumulated experience of probation officers in such questions as where, how often and when to see persons under supervision, how to make the arrangements for such meetings, and how to review progress in each case. Probation Rules govern these matters, and if these are applied by local authority social workers they will be of great assistance, pending Regulations to be made.

Supervision orders may be discharged or varied on application under s. 15; until the supervised person is 18. When a supervision order is discharged the court may make a care order, but only if the care or control test is applied. The care or control test is in fact to be applied in all applications for discharge or variation of supervision orders whether the result will be favourable or unfavourable to the supervised person. But when the result will be favourable to him, or when the variation is purely technical, the supervised person need not be brought before the court (140, 146). When the application is not opposed, however, the court must consider the representation of the child if the order arose from care proceedings. Sections 32A(2) and 32B(1) of the Act apply.

After the age of 18, only supervision orders made in criminal proceedings can still be in force. The power to discharge or to make minor variations is thus confined to adult courts which are not required to consider the care or control test, and may impose the penalties for non-compliance set out at the beginning of this chapter.

There are cross-border arrangements to meet cases in which the supervised person moves lawfully from one part of the United Kingdom to another. See para. 247 of the "Guide" and the Social Work (Scotland) Act 1968, operative from April 1971.

2. THE COURTS

The Children and Young Persons Act 1933, did not make Children's Committees responsible for Part I of the Act (prevention of cruelty and exposure to moral and physical danger) or for Part II (regulation of employment). Prosecutions under these Parts of the Act were, therefore, left in the hands of the Police, the N.S.P.C.C. and the local Education Authority. It is now provided additionally that the local authority may institute proceedings in respect of offences under either Part I or Part II of the Act (*e.g.* neglect or cruelty, or offences against employment statute or by-laws).[3] Social workers may at times appear at the adult court either as a witness or to make a report. They may also appear in the magistrates' domestic court and in the county court and crown court, where procedures are not the same as in a juvenile court (see "The Social Worker and the Courts", C.C.E.T.S.W. 7).

3. THE JUVENILE COURT

Social workers will frequently represent their local authority in the juvenile courts in their own area and at times in other areas. They will often be expected to supply reports in proceedings and to recommend to courts the making of appropriate orders.

The institution of proceedings is however a rather different matter, as they are to be instituted by the authority, not by an individual. Unless the Director of Social Services has the delegated authority to institute proceedings, he would seek the authority of his committee, or at the very least the authority of his chairman subject to confirmation by the committee. This is a matter for each local authority to determine, but if a Director has delegated powers it makes possible the freedom of action which is sometimes essential in emergencies, and would be expected to lead to a situation where an individual officer could be authorised to institute proceedings under the authority of the Director.

An officer of a local authority who is not a solicitor may conduct proceedings if authorised to do so, under the Local Government Act 1972, s. 223, but usually it is necessary for the case to be conducted by a solicitor on behalf of the authority, especially in view of the wider provisions for legal aid to be available for persons concerned in care and similar proceedings. The partnership between local authority lawyers and social workers has been referred to in earlier chapters. Though a social worker may have a clear idea of the purpose to be achieved by legal means, the solicitor can play an equal part in the decision by advising how the interests of the child can best be served; he will often be able to consider measures other than an application to a juvenile court.

4. REPORTS TO COURTS

A social worker may be present in court for various reasons: to act as a supporter to someone who is appearing as a defendant, to act as a guardian *ad litem* or advocate, to give evidence as a witness in proceedings, or to present a report. These functions must not be confused. A report is only put into the court after it is satisfied that the case has been made out, and is not in itself evidence. There are several other points of importance. In the juvenile court, proceedings are governed by the Magistrates' Court (Children and Young Persons) Rules 1970, as amended, but it will be found that practice varies from one court to another. For example, some courts expect a report to contain references to any police cautions which have been administered prior to the present case; others do not. Some courts follow the Rules precisely by disclosing to defendants and parents the salient points of a social report; others require a copy of the report to be handed to the parties; yet others read the report aloud but paraphrase it as they read. These are all ways of ensuring natural justice. No social report is entirely confidential. If parts of it are very delicate, they can be suitably marked to draw the attention of the court to those matters which would cause concern.

The writing of a social report is in itself a most important task, since it will often lead to a recommendation that a certain course should be followed. The actual content is not prescribed, but must include the basic facts clearly distinguished from opinion. The language used should be clear, concise and free from jargon, so that it can be understood by all concerned. A brief outline of the minimum content of a report is given in "The Social Worker in the Juvenile Court"[4] along with other helpful suggestions for training in the task. Social workers will make reports to adult courts less frequently than to juvenile courts, and will find that the report itself will be handed to the parties, or their legal representatives. In the event of statements being challenged, the social worker may be called upon to give sworn evidence.

Quite apart from the submission of reports to assist courts in the disposal of a variety of criminal and civil cases, periodical reports on progress are a valuable means of promoting understanding and confidence between courts and social workers. Reports to juvenile courts have already been mentioned, but much could be done to stimulate the interest of other courts in the effect of the orders they have made. The increase in divorce for instance means that more children are now placed under supervision, but that the supervisors often have little understanding of the purpose of the order which can drift on until it lapses, even if it is no longer needed.

On the other hand, it may be inadequate; it may be that the child will be seen to be in need of care and the question of care proceedings under the 1969 Act may arise. If the court were kept informed of the position by periodical reports, it would be alerted to the child's position and could itself make an appropriate order without delay. Similar considerations apply to supervision orders made in other types of proceedings.

5. CONVEYING

A further responsibility undertaken by local authority social workers in the courts—and this may arise in adult and in higher courts—is that of conveying to and from courts children and young persons subject to a care order, interim order, supervision order, remand warrant or, in some cases, detained in a place of safety. This responsibility extends also to conveying children and young persons from one type of accommodation to another, and recovering those who abscond—officially to be known as absentees.

The main burden of all conveyals falls upon the local authority as the probation service is no longer concerned in it, but the police may be willing to assist by arrangement, such as that suggested in *Social Work Today* for 3 June 1971.

The police will still be responsible for conveying to and from courts those persons sent to detention centres, remand centres, borstals and prisons.

6. INVESTIGATIONS AND REPORTS

As we have seen, every part of the country has a Social Services Department and because of the excellent co-operation which usually exists it is possible for one department to obtain reports from another department in any part of the British Isles, or to exercise supervision over children through this agency service wherever they may be. A Social Service Department, therefore, receives a number of enquiries from other departments and it is essential that work carried out on behalf of other authorities or voluntary societies, which is considerable, should receive the same careful attention as is given to the authority's own duties towards the children in its care. It is frequently necessary for enquiries to be made or for supervision to be carried out in respect of children outside the British Isles and in such cases authorities often make use of International Social Service which, in turn, asks for the co-operation of English authorities in undertaking work on behalf of social agencies overseas. I.S.S. charge a fee for each enquiry and report.

A social worker today may thus be called upon to carry out duties not only for his own authority but for voluntary organisations, other local authorities and social workers in other countries. This work is carried out under the various Acts and Rules and is summarised at the end of this chapter.

7. ACCOMMODATION OF CHILDREN SUFFERING FROM MENTAL DISORDER

Such children, if otherwise eligible, may be received into care or committed to care.

It should be noted, however, that a local authority may also accommodate in its homes such a child under the age of 18 who is not in the authority's care under the Children Act. An arrangement of this kind will be readily made by the Social Services Department which is responsible for such children whether in care or not.

8. RELATIONSHIP BETWEEN LOCAL AUTHORITIES AND VOLUNTARY SOCIETIES

We have so far been concerned with local authority departments. It will be remembered that in addition to local authorities there are a number of voluntary societies which provide a separate child care service, either in part or in whole.

The best known of the national societies are Dr. Barnardo's, the National Children's Home, the Catholic Crusade of Rescue and the Church of England Children's Society, but there are others operating on a smaller scale and concentrating on a particular aspect of child care work, such as adoption, whereas the larger societies provide nurseries, children's homes, hostels and special schools and also arrange adoption and the boarding-out of children.

The Children Act 1948 recognised the importance of the voluntary bodies and empowered the Secretary of State to make grants to voluntary organisations for improving premises; it also empowered local authorities to make contributions to any voluntary organisation which has as its main object the promotion of the welfare of children.

The great virtue of the voluntary organisation is that it is not governed by the Children Act in deciding which child to admit to care and it may, therefore, admit any child—usually at the request of a parent—and in some cases children may not be regarded as eligible to be received into the care of a local authority. It is now usual for a voluntary organisation to consult a local authority before offering care or other services.

A disadvantage from the point of view of the voluntary organisation is that it cannot enforce contributions from a parent and relies on the collection of money by agreement. Nor has it yet power to assume parental rights though there are restrictions on the power of a parent to remove from care, as in the case of a local authority.[5]

In recent years local authorities have increasingly sought the help of voluntary organisations in accommodating children in public care especially through the community homes system. The voluntary societies are continuing to pioneer new schemes for the support of children and their families as they have always done in the past.

Because of the two parallel systems of child care, the statutory and the voluntary, there is a great need for continuing co-operation between the officers of local authorities and voluntary organisations. There is already a close link between the Secretary of State, local authorities and voluntary organisations, the main provisions of the Act and Regulations being as follows:

A   CHILDREN'S HOMES

The Children and Young Persons Act 1969, s. 58 empowers the Secretary of State to "cause to be inspected" any premises where children in care are accommodated, including foster homes.

Since 1948 it has been necessary for every voluntary home (whether administered by one of the large voluntary societies or not) to be registered by the Secretary of State, who has power to remove any particular home from the register if it is not carried on properly, subject to the right of the home to appeal to a tribunal.[6] (This does not now apply to these homes which are community homes.)

The Secretary of State notifies the local authority of any voluntary home in its area which has been registered and the local authority then has a duty to cause the children in that home to be visited and to authorise its officers to enter the voluntary home for this purpose.

With regard to voluntary homes outside its own area, the local authority has the right to visit any of the children in its care who are accommodated in such a home, but may delegate the duty of visiting to the local authority for the area of the home.

Local authority officers are, therefore, required to visit voluntary homes in the discharge of their duties and should have a proper form of authority which they can produce if required; it is an offence for any person to obstruct the entry of a properly authorised officer, under a penalty of £5 for the first offence and £20 for the second.

In order to control the conditions in children's homes the Secretary of State issued the Administration of Children's Homes Regulations in 1951—these apply to voluntary homes which are not community homes within the regional plans.

B   BOARDING-OUT

In arranging boarding-out the Regulations of 1955 require a considerable degree of co-operation between the local authority and the voluntary society. Before placing a child in a foster home the voluntary society must enquire of the local authority if there is any reason to suppose that the placing would be detrimental to the child. Fourteen days' notice is required for this enquiry and the local authority is not required to visit the home but merely to supply information from official sources. The local authority does not approve or disapprove of the home which it is proposed to use but must give the voluntary society any information it has on which they can make their own decision. When the placing has been arranged the voluntary society must inform the local authority of the name, sex, date of birth and religious persuasion of the child, full names and religious persuasion of each foster parent and their address and the date of placing. They must also state clearly what arrangements have been made for supervision and in the event of the child's removal must report the fact, together with the reasons.

All placings by voluntary societies within an authority's area are recorded by the authority in its boarding-out register along with details of its own children placed in the area.

A local authority has also a duty to enquire from time to time what staff and facilities a voluntary society has for carrying out its statutory duties and, if not satisfied that they are adequate, must itself take over the supervision and relieve the voluntary society of its duties.[7]

As we have seen, it is possible for a local authority to place children in its care with a voluntary society which may decide to place the child in a foster home. In such cases the society is required to notify the authority in whose care the child is and to keep it informed of the child's progress.

C   AFTER-CARE

When a child over compulsory school age ceases to be in the care of a voluntary organisation, either in a home or otherwise, the organisation must inform the local authority for the area in which the child proposes to live and must state whether or not the organisation has the facilities for advising and befriending the child or whether it wishes the local authority to do so. This is the same provision as exists for children formerly in the care of a local authority under the Children Act 1948 and the after-care continues until the child is 18 or until it is felt that it is no longer necessary.[8]

D   ADOPTION

Voluntary bodies acting as adoption agencies must make certain enquiries of the local authority before placing a child with prospective adopters, and must be registered with the authority in whose area their office is situated; they must supply details of their accounts for inspection at the end of each financial year.[9]

9. SEPARATE REPRESENTATION OF THE CHILD

This is a social work task which seems likely to become more and more important as a means of providing protection for a child and his interests in the legal and administrative complex that surrounds him. Anyone representing a child must clearly be independent of any local authority concerned in dealing with him, and some representative work is being done by voluntary organisations. But a local authority social worker is always liable to be called upon to act in this way, either as a guardian *ad litem* in adoption or matrimonial cases, or in unopposed applications for the discharge of a 1969 Act care order or supervision order. Ultimately it will be possible for a guardian *ad litem* to be appointed in any type of care proceedings, and in guardianship or s. 2 Resolution proceedings.

Social workers acting on behalf of children will above all else need the capacity for understanding their wishes and feelings and the ability to express these in all circumstances. Though these qualities are needed in all dealings with children in care, they are of special importance in those many situations where the social worker is—or will be—required to be the voice of the child.

Guidance on the duties and responsibilities of the guardian *ad litem* is set out in Circular LAC 20/1976, H.O. Circular 178/1976, and an explanatory letter from the Chief Social Work Officer of March 1977.

10. COUNSELLING OF ADOPTED PERSONS, AND ADULTS FORMERLY IN CARE

The Children Act 1975 added a new s. 20A to the Adoption Act 1958; this makes it possible for an adopted person over the age of 18 to obtain a copy of his original birth certificate. Because of the concern aroused at the time, however, the Section requires that any person adopted before November 1976 must be interviewed by a counsellor who will pass to him the information which he will need to make his application to the Registrar General. Persons adopted after that date will be able to obtain the information direct from the Registrar General, but will be offered counselling without being required to accept it.

This new provision was publicised at the time and provoked a number of enquiries. Few are now being made, following the experience of Scotland where such a provision has existed for many years. Guidance on the precise procedure is contained in booklets for counsellors available in Social Service Departments. The depth of counselling and the involvement of adoption agencies and courts will vary in each case, but it should be remembered that the basic intention is that an adopted person should be in the same position as any person who wishes to obtain a copy of his birth certificate. Counselling so far undertaken has revealed a number of points on which adoptees have anxieties, and it is to be hoped that their disclosure will have a beneficial effect on future placings by local authorities and other agencies.

There has been a good deal of research into the feelings of adoptees by Raynor, Treseliotis, McWhinnie and others, and a short account of a survey appeared in *Adoption and Fostering* in 1977 (No. 3). Much of the material applies equally to adults who have been brought up in care and who sometimes seek information and support from Social Services Departments or from voluntary child care organisations.

11. DUTIES OF LOCAL AUTHORITY SOCIAL WORKERS

The main duties may be summarised as follows so far as children's legislation is concerned:

1. INVESTIGATION OF:

A   applications for admission to care;

B   allegations that children are in need of care or control (involving consultation with police, education authority and N.S.P.C.C.);

C   circumstances of children at request of divorce court or magistrates' court: Such investigations are more frequently made by the probation service. They should be made at the request of the court, not at the request of solicitors or parties to a case. There is an agreed procedure by which probation officers (acting as Court Welfare Officers) and local authority officers should consult one another in divorce court cases. For details consult "Memorandum of Guidance for Divorce Court Welfare Officers" (August 1968). This deals with consultation when children are known to the local authority.

D   applications for other orders, such as custodianship;

E   circumstances of children under 13 who are to appear before a court, of those over that age who are to be brought before the court by the local authority in care proceedings; of those over 13 appearing in criminal proceedings if requested to do so;

F   cases referred for advice, guidance and assistance;

G   applications for approval as foster parents or prospective adopters or child-minders;

H   applications for adoption order (guardian *ad litem*).

Some investigations may also be made at the request of other local authorities or voluntary societies.

2. SUPERVISION OF CHILDREN UNDER EIGHTEEN:

A   boarded-out in foster homes, including on request those placed by other authorities or voluntary societies;

B   placed privately in foster homes;

C   placed by third party for adoption with a person who is not a parent, guardian or relative;

D   placed with prospective adopters who have given notice of intention to adopt;

E   in care but under charge of parent guardian, relative or friend;

F   under statutory supervision orders made by juvenile courts, magistrates' courts or higher courts under relevant statutes;

G   discharged from the care of a local authority or voluntary society after school-leaving age;

H   placed in voluntary homes within the authority's area;
I   placed in voluntary homes outside the area;
J   placed elsewhere while remaining in care.

Again, some of the foregoing duties may be undertaken at the request of another authority or organisation.

3. GENERAL DUTIES:

A   case work with families whose children are in care, have been in care or are at risk;
B   maintaining contact with children in residential care;
C   attendance at juvenile and county courts and presentation of reports;
D   conducting proceedings in juvenile courts in respect of children alleged to be in need of care or control;
E   arrangement for provision of accommodation for children remanded to care or committed to care on interim orders;
F   visitation of voluntary children's homes within the area, whether they are accommodating children in the care of the authority or not;
G   assessment of family situations and of needs of individual children in cases arising under the 1969 Act, and applying the care or control test;
H   assessment of those situations and needs when criminal proceedings are being considered;
I   conveying children and young persons in care from one type of accommodation to another, recovering absentees, conveying persons to and from juvenile and adult courts;
J   maintaining adequate case records of all work undertaken with families and children;
K   taking part in six-monthly reviews of children in any form of care (ideally there should also be periodical reviews in respect of children under voluntary or statutory supervision, though this is not at present required);
L   making reports to juvenile court justices on persons subject to care or supervision orders, as advocated in para. 107 of the Guide to Part I of the Act; and reporting to other courts in the same way;
M   stimulating and encouraging community activity in the interests of families and children; promoting group work as a supplement to individual case work with children, parents, and prospective foster parents or adopters, or with other groups within the community;
N   representing children in care and other proceedings in the capacity of guardian *ad litem*;
O   counselling adults who have been in care or have been adopted and who need information about their origins and life history;
P   counselling parents who are considering placing a child for adoption, and would-be applicants for an adoption order;
Q   giving evidence to courts, when required to do so in a wide range of proceedings.

(NOTE: Case records kept under the Boarding-Out of Children Regulations 1955 are statutory records, confidential and privileged. In *Re D (infants)*, [1970] 1 All E.R. 1088 the Court of Appeal held that such records should not be produced in Wardship proceedings, and that there was no cause for an exception to be made to the privilege attaching to such records.)

The whole question of confidentiality, both personally, and in relation to records is one of great importance to a social worker, especially in a situation in which he becomes aware that an offence has been committed, and that criminal proceedings may be under consideration. The subject is complex, but some guidance may be found in the following publications by B.A.S.W.:

Confidentiality in Social Work; A Code of Ethics for Social Work; Advice to Members who are Questioned by the Police about Clients; Disclosure of Confidential Information.

NOTES

1. *Intermediate Treatment Project and Intermediate Treatment Guide (Appendix B)*, D.H.S.S., H.M.S.O.
2. Social Work Service Development Group 1978.
3. Children and Young Persons Act 1963, s. 56, as amended.
4. C.C.E.T.S.W. No. 3.
5. Children Act 1948, s. 33A.
6. Children Act 1948, ss. 29 and 30.
7. Boarding-Out Regulation 15.
8. Children Act 1948, s. 34.
9. See Chapter 15.

Chapter 15

CUSTODIANSHIP AND ADOPTION

SUMMARY

The Children Act of 1975 arises largely from the recommendations of the Houghton Committee,[1] but does not fully implement them. It also contains some sections arising from the Colwell Report[2] calling for the separate representation of the child in care proceedings. Other sections amend the legislation dealing with children in care and, so far as they are operative, these have been taken into account in previous chapters.

Custodianship and adoption are both intended to supply long-term security to children and were mentioned in Chapter 11 as possible methods of treatment available to children in care. They may also be available to children not in care, and for this reason must be dealt with in isolation from that chapter.

The main purposes of the Children Act 1975 are to establish a comprehensive adoption service as an integral part of child care, to simplify the procedure for obtaining parental agreement (if the parent so desires), and to clarify the essential nature of an adoption order. The Act is designed to discourage the use of adoption by the natural parents, relatives, or step-parents of a child, though not prohibiting it altogether. It offers instead legal custody, either solely or jointly with a parent, as being more appropriate than adoption. Moreover, it enables a court hearing an application for guardianship or for adoption, even by persons unrelated to the child, to treat the application as though it had in fact been made for a custodianship order. It would appear therefore that custody—under a custodianship order or otherwise—will have a great part to play in providing for many children when Part II of the Act comes into operation. In the meantime the concept of custody, as the alternative to adoption, has brought about changes in the application of the Adoption Act 1958, as modified by the 1975 Act, which still governs the procedures.

The Children Bill, which preceded the 1975 Act aroused a great deal of controversy which may be revived when the "freeing procedure" in Sections 14-16 are implemented. On the one hand, there are those who consider that everything possible should be done to strengthen family life by putting in support of all kinds to enable parents, including single parents, to bring up their own children satisfactorily without recourse to care or adoption or other substitutes for family care. On the other hand are those who, while recognising the need for supporting natural families, consider that children have needs and rights of their own, and that not all parents are fitted for the upbringing of children however much support they may be given. There is thus a conflict between the upholders of parental rights, and the advocates of parental duties, and (failing their fulfilment) of a child's *rights* to benefit from love and care from someone other than the parent.

The *main* points of dissension are commented upon below; it will be seen that the "pros" and "cons" broadly follow the two schools of thought set out in the previous paragraph.

Pro	Con
SECTIONS 1 AND 2 AND 4-7	
These sections provide for a nation-wide adoption service, including the counselling of children, their parents and actual or prospective adopters.	It is necessary for adoption services to be provided, but there is a danger that adoption may still be seen as something apart from the main stream of child care alternatives.
SECTION 3 (In operation)	
This section seeks to ensure that in adoption matters, the first consideration is to be the promotion of the welfare of the child *throughout his childhood* i.e. up to age of 18, and	The best way of providing for a child throughout childhood is by enabling his family to bring him up. "Rescuing" a child from his family is not by any means always

Pro

provides that as far as possible the child's views shall be taken into account. (This principle is included again in s. 59 where it relates to a child in the care of a local authority.) "First consideration" does not make the child's welfare paramount, but makes it weightier than any other consideration.

Con

the right answer. Adoption is not an unqualified success, foster home breakdowns are all too frequent, and residential care rarely provides a child with satisfying personal relationships. Adoption in particular extinguishes the parent-child relationship for ever, and in the case of babies the child's point of view is ignored.

SECTIONS 14-16

These sections set out a procedure by which a parent may relinquish parental rights to a local authority or adoption agency, and a court may declare a child "free for adoption". This procedure is meant to be used as an alternative to the practice of agreeing to adoption by specified persons, as at present carried out. The sections contain certain safeguards for the parents who choose this method.

This change will benefit prospective adopters, but the Act makes no provision for new services which would help a natural parent to maintain his or her own child adequately, without feeling the need, for the child's sake, to seek adoption arrangements.

SECTION 12 (In operation)

If a child has not been declared "free for adoption" and the parent's consent to adoption is required, the grounds for dispensing with it are widened to include serious ill-treatment, but only if the rehabilitation of the child with the parent is "unlikely"

The other grounds for dispensing with consent are not subject to the proviso about rehabilitation being "unlikely". How is the decision as to whether it is likely or not to be made? The failure to make this decision in respect of children in long-term but indeterminate care is possibly the nub of the whole present problem of "Children who Wait". Will the Act make it any easier for the decision to be made?

These provisions are thought to be helpful in cases of children who have languished for years in care because parents will neither agree to adoption, nor make their own plans for rehabilitation.

It is doubtful whether children who are no longer babies will benefit from this provision. Languishing in care is probably due to the low priority which social workers give to the maintenance of contact between parents and children in care, and also to the failure to use s. 2 resolutions in all appropriate

Pro	Con
	cases. There has never been anything to prevent the placing of such children in long-stay foster homes, where adoption or custodianship might well follow later.

SECTION 29 (In operation)

Pro	Con
This section empowers a person, including a foster parent, who has cared for a child for *5 years* to apply for an adoption order, and to retain the child against any claim by a parent until the application is made, or 3 months have elapsed since notification to the local authority of intention to adopt.	This appears to apply to children who are in the care of a local authority or voluntary agency and are boarded out with foster parents. The application may be made without the consent of the parent. "Private" foster parents who have cared for a child for 5 years may use this power.

SECTIONS 33 TO 46

Pro	Con
These sections set out the new concept of custodianship. A court may give legal custody to a relative or other person (including a foster parent, but excluding a parent or a natural father); if the child has been living with the applicant for 3 years, the consent of the parent is not required. A custody order does not convey parental rights to the custodians, who may apply to be relieved of their powers. Custodianship is designed to give a child long-term protection without adoption, and without depriving parents of their right to apply for access or discharge or of their liability to maintain the child if an order is made for that purpose. A local authority may make a maintenance allowance to a custodian who is not a step-parent of the child.	Custodianship falls short of guardianship and if the child concerned were in the care of a local authority or voluntary agency, the order might create a very difficult situation. The objection to this provision is that if the child has lived with the prospective custodian for three years, the application can be made without the consent of either the parent or the local authority (if the child is in fact in care).

The Act which emerged from these conflicts could not be brought fully into operation without additional resources of finance and staff; there is as yet no "comprehensive adoption service" though planning for it is in progress; nor is it possible for the custodianship procedure, or the freeing procedure, to be used at present. Adoption legislation has been consolidated into the Adoption Act 1976 but this cannot be implemented until such time as the remaining sections of the 1975 Act have been brought into force. Adoption is therefore still dealt with largely under the Adoption Act of 1958, with some provisions of the 1975 Act, and under the Adoption Rules of 1976.

PRELIMINARY ARRANGEMENTS

Legal adoption is effected by an order made by an authorised court, that is the High Court, a county court or a magistrates' court within the "commission area".[1]

The effect of an adoption order is to bring the child into a relationship with the adopters such as he would have had if he had been born to them in marriage. It transfers parental rights and duties from the parents to the adopters and prevents an adopted person from being illegitimate.[2]

Adoption orders once made are irrevocable, except those set aside on appeal or by legitimation, or by re-adoption.

Affiliation orders in respect of the child cease to have effect. The rights and powers of local authorities under care orders, except interim orders, and resolutions passed under s. 2 of the Children Act 1948, are extinguished as are parental rights vested in a person by order of any court.[3]

An adopted child who was not a citizen of the United Kingdom and Colonies prior to the adoption acquires such citizenship if the adopter, or male adopter is a citizen of the United Kingdom and Colonies.[4]

PLACING FOR ADOPTION

A child may be placed for adoption:

A by a registered adoption society;[5]
B by a local authority;[6]
C by a "third party" (Chapter 7);[7]
D by the parent or guardian direct.

Adoption societies and local authorities are adoption agencies and as such must observe s. 3 of the Children Act 1975, containing the welfare principle, and s. 13 which requires them to have regard to any wishes parents may have as to the child's religious upbringing. Restrictions on placings by third parties and parents (s. 28) are not yet in operation, so that such placings may be made without regard to ss. 3, or 13.

TYPES OF ORDER

The most common type of order is that made under s. 1 of the Adoption Act 1958, where the applicants are *resident and domiciled* in England or Wales.[8]

A Convention adoption order may be made under s. 24 of the Children Act 1975, but only in the High Court. The number of such orders is expected to be small.

Section 53 of the 1958 Act authorises the making of a "Provisional Order" in the case of applicants who are not domiciled in England or

Wales. Such an order can only be made by the High Court or a County Court (not a magistrate's court) and permits the removal of the child to the country of domicile for adoption in accordance with the law of that country. The applicants must give *six months'* notice to the local authority of their intention to apply for a provisional order and must have the care and possession of the child for *at least six months* before the date of the order (sub-s. (5)).

An interim order gives applicants the custody of the child for a probationary period of up to two years. It is not an adoption order within the meaning of the Act and has the effect of postponing the determination of the application if the court is not satisfied that an adoption order should be made immediately. It cannot be made unless a full adoption order could lawfully be made and should not be made without regard to the welfare principle contained in s. 3. In making an interim order a court may specify such terms as it thinks fit with regard to the maintenance, education and supervision of the child.[9]

Before the expiration of the interim order the court will fix a date for the hearing of the original application for an adoption order.[10]

NOTIFICATION TO LOCAL AUTHORITY

Unless the child is above compulsory school-leaving age or one of the applicants is the father or mother of the child, an adoption order may not be made until after the expiration of at least *three months* from the date on which the applicants notified the local authority, in writing, of their intention to adopt the child.[11] This requirement is different in the case of applicants under s. 53 who must give *six months'* notice instead of three months.

One important effect of this notification is that the child becomes a "protected" child and therefore liable to supervision by the local authority (Chapter 7).[12] (But as applicants who are parents are not required to notify intention (until s. 18 of the Children Act is implemented) there is no such supervision, and the application for an adoption order may be made at once. This has implications for courts, local authorities and persons appointed as guardians *ad litem*, and will be referred to later in this chapter.)

Other applicants desiring an early hearing should understand the necessity for an early notification.

Applicants are sometimes under the impression that application to the court cannot be made until the three months has expired. This is not so, as the application can be made as soon as all the requisite court documents are completed[13] but the hearing will not take place until the three months' period has expired. The notification is to be made to the local authority within whose area the applicants are resident. If they change their address before the court hearing they must notify the local authority and if the new address is in the area of another local authority then the first-named local authority must inform the other local authority concerned.[14]

Notification is important also as, in the case of children who are in the care of the local authority, the contributions from the parents in respect of the maintenance of the child cease to be payable and a further point is that the local authority lose the right to require the child to be returned to their care under the Boarding-Out Regulations.[15]

ACTUAL CUSTODY

At the date of hearing the child must have been in the actual custody of the applicants for at least three months not counting any period during which the child was less than six weeks old.[16] If the applicants are not ordinarily resident in Great Britain, the child must have been in the care and possession of both applicants for one month and in the care of one of the applicants for three months.[17] The corresponding period for provisional orders is six months for both applicants. Care and possession (now actual custody) is not disturbed by temporary absence, *e.g.* at boarding school. *Re B. (G.A.)*, [1963] 3 All E.R. 125).

CHILD

For the purpose of the Act a child is a person under 18 years of age who is not, and has not been, married.[18] (Persons under 18 may be described as "minors"; Family Law Reform Act 1969, s. 12.)

AGREEMENTS

Subject to the court's powers to dispense with agreements, every person who is a parent or guardian of a child must give agreement to the making of an adoption order.[19] Agreement may be given on personal attendance at the court hearing but is in nearly all cases given on the appropriate court form, which is an integral part of the application for the order.[20]

The agreement of a local authority, even if the authority hold parental rights or powers under a s. 2 resolution or a care order, is not required.[21]

"Parent" is not defined in the Adoption Act 1958, but "guardian" means a person appointed by deed or will in accordance with the provisions of the Guardianship Acts, or by a court of competent jurisdiction to be the guardian of the child. It now includes a natural father who has custody.[22]

The term "parent" does not include the natural father of an illegitimate child (*Re M. (An Infant)*, [1955] 2 All E.R. 911).

Agreement must be to a *particular* application as evidenced either by the names of the applicants or by a serial number, and must be unconditional.

In giving agreement to an application which is made under a serial number the parent or guardian no longer has the right to make a stipulation with regard to the religious persuasion in which the child is to be brought up.

A form of agreement is invalid if it is signed before the infant is 6 weeks old[23] or not attested on the date of signature.[24]

Forms of agreement must be attested in the manner set out in the Adoption Rules (usually by a Justice of the Peace, Clerk to Justices or an authorised County Court Officer), and in the case of at least one of the parents must be accompanied by a birth certificate of the infant similarly attested. Shortened forms of birth certificate are accepted for this purpose by some courts but it is usual for a full copy of the birth certificate to be used.

Difficulties sometimes arise where the mother of the child is a married woman who was married at the time of the conception of the child. In such a case the child is presumed to be the child of the marriage unless the contrary is proved and agreement would, therefore, be required from the husband. (But see Family Law Reform Act 1969, s. 26.) If the husband is unaware of the child's existence or is unwilling to sign the agreement courts will sometimes accept an affidavit from the mother with regard to the paternity of the infant.

The court has power to dispense with the agreement of any person if it is satisfied:

A that the person cannot be found or is incapable of giving agreement;
B that he is withholding his agreement unreasonably;
C that he has persistently failed without reasonable cause to discharge the parental duties in relation to the child;
D that he has abandoned or neglected the child;
E that he has persistently ill treated the child;
F that he has seriously ill treated the child and that for that or any other reason the rehabilitation of the child within the household of the parent or guardian is unlikely.[25]

Agreement may be withdrawn at any time before the date of hearing but the child may not be restored to the parent concerned without the leave of the court once the application has been made.[26] The person withdrawing agreement would normally attend the court hearing to explain his request to the court and unless the court dispenses with the agreement the application for an adoption order would fail and the child would then return to the parent or guardian. Even if there has been no parental agreement to adoption the child may not be removed, without the leave of the court, if he has had his home with the applicants for a period of 5 years when an application for an adoption order is made, or when the intention to apply for one is notified to the local authority. This does not, however, obviate the need for the parental agreement to be either obtained or dispensed with in the usual way. The restriction on removal applies also to an adoption agency which has placed the child with the applicants. It should be noted that a parent opposing an adoption application or seeking to remove his child may now be given legal aid.

APPLICANTS

Applicants for adoption orders must fulfil certain conditions if they are to have an order granted to them:[27]

A In a joint application the applicants must be married to each other.

B Both applicants must be 21 or over and must be domiciled in the United Kingdom, the Channel Islands or the Isle of Man (except in Convention Order cases).

C In other applications, the applicant must be aged 21 and unmarried.

D Or, if married, be 21, and be able to satisfy the court that his spouse cannot be found, or is permanently separated from him or is incapable of joining in the application because of physical or mental illness.

E He must be domiciled as in B above.

F A father or mother of a child may not apply alone for an adoption order unless the other natural parent is dead or cannot be found, or there is some other reason to justify his or her exclusion from the application.

These legal qualifications are however subject to ss. 10(3) and 11 which are meant to discourage adoption by parents, step-parents and relatives. Though a married couple, of whom one is a parent of the child and the other a step-parent, may apply for an adoption order the court must dismiss the application if it considers that the matter would be better dealt with under an existing custody order under the Matrimonial Causes Act 1973, s. 42. Similarly an application by a step-parent alone may be dismissed for the same reason. This information is contained in para. 22 of the notes to the County Court Rules and para. 16 of the notes to the Magistrates' Courts Rules which appear in the forms of application. Both Rules provide that when an application of this nature is received the attention of the court should be drawn to it and no further steps should be taken until the court has given directions as to whether or not the application should proceed. The varying practices of courts in dealing with such applications have an effect on local authority practice; the difficulties are explained in the Annex to Circular LAC (76)22. It has been found helpful for a social service department to have an arrangement with the courts whereby would-be applicants are referred for social work advice if they appear to be affected by ss. 10(3) and 11(4).

COURT PROCEDURE

Applications for adoption orders are made by completing the appropriate court forms and delivering them or sending them to the court office.[28] There is an explanatory memorandum which courts are asked to give to applicants. This explains the procedure, and points out the rights of an adopted person to have access to his birth record at the age of 18.

SERIAL NUMBER

Applicants may obtain from the court a serial number which is inserted on the form of application and forms of agreement in order to prevent the parents or guardians of the child from learning the applicants' identity.

Once an application is lodged in the court a parent or guardian of the child who has agreed to the application cannot remove the child from the actual custody of the applicants without the leave of the court.[26] This restriction also applies to local authorities and registered adoption societies who have arranged placings.[29]

The actual forms used in county courts are in the Appendix.[30] The forms should be very carefully completed and the explanatory notes given on the forms should be studied to ensure that the documents are in order.

NOTICES OF HEARING

Notices of hearing of the application must be served by the court on the guardian *ad litem* and on the respondents:[31]

A　Every person not being an applicant whose consent to the making of an order is required under the Act.

B　Any person having the rights and powers of a parent of the child.

C　Any person liable by an order or agreement to contribute to the maintenance of the child.

D　The local authority to whom notice of intention to adopt has been given.

E　The local authority or adoption society taking part in the arrangements for the adoption.

F　The spouse of any sole applicant.

G　Any other person not being the child who in the opinion of the court should be served with notice of hearing.[32]

COURT ARRANGEMENTS

Applications to magistrates' courts are to be heard in the domestic court from November 1979. Section 73(1) of the Domestic Proceedings and Magistrates' Courts Act 1978 extends s. 21(1) and 21(2) of the 1975 Act to cover the privacy of all adoption proceedings arising under the Adoption Acts and the Children Act 1975.[33]

ATTENDANCE OF PARTIES

The court requires the personal attendance of the applicants before making an adoption order except that in the case of a joint application the court may dispense with the attendance of one spouse provided he has verified the application by affidavit.[34]

Where the guardian *ad litem* reports to the court that in his opinion the child is old enough to understand the nature of an adoption order, the court must serve a notice on the applicants requiring them to bring the child to the court hearing.[35]

APPOINTMENT OF GUARDIAN AD LITEM

The guardian *ad litem* of the child must be appointed by the court as soon as practicable after the application is made.[36]

DUTIES OF COURT

In making a decision relating to adoption, a court is now subject to s. 3 of the Children Act 1975 as regards the welfare of the child and consideration of his wishes and feelings.

In addition, in making an adoption order the court must be satisfied:[37]

A   that all necessary agreements have been obtained and that the persons concerned understand the nature and effect of an adoption order or that an agreement may be dispensed with on stated grounds;

B   that the applicant has not received or agreed to receive and that no person has made or given or agreed to make or give to the applicants any payment or other reward in consideration of the adoption except such as the court may sanction (for "reward" see Adoption Act 1958, s. 50). The new sub-s. 3A, introduced by the Criminal Law Act 1977, establishes that payments by agencies towards adopters' legal costs or medical costs, or payment of fees for inter-agency placements are legal, and that s. 50 has never applied to them.

The court when making the order may impose such terms and conditions as the court may think fit.

IDENTIFICATION OF CHILD

In the county court a child is sufficiently identified by the birth certificate attached to the form of consent[38] but in the magistrate's court proof of identity may be made by affidavit and the court may still require the attendance of a witness in special circumstances.

PREVIOUS APPLICATIONS

If a previous application or applications to adopt the same child have been dismissed by any court on their merits the court will not proceed to hear a further application unless satisfied that there has been a substantial change in the circumstances since the date of the previous application.[39]

REFERRAL TO HIGH COURT

If a magistrate's court considers that it would be more fit for an application to be dealt with in the High Court it may refuse to deal with the application.[40]

The High Court may remove an application from the County Court including one made under ss. 34 or 34A.

RESULT OF HEARING

The court must notify the result of the application to all respondents.[41]

INFORMATION

Information in connection with an application for an adoption order must be treated in confidence and must not be disclosed except as far as is necessary in the proper execution of business, or at the request of a court, or to a person engaged in research with the written authority of the Secretary of State or enquiring about his original name.[42]

COMPLETION OF ADOPTION

RE-ADOPTIONS

An adopted child may be the subject of a second or further application, in which case the previous adopters are regarded as the parents of the child.[43]

LEGITIMATION FOLLOWING ADOPTION

An adoption order may be revoked when the person adopted has been legitimated by the marriage of his parents.[44]

BAPTISM

Section 25 of the Adoption Act 1958 dealing with baptism after adoption is now repealed.[45] New certificates of baptism may be obtained in respect of children who had been baptized before adoption. Children may now be baptized in their adoptive names.

FORM OF ORDER

The forms of adoption order and abridged adoption order are set out in the rules. A copy of the full order is sent by the court to the Registrar General and a copy of the abridged order is sent to the applicants, within seven days of the order being made.[46]

CHILD BENEFIT

Child benefit is payable from the date of placing, unless a boarding-out allowance is being made.

APPEALS

Appeals against decisions in magistrates' courts[47] lie to the High Court and from county courts to the Court of Appeal.[48]

COSTS

The court may make orders as to costs and in particular may direct the applicant to pay the out-of-pocket expenses of the guardian *ad litem* and the expenses incurred by a respondent in attending the hearing.[49] Local authorities do not usually claim expenses in respect of their duties as guardian *ad litem* and orders in favour of respondents for other costs are rare.

ADOPTION RULES

The references are to the Adoption (County Court) Rules 1976. The Magistrates' Courts (Adoption) Rules 1976, and the Adoption (High Court) Rules 1976, are very similar to the County Court Rules, but for the sake of simplicity the references have not been triplicated. Rules concerning adoption were amended in 1976 and 1978.

SCOTLAND, IRELAND, ISLE OF MAN, AND CHANNEL ISLANDS

The Adoption Act 1958, applies to Scotland but the provisions of the Act relating to Scottish law have not been dealt with in this chapter. For most purposes of English law adoption orders made in Scotland or Northern Ireland have the same effect as orders made in England, as do orders made in the Isle of Man or in the Channel Islands (Adoption Act 1964).

ADOPTION ORDERS MADE OVERSEAS

The Adoption Act of 1968 provides *inter alia* for the recognition in the United Kingdom of orders previously made in certain overseas countries whose adoption laws are similar to our own. This provision makes it unnecessary for new adoption applications to be made in such cases of children already adopted elsewhere.

ADOPTION OF CHILDREN FROM OVERSEAS

For some years past there have been various schemes under which children from other countries have arrived in the United Kingdom to be placed with families, sometimes with the intention that they should be adopted. Cases of this kind raise questions on such matters as the legality of the placing, the involvement of the local authority in supervision, and the requirements of adoption law if in fact an application for an adoption is made. General guidance on the position is available in a D.H.S.S. Circular, D.S.W.S. 79(3) of April 1979.

REGISTERED ADOPTION AGENCIES

POWER TO ARRANGE ADOPTIONS

Local authorities (*i.e.* the councils of counties and county boroughs acting through their social service committees) have power to arrange adoptions whether the children concerned are in the care of the local authority or not.[50]

The only other *body* of persons empowered to arrange adoptions is a registered adoption society.[51] The arrangement of adoptions by any other body of persons is unlawful and anyone taking part in such arrangements becomes liable to a fine of not more than £100 and/or six months' imprisonment. Arrangement of adoptions by individuals is not yet illegal.

REGISTRATION OF ADOPTION SOCIETIES

Adoption Societies wishing to be registered under the Adoption Act 1958, must apply to the local authority for the area in which their administrative centre is situated, enclosing the statutory fee of £1 and a completed form giving details of the society as required by the Act and Regulations. [52]

The local authority may refuse to register an adoption society if it does not consider it to be a charitable association, or for other reasons defined in the Act relating to the unsuitability of members or staff of the society.

APPEAL

An Adoption Society may appeal to the Crown Court against a refusal to carry out registration or against a cancellation of registration.[53]

REGULATIONS

Acting under the power given to him by the Adoption Act, the Secretary of State made regulations governing the conduct of registered adoption societies and local authorities in making arrangements for adoption. The regulations concerned are the Adoption Agencies Regulations 1976.

ANNUAL RETURN

Registered adoption societies are required to provide the appropriate local authority with an annual return containing accounts, statistics and a copy of their annual report.[54]

BEFORE PLACING

Before a child is made available for adoption a society or local authority (known as an "agency") must provide the parent, or parents, with a memorandum in the form set out in the Regulations, and the parent must sign an acknowledgment to the effect that he, or she, has read and understood the memorandum.[55] This explains, *inter alia*, that the child will have a right at the age of 18 to have access to his original birth record. Agencies before placing a child for adoption are required by the Regulations:—[56]

A to obtain details of the proposed adopters in a form prescribed by the Regulations, to interview the adopters and inspect their home;

B to obtain a medical report on the child in a form prescribed by the Regulations, including blood tests for syphilis for babies more than 6 weeks old and a test for phenylalanine for children between the ages of 6 days and 2 years;

C to enquire of the local authority for the area where the applicants reside whether there is any reason to believe that it would be detrimental to the child to be kept by the applicants in the particular premises.

After considering all the information relating to the applicants and the child the case committee of the agency must approve the particular placing.

AFTER PLACING

After the child is placed the agency must provide the proposed adopters with full information about the child and make adequate arrangements for supervision until such time as the applicants notify the local authority of their intention to adopt the child.[57] When this notification is received the responsibility for visitation passes to the local authority as the child becomes a "protected" child within the meaning of the Act.

All information received by adoption societies and local authorities in connection with adoption must be treated as confidential and documents must be preserved for at least 75 years.[58]

THE GUARDIAN AD LITEM

Until s. 20 of the Children Act 1975 comes into operation, the court must appoint a person to act as the guardian *ad litem* of the child in any application for an adoption order, or provisional adoption order. (Adoption Act 1958, s. 9(7).) Except in High Court cases, the person so appointed may be an officer of the local authority (*i.e.* county or metropolitan district councils acting through their Directors of Social Services), provided the local authority agree, or a probation officer, or in the event of the court considering the appointment of either of these two persons undesirable in the circumstances, some other person to be appointed by the court. An officer of a local authority may not be appointed guardian *ad litem* if the authority holds parental rights and powers over the child or has taken part in the arrangements for the adoption.

The Director of Social Services may carry out guardian *ad litem* duties personally or may appoint a member of his staff for the purpose.

The duty of the guardian *ad litem* is to "safeguard the interests of the child before the court" so that he remains in office during the existence of any interim order, or while any appeal is being made. His office has been described as "forensic"; added significance is given to it by the increasing number of applications involving children old enough to be able to express their wishes and feelings in accordance with the welfare principle in s. 3.

Although the guardian may be a local authority social worker or a probation officer responsible to his employing committee, once appointed he is responsible to the court. He may therefore seek directions from the court at any stage of the proceedings and should not hesitate to do so. In certain matters he is specifically required to inform the court of any opinion he has formed; for instance whether a child is old enough to understand the nature of an adoption order, or whether any respondent is "under a disability". The purpose of such reports to the court is to enable it to decide whether or not persons who are not respondents should be made respondents or, in some instances, whether they should themselves have a guardian *ad litem* to represent them.

The court may authorise a local authority to incur any expenditure necessary to the prosecution of its officer's enquiries as guardian *ad litem*.

The *particular* duties of the guardian *ad litem* are set out in the second Schedule to the Adoption (County Court) Rules 1976 and the Magistrates' Court (Adoption) Rules 1976. The Schedules are similar, but not identical.

The Schedule to the County Court Rules is set out at the end of this chapter. Many authorities use a proforma to ensure that all the points are covered by the guardian *ad litem* in the final report to the court; this may be helpful, though it should be remembered that the work involved primarily concerns the welfare of the child and is more onerous than the answering of a number of questions. Detailed explanation of the issues is contained in an A.B.A.F.A. booklet *The Guardian ad Litem and Adoption*.

Persons appointed as guardian *ad litem* require a broad knowledge of the law concerned, including that relating to protected children, foster children, and adoption procedure. They also require the capacity of working with children in a helpful relationship, when—as will be more often the case—they are of an age to understand their position.

In the process of working through the Schedule the guardian will be dealing with applicants, natural parents and other respondents as well as with the child and will be able to piece together the picture which he will ultimately present to the court. In some cases there will be legal issues, especially those concerning the withholding or withdrawal of agreement on the part of a parent; the range of cases already decided is so wide that legal advice may be essential and legal representation may be necessary.

Pending further implementation of the Children Act 1975, applicants for adoption orders will have greatly varying understanding and appreciation of the work of the guardian. When the child has been placed by an agency, either directly or following boarding out, the applicants will have been well informed and supported by a social worker; while preserving independence the guardian should in such situations be able to put faith in the assessments which have been made by the agency. In third party and direct placings there will usually have been no social worker involved in the application and it may fall to the guardian *ad litem* to explain and expound the consequences of adoption before he can examine whether it is legally possible or desirable for the child concerned. Similar considerations apply when the applicants are relatives.

The greatest concern arises however from applications involving step-parents, either solely or jointly with a parent. In such cases the court may have appointed a guardian *ad litem* to report on whether the application should be heard, or may have decided that it should be heard and have appointed a guardian *ad litem* in the usual way. The issue then becomes one of recommending adoption or custody and of considering the decision in *Re S.* (1977), which requires the guardian *ad litem* to "draw the attention of the court to the disadvantages as well as the advantages of adoption". There are of course some cases in which the possibility of joint custody does not exist and in which a step-parent cannot yet apply with the parent's consent for a custodianship order under Part II of the Children Act 1975.

Helpful guidance on these matters will be found in the A.B.A.F.A. booklet *Stepchildren and Adoption* which has been widely distributed to local authorities and to courts.

Having completed his enquiries the guardian *ad litem* must make a written report to the court which appointed him; he should follow any suggestions by the court as to the way in which the report should be set out and will need to know whether or not he is expected to make a recommendation as to whether or not the order should be made. The report is confidential to the court, which has the duty of making the final decision on the application. For a suggested outline report see Appendix H.

ADOPTION (COUNTY COURT) RULES 1976, SCHEDULE 2

SCHEDULE 2   Rule 11(1)(a)

PARTICULAR DUTIES OF THE GUARDIAN AD LITEM

1. The guardian *ad litem* shall interview the applicant and shall ascertain:—

   (a) why the applicant wishes to adopt the child;

   (b) whether the applicant understands the nature of an adoption order and, in particular, that the order, if made will render him responsible for the maintenance and upbringing of the child;

   (c) in the case of an application by the mother or father of the child alone, what reason there is justifying the exclusion of the other natural parent;

(d) in the case of an application by one only of a married couple, why the other spouse does not join in the application;

(e) in the case of an application by a married couple, the state of the marriage, and, in particular, whether it has the stability which is likely to provide a sound basis for a secure parental relationship with an adopted child;

(f) such other information, including an assessment of the applicant's personality and, where appropriate, that of the child, as has a bearing on the mutual suitability of the applicant and the child and on the ability of the applicant to bring up the child;

(g) whether the applicant suffers or has suffered from any serious illness and whether there is any history of tuberculosis, epilepsy or mental illness in the applicant's family;

(h) particulars of all members of the applicant's household and their relationship (if any) to the applicant;

(i) particulars of the accommodation in the applicant's home and the condition of the home;

(j) the means of the applicant and, where appropriate, the rights to or interests in property (under dispositions already made) which the child stands to obtain if adopted;

(k) the applicant's religious persuasion, if any;[59]

(l) whether any person specified in the application as a person to whom reference may be made is a responsible person and whether he recommends the applicant with or without reservations.

2. Except in the case of an application for a provisional adoption order, the guardian *ad litem* shall forthwith inform the court if it appears to him that the applicant or both applicants may not be domiciled in a part of the United Kingdom, the Channel Islands or the Isle of Man.

3. The guardian *ad litem* shall ascertain and inform the applicant:—

(a) whether the child has been baptised and, if so, the date and place of baptism;

(b) what treatment the child has received with a view to immunising him against disease;

(c) what, if any, rights or interests in property the child stands to retain or lose if adopted;

(d) whether an insurance policy for the payment on the death of the child of money for funeral expenses has been effected.

4.—(1) The guardian *ad litem* shall, as soon as is reasonably practicable, ascertain whether the child is able to understand the nature of an adoption order.

(2) If, in the guardian's opinion, the child is able to understand the nature of an adoption order, the guardian shall forthwith inform the court.

(3) The guardian shall, so far as practicable, ascertain the wishes and feelings of the child regarding the decision.

5.—(1) The guardian *ad litem* shall interview either in person or by an agent appointed by him for the purpose every individual who is a respondent or who appears to him to have taken part in the arrangements for the adoption of the child.

(2) The guardian shall forthwith inform the court if, in his opinion, any respondent is under the age of majority.

6.—(1) The guardian *ad litem* shall obtain from every respondent, not being an individual, such information concerning the child as they have in their possession and which they consider might assist the court in deciding whether or not the child should be adopted by the applicant.

(2) Where such information is given in the form of a written report, the guardian shall append it to his own report to the court.

7. The guardian *ad litem* shall ascertain who has had actual custody of the child throughout his life and for what period or periods.

8. The guardian *ad litem* shall ascertain that every agreement to the making of an adoption order in pursuance of the application is freely and unconditionally given and with full understanding of what is involved.

9. Where either parent of the child is dead, the guardian *ad litem* shall forthwith inform the court if he learns of any relation of the deceased parent who wishes to be heard by the court on the question whether an adoption order should be made.

10. Where the child is illegitimate but the putative father is not the guardian of the child or is not liable to contribute to his maintenance by virtue of any order or agreement the guardian *ad litem* shall forthwith inform the court if he learns of any person, claiming to be the father, who wishes to be heard by the court on the question whether an adoption order should be made.[60]

11. The guardian *ad litem* shall forthwith inform the court if he learns of any person who is or has been married to the mother or father of the child and who may have to be joined as a respondent.

12. The guardian *ad litem* shall forthwith inform the court if he learns of any other person or body who wishes or ought in his opinion to be heard by the court on the question whether an adoption order should be made.

13. Where appropriate, the guardian *ad litem* shall endeavour to obtain a report on the applicant's home and living conditions from a suitable agency in any country outside Great Britain in which the applicant is or has been living or resident.

EXPLANATORY NOTE

(This Note is not part of the Rules.)

1. These Rules consolidate with amendments the Adoption (County Court) Rules 1959 and subsequent amending instruments. In addition to drafting changes, the rules make the amendments rendered necessary by

the changes in statute law effected by the provisions of the Children Act 1975 which are in force on the date of commencement of the rules.

2. The main alterations of substance in the rules are as follows:—

(1) directions by the judge for the further conduct of an adoption application will be required where it may be that the application should be dismissed on the ground that custody proceedings under section 42 of the Matrimonial Causes Act 1973 would be more appropriate (rule 9(a));

(2) no provision now appears to enable a judge to refuse to proceed with an application because it would be better dealt with by the High Court: this is now regulated by section 101(1) of the Children Act 1975;

(3) provision is made in the rules relating to the determination of the place and date of birth of the child (rule 19(3) and (4));

(4) provision is made (for cases where an adoption order is refused and the court proposes to commit the child to the care of a local authority) for the hearing of any representations from the local authority concerned (rule 20);

(5) the rules provide for the making and conduct of applications to remove, to restrain the removal of or for the return of a child who is the subject of an actual or proposed adoption application (rule 21);

(6) the rules permit the identity of the local authority or adoption agency which was involved in the adoption proceedings to be disclosed from court records at the request of the Registrar-General or anyone authorised by him (rule 30(2)(*b*)(ii)).

3. Apart from changes rendered necessary by the new legislation, the main modifications in the forms are as follows:—

(1) Form 1 no longer contains material relating to a provisional adoption order for which a separate form (Form 7) is prescribed;

(2) the form of agreement is now Form 7 rather than Form 5;

(3) forms are no longer separately prescribed for notice of a further hearing following an interim order;

(4) the forms of order now contain an Appendix in which certain information is specified for the purposes of the records held by courts and by the Registrar-General;

(5) an abridged form of interim order is prescribed (Form 12).

4. There are some changes in the duties which are prescribed for the guardian *ad litem*, particularly at paragraphs 1(*e*), 2, 7 and 11 of Schedule 2.

NOTES

1. Children Act 1975, ss. 8(1) and 100.
2. *Ibid.*, Schedule 1, Part II.
3. *Ibid.*, s. 8(3).
4. Adoption Act 1958, s. 19.
5. *Ibid.*, s. 29.

6. *Ibid.*, s. 28.
7. *Ibid.*, s. 37.
8. Children Act 1975, s. 10(2)(*a*).
9. Adoption Act 1958, s. 8.
10. Adoption (County Court) Rules 1976, r. 29.
11. Adoption Act 1958, s. 3.
12. *Ibid.*, s. 37(1)(b).
13. Adoption (County Court) Rules 1976, r. 4.
14. Adoption Act 1958, s. 40(4).
15. Adoption Act 1958, s. 36.
16. *Ibid.*, s. 3.
17. *Ibid.*, s. 12.
18. Adoption Act 1958, s. 57, as amended.
19. Children Act 1975, s. 12.
20. Adoption (County Court) Rules 1976, r. 6.
21. Adoption Act 1958, s. 4(3) and Children Act 1948, s. 2(11).
22. Children Act 1975, s. 107.
23. Adoption Act 1958, s. 6.
24. *Ibid.*
25. Children Act 1975, s. 12.
26. *Ibid.*, ss. 34 and 34A.
27. Children Act 1975, ss. 10 and 11.
28. Adoption (County Court) Rules 1959, r. 4.
29. Adoption Act 1958, ss. 35 and 36.
30. Adoption (County Court) Rules 1976, Schedule 1.
31. *Ibid.*, r. 12.
32. Adoption (County Court) Rules 1959, r. 4(3).
33. Children Act 1975, s. 21.
34. Adoption (County Court) Rule 15.
35. *Ibid.*, r. 16.
36. *Ibid.*, r. 10.
37. Children Act 1975, s. 12.
38. Adoption (County Court) Rules 1976, r. 19.
39. Children Act 1975, s. 22(4).
40. Children Act 1975, s. 101.
41. Adoption (County Court) Rules 1976, r. 24.
42. *Ibid.*, r. 30. See also Adoption Act 1958, ss. 20 and 20A for information to adopted person.
43. Children Act 1975, Schedule 1.
44. Adoption Act 1958, s. 26 and Adoption Act 1960, s. 1.
45. For information regarding children baptised before adoption, see letter addressed to clergy by Archbishops in 1966.
46. Adoption (County Court) Rules 1959, r. 25.
47. Children Act 1975, s. 101(2).
48. County Courts Act 1959, s. 109.
49. Adoption (County Court) Rules 1976, r. 23.
50. Adoption Act 1958, s. 28.
51. *Ibid.*, s. 29.
52. *Ibid.*, s. 30.
53. Adoption Act 1958, s. 31.
54. Adoption Agencies Regulations 1976, r. 5.
55. *Ibid.*, r. 7.
56. *Ibid.*, r. 8.
57. *Ibid.*, 1976, rr. 9 and 14.
58. *Ibid.*, r. 10.
59. Particular difficulties may arise if the adoptive parents are of the Jewish faith. They should be advised to consult the Beth Din (Jewish Ecclesiastical Court) before adopting a child.
60. A Practice Direction states that the guardian *ad litem* has no *duty* to seek out

the natural father; literal compliance with this Rule is sufficient. (*Re W (An infant)*, [1963] 3 All E.R. 459, Wilberforce, J.)

APPENDIX

SUMMARY

A. SPECIMEN COMMUNITY CARE PROGRAMME AREAS AND OBJECTIVES

This outline structure consists of an overall objective which states the philosophy, five first-level objectives which serve the overall objective, and a number of separate activities which are undertaken to achieve the stated objectives. Where activities are actually carried out within another programme area, and by another local authority department, there is a note in the margin to that effect. Probation activities, though not strictly local authority services, have been included because expenditure on them serves the community care objectives. Similarly, Area Health Authority activities are included in those activities which serve the objectives of this programme.

The word "care" where it is used means accommodation and maintenance, and is thus separated from "support". It will be noticed that short-term care of various types is included in Programme C, among those activities which are used to minimise the prospect of long-term dependence on care or treatment of different kinds.

Very simply, the concept is that everything should be done to promote an environment which is helpful (A), but that there will be those who will nevertheless be at risk of long-term care; there must be ways of detecting them (B) and of providing ways of supporting them in the community (C), but finally there will be some who need long-term care or treatment, which is provided under (D), but with the intention of rehabilitation into the community wherever this is possible. All activities in support of these objectives, such as travelling, and clerical work, are deemed to be part of the actual activities themselves. Other administrative activities, which should be minimal, are provided for in (E).

OVERALL OBJECTIVE

To build up a community of families and individuals able to lead a full personal life, supported, when required, by appropriate social measures.

FIRST-LEVEL OBJECTIVES

A. To contribute towards the creation of a physical and social environment favourable to human development.
B. To detect those families and individuals who are at risk of becoming dependent upon the community.
C. To provide, and deploy, resources to minimise long-term dependence on community care.
D. To provide long-term care or treatment for those families and individuals who need it.
E. To provide general administration and support services.

Note: Headings in the left-hand margins refer to other major programmes served by the activity on the right.

A	To contribute towards the creation of a physical and social environment favourable to human development

PLANNING	1	By influencing the physical environment in the light of social factors, through:
and		(a) Social element of allied County plans
TRANSPORTATION		(b) District councils
		(c) Voluntary housing provision
DISTRICT COUNCILS	2	(a) By liaising with the housing authorities for the provision of suitable and sufficient housing especially for the handicapped and homeless
		(b) By providing grants for special housing schemes
	3	By encouraging the community to involve itself in the construction of a healthy social environment, through:
EDUCATION		(a) Education in personal relationships and in citizenship
EDUCATION		(b) Training in domestic skills

DISTRICT
COUNCILS

   (c)   Community relations
   (d)   Community centres, adventure play-
       grounds, etc.
   (e)   Involvement of local interest in homes
       and other establishments provided by
       the authority
   (f)   Village or area community schemes
       and street warden schemes

POLICE, EDUCATION
and PROBATION
PROBATION D.H.S.S.

4 By providing an advisory service:
   (a)   General advice and guidance

   (b)   Information about rights
   (c)   Information about services

5 By research:
   (a)   Research into personal and community
       factors causing problems
   (b)   Devising and executing surveys
   (c)   Processing routine flows of information
   (d)   Circulation of research findings

6 By interpretation and reappraisal of social
  policy in the light of research findings

B To detect those families and individuals who are at risk of
becoming dependent upon the community

---

1 By encouraging self-referral:
   (a)   Publicity to encourage referral
   (b)   Accessible facilities in areas

AREA HEALTH
AUTHORITY

   (c)   Accessible facilities in hospitals

   (d)   Provision of an on-call system

2 By establishment of early warning systems:

PROBATION, POLICE

   (a)   Police and courts:
       Police; probation service; juvenile
       courts; divorce courts; magistrates
       courts; county courts; crown courts;
       prisons

PROBATION, POLICE
AREA HEALTH
AUTHORITY

   (b)   Juvenile bureau
   (c)   Medical; area health authority; general
       practitioners and health visitors

EDUCATION
DISTRICT
  COUNCILS,
  ETC.

   (d)   Education:
       Schools; education welfare officer
   (e)   Financial need:
       Housing authorities and building
       societies; Department of Health and
       Social Security; Department of
       Employment and Productivity; elec-
       tricity and gas boards

(f)   Community services:
       Citizens advice bureau; clergy; home
       helps;   volunteers—meals   service,
       W.R.V.S., village or area commun-
       ity scheme; voluntary agencies—
       children, elderly, mental health,
       handicapped children

C   To provide, and deploy, resources to minimise long-term
    dependence on community care

PROBATION/
EDUCATION

1   By initial assessment of need:
     (a)   Reports to courts

     (b)   Reports on all other cases detected
           under Programme B

2   By periodical reviews of all cases receiving
    supervision or support so that:
     (a)   Any unmet need can be identified
     (b)   Support is given only as long as it is
           necessary

EDUCATION

EDUCATION/
   PROBATION
PROBATION

PROBATION
PROBATION

AREA HEALTH
   AUTHORITY

3   By counselling:
     (a)   Consultation with nuclear and ex-
           tended family
     (b)   Provision   of   individual   casework
           support/supervision
     (c)   Group therapy
     (d)   Legal supervision of persons under
           court orders
              (i)   Persons under 17
             (ii)   Persons over 17
     (e)   Supervision of children placed for
           adoption
     (f)   Supervision of private foster homes, etc.
     (g)   Counselling in hospital

DISTRICT
   COUNCILS

PROBATION

EDUCATION

4   By counselling plus material and financial
    assistance:
     (a)   Homelessness prevention
     (b)   Assistance in cash or kind to diminish
           need for care (for children)
     (c)   Minimising long-term dependence or
           community   care   through   financial
           assistance
     (d)   School meals and clothing

5   By counselling plus support services including
    voluntary services, in managing the home:
     (a)   Training in domestic management
           within the home

DISTRICT COUNCILS	(b)	Meals on wheels
	(c)	Home helps
	(d)	Family aids and night sitters
	(e)	Aids and equipment to improve mobility
	(f)	Adaptation of property
	(g)	Telephones
	(h)	Television and radio
	(i)	Use of young volunteers
	(j)	Car badges

6 By counselling plus personal support services:

EDUCATION	(a)	Social counselling in child guidance
	(b)	Home tuition
	(c)	Services for the blind: teaching, talking books, mobility teaching, vocational guidance, etc.
	(d)	Services for the deaf and hard of hearing: teaching, communication, vocational guidance, etc.
	(e)	Services for the handicapped: occupational therapy, instruction, vocational guidance, etc.

7 By counselling plus support services outside the home:

PLANNING and TRANSPORTATION, HEALTH	(a)	Transport
	(b)	Child-minders
EDUCATION	(c)	Playgroups
EDUCATION	(d)	Day nurseries
EDUCATION	(e)	Nursery schools
EDUCATION	(f)	Adventure playgrounds
EDUCATION	(g)	Youth clubs and organisations
	(h)	Day care
	(i)	Day centres and clubs
	(j)	Luncheon clubs
	(k)	Social clubs and activities
	(l)	Provision of holidays
PROBATION	(m)	Community training centres (Probation)

8 By counselling and facilities for employment or training:

EDUCATION	(a)	Special day schools
	(b)	Workshops
	(c)	Industrial out-work
	(d)	Adult training centres

9 By counselling and the provision of temporary "care":

EDUCATION	(a)	Residential assessment of social need
		(i) Community homes (for children and young persons)
		(ii) Homes for the elderly
		(iii) Homes for the handicapped
	(b)	Short-stay foster homes
	(c)	Mother and baby homes
	(d)	Training units for mothers and children
	(e)	Intermediate treatment under Children and Young Persons Act 1969
EDUCATION	(f)	Residential special schools
EDUCATION	(g)	Boarding school education
	(h)	Short-stay accommodation
	(i)	Temporary accommodation (Part III)
PROBATION	(j)	Probation and voluntary hostels
	(k)	Rehabilitation units
		(i) Blind
		(ii) Families
		(iii) Handicapped
HEALTH	(l)	Admission to hospital

PUBLIC PROTECTION   10   By providing community care during and after civil emergencies

---

D   To provide long-term care for those families and individuals who need it

---

1   By the provision of long-term care:
    (a)   Long stay foster homes
    (b)   Voluntary homes
       (i)   Children
       (ii)   Others
    (c)   Training establishments

EDUCATION   (d)   Community homes (for children and young persons)
    (e)   Homes for the aged
    (f)   Hostel homes:
       (i)   Young people up to the age of 21
       (ii)   Mentally ill
       (iii)   Mentally handicapped

2   By the enforcement of care and/or treatment where necessary, failing voluntary agreement:

EDUCATION   (a)   Children/young people
PROBATION   (b)   Offenders in breach of probation orders and statutory licences
    (c)   Elderly
    (d)   Mentally disordered

3   By the provision of support services:
    (a)   Development of foster care for children, elderly and mentally handicapped

| | (b) | Development of adoption service and placing for adoption |

(c) Homes services
    (i)   Casework
    (ii)   Local community interests

HEALTH
HEALTH
    (iii) Medical services
    (iv) Dental services
    (v)   Spiritual guidance
    (vi) Leisure activities/holidays
    (vii) Occupational therapy
    (viii) Property protection
    (ix) Receiverships

PROBATION   (d) Prison welfare
PROTECTION   (e) Registration and inspection of or advice to homes

(f) Visiting voluntary children's homes
(g) Providing official visitor for certain children

AREA HEALTH   (h) Liaison arrangements with hospital
AUTHORITY   service

4 By encouraging rehabilitation:
   (a) Using powers to allow children in care under Orders or Resolutions to live at home under supervision
   (b) Acting as Guardian *ad litem* in adoption cases
   (c) Allocating social work support to each client or family in long-term care

PROBATION   (d) Group work (probation)
   (e) Making and maintaining contact with the wider family
   (f) Periodically reviewing each case with a view to ensuring that care is not continued longer than essential for the client's well-being
   (g) Providing support services (as in Programme C) as required after discharge from care

PROBATION   (h) Providing after care support for persons released from prisons, borstals and detention centres
PROBATION   (i) After care support (probation)

E   General administration and Support Services

---

1 Training and development of staff, through:
   (a) Training
      (i)   Induction training
      (ii) Post-entry training and trainees

PERSONNEL

        (iii) Refresher training
        (iv) Management training
        (v) Training or personnel placed for practical experience

PROBATION

        (vi) Training of volunteers (probation)
  (b) Staff development

PROBATION

2 Maintaining contact with voluntary agencies and training of individual volunteers, in order to provide voluntary support and assistance to probation officers and other social workers.

3 Liaison at all levels with area health authority.

4 General administration and support services.

B. PLACE OF SAFETY ORDER

The order is set out in due form, which should be completed, stating precisely what the grounds for the application are in accordance with the Act, so that the Justice of the Peace can see what is the basis of the informant's "reasonable cause to believe that . . .".

The name of the Petty Sessional Division, and the name and office address of the informant should also be completed. The form of order should then be taken personally to a Justice of the Peace, and the informant should be prepared if asked to show that he is an officer of the local authority and authorised to make the application.

As the application is *ex parte*, the parent or guardian has no legal right to be present, but may attend if so desired.

The informant should be prepared to give details of his cause for concern about the child, and should be prepared to answer questions arising from his statement.

If the Justice of the Peace is satisfied that the application is well founded, he will sign the order authorising detention for a period not exceeding twenty-eight days. The period for each case may be suggested, within that limit.

The informant is then authorised to remove the child to whatever place of safety has been arranged, and must inform the parent or guardian (if not present at the application) of the reason for the detention and of the making of the order.

It will then be necessary to take action to ensure that a decision as to the next stage is reached with as little delay as possible.

Copies of the order should be served on the parent or guardian and on the person who will actually be in control of the child while detained.

If a child is already in a safe place, *e.g.* a hospital, a place of safety order should normally be obtained only if there are grounds for supposing that without such an order he will be removed by a parent or unauthorised person.

AUTHORITY TO REMOVE TO A PLACE OF SAFETY
CHILDREN AND YOUNG PERSONS ACT 1969 (SECTION 28(1))

In the County of

Petty Sessional Division of: ....

(Name of Officer applying for Place of Safety Order): ....

of (Office address): ....

....
(hereinafter called the Applicant) has this day applied under section 28(1)
of the Children and Young Persons Act 1969 for authority to detain and
take to a Place of Safety

(Name of relevant Infant) ....

of (address of relevant Infant) ....
a child or young person (hereinafter called the relevant Infant).

AND I, the undersigned Justice of the Peace, am satisfied that the
Applicant has reasonable cause to believe that (specify belief in terms of
section 28(1) (a), (b) or (c)).

and hereby grant the said Application.

AND the relevant Infant may be detained in a Place of Safety by virtue
of this authorisation for a period of .... days beginning
with the date hereof.

Dated this .... day of 197

.... J.P.

Justice of the Peace for the County aforesaid

C. A SUGGESTED PROCEDURE FOR PRELIMINARY INVESTIGATION OF PROSPECTIVE ADOPTERS, PRIVATE AND LOCAL AUTHORITY FOSTER PARENTS, AND CHILD-MINDERS

Anyone undertaking the care of a child, or children, in one of these ways is providing a service; in all, this represents a considerable resource to the department which is specially valuable because the service is offered within private homes, and within a defined locality, which may be identical with the place in which the need for the service arises.

This opens up the possibility of using these services, or some of them, for different purposes at different times. A person registered as a child-minder may be willing to act as a short-term foster parent for instance, or someone who has adopted a child may be willing to provide day care to a child living near by. Not everyone of course will be willing to assist in more than one capacity, but the possibility can be encouraged.

One apparent difficulty is the slightly different criteria for "approval" as between registered child-minders and local authority foster parents. In addition there are no regulations laying down precisely what enquiries should be made in the cases of people intending to act as private foster parents, or to have children placed with them with a view to adoption. But in the last two situations, there is a duty to notify the local authority under the Children Act 1958 and the Adoption Act 1958 respectively; the authority has power to prohibit the placing and could only do this if it had made enquiries as to the suitability of the persons making the notification. Similarly, if there is a failure to notify before placing, enquiries should be made after the placing becomes known, as the authority has the power to apply for an order for the removal of the child; here again enquiries would have to be made to justify this action.

The procedure for enquiry in the case of a child-minder is laid down in an old Circular, Ministry of Health 36/68, and surprisingly seems rather better than the procedure for foster parents under the Boarding-Out Regulations 1955.

The recommended procedure is for a general discussion of the position first, with explanation of what is entailed; this is followed by an application completed by the person wishing to be registered, with a declaration containing a number of statements all of which can be verified, and a declaration of health. The Circular recommends verification by means of enquiries to various sources, including the police and probation services. No visit by a member of staff is needed until all this preliminary work has been carried out and the ground has then been cleared for a real assessment of the personal qualities of the applicant.

There seem to be advantages in using the application method in all four types of case set out above, but only as a means of establishing certain *facts* before the assessment, which is a matter of *opinion*, takes place.

In this way everyone would first apply, or enquire, and be given advice or counselling, which can be done individually or—probably better—in groups. After this, those who still wish to continue would be invited to complete a simple form of application (A and B) and the statements in it would be verified by a series of form letters to the persons mentioned at the head of form C. When all the replies have been received, and marked off, the social worker concerned could begin the necessary detailed enquiry knowing that there was no basic objection to acceptance on *personal grounds.* If the replies disclosed any adverse facts, such as a conviction, the weight of this could be considered, but need not necessarily lead to rejection; if it does there would be some good reason. (The likelihood of rejection would be greatly minimised by the initial discussion before the application is made, as in the course of it applicants would be told of the *kind* of enquiries which would be instituted in the event of an application being received. Self-rejection would be specially likely if the preliminary discussion took place in a group.)

The requirements for registration as a child-minder are more detailed and more precise than those for a foster parent, local authority or otherwise, so that given the basic information, two different assessments of *opinion* may be required, form C or D being used as appropriate.

In using this method, the department would treat in the same way everyone who wishes to offer a home for a child whether for two hours a day, or for life, and the basic facts would be established before the particular kind of personal assessment was embarked upon. This would make a later "change of use" possible without a repetition of enquiries already made. A further advantage is that the basic work, after initial counselling, would be purely an administrative matter until such time as the way was clear for fuller social work investigation. The suggested Forms A, B, C and D are set out in the following pages; the form letters at present used for foster parents would be suitable, after slight amendment to take in the whole of the suggested scope of enquiry.

Appendix

FORM A

COUNCIL

SOCIAL SERVICES DEPARTMENT

Information given by persons wishing to care, in their
own home, for a child or children under the age of 18

	Wife (or lady householder)	Husband (or other householder)
1. Full Name		
2. Maiden or former Name		
3. Date of Birth		
4. Married/Single/Widowed Divorced/Separated		
5. If married date of marriage		
6. Address and Tel. No.		
7. How long here		
8. If less than two years previous address		
9. Any qualifications (Child Care, Nursery etc.)		
10. Religion		
11. Occupation		
12. Approx. Income per week		
13. Name and address of G.P. Telephone Number		

14. Family and Household
    (1) Other persons *over 16*   All members of the family (*under 16*)
       living here
       Full Name   *Age* *Full Name*   *Address*

    (2) The following persons would assist in the care of the children:

Name	Address	Age
Name	Address	Age
Name	Address	Age

15. Brief description of home—owned or rented, from landlord or
Council, how many rooms, main Services, whether there is a
garden, etc.

I DECLARE that neither I nor any of the persons named overleaf has had made against him or her an order under any of the following enactments:

(a) Part 1 of the Children Act 1958 removing a child from his or her care.

(b) The Children and Young Persons Acts 1933–1969 or the Social Work (Scotland) Act 1968 in respect of any child found to be in need of compulsory care, being an order by virtue of which the child was removed from his or her care.

(c) Section 1(4) of the Nurseries and Child-Minders Regulation Act 1948 refusing his or her registration under that Act or an order under Section 5 of that Act cancelling his or her registration under that Act or the registration under that Act of any premises occupied by him or her.

(d) Section 43 of the Adoption Act 1958, (removal of protected children from unsuitable surroundings) for the removal of a child from his or her care.

I FURTHER DECLARE that neither I nor any of the persons named overleaf have been convicted of any of the following offences:

(a) The murder or manslaughter of a child or young person, also aiding, abetting, counselling or procuring the suicide of a child or young person.

(b) Infanticide.

(c) Any offence under section 27 or 56 of the Offences against the Persons Act 1861, and any offence against a child or young person under section 5, 42 or 43 of that Act.

(d) Any offence under sections 1, 3, 4, 11 or 23 of the Children and Young Persons Act 1933.

(e) Any offence against a child or young persons under any of the following sections of the Sexual Offences Act 1956, that is to say sections 2 to 7, 10 to 16, 19, 20, 22 to 26 and 28, and any attempt to commit against a child or young person an offence under sections 2, 5, 6, 7, 10, 11, 12, 22 or 23 of that Act.

(f) Any offence specified in the First Schedule to the Children and Young Persons (Scotland) Act 1937.

(g) Any other offence involving bodily injury to a child or young person.

I FURTHER DECLARE that neither my rights and powers nor any of the rights and powers of the persons named with respect to a child have been vested in a local authority under section 2 of the Children Act 1948.

I understand that the   Council has a duty to make enquiries about the members of a household in which children may be cared for away from their parents. I therefore authorise the Council to verify any of the information I have given above.

I also authorise the Council to make enquiries of the following persons who are willing to act as referees in this application:

(1) *Name and Address*

(2) *Name and Address*

Signed........................ Date........................

Signed........................ Date........................

FORM B
.... COUNCIL SOCIAL SERVICES DEPARTMENT
BOARDING-OUT OF CHILDREN REGULATIONS 1955
CHILDREN ACT 1958
as amended by the
CHILDREN'S AND YOUNG PERSONS ACT 1969
ADOPTION AGENCIES REGULATIONS 1959
NURSERIES AND CHILD-MINDERS REGULATION ACT 1948
as amended by the
HEALTH SERVICES AND PUBLIC HEALTH ACT 1968

DECLARATION OF HEALTH

Name ....

Address ....

.... Date of
Birth ....

Are you in good health at present? ....

Are you at present attending the doctor
for any reason? (If so, state reason) ....

Do you have any treatment prescribed
regularly by the Doctor? (If so, give details) ....

Have you ever suffered from nervous or other
similar illness and, if so, what age were
you when this happened? ....

Have you ever suffered from epilepsy or fits? ....

Have you ever suffered from tuberculosis or
have you been in close contact with a known
case of tuberculosis? (If yes, please give details) ....

When did you last have a chest X-ray and with
what result? ....

Is everyone else living in your household
(including lodgers) as far as you know in
good health? ....

I agree that an authorised Medical Officer of the Area Health Authority may seek medical information from any doctor who has at any time attended me and I authorise the giving of such information.

My general practitioner is: Name ....

Address ....

....

I certify that the above statements are true.

Signature ....

Date ....

ASSESSMENT OF APPLICATION TO CARE FOR A CHILD

1. Enquiries regarding ....

	Date sent	Date Reply		Date sent	Date Reply
Police			Personal Ref. (1)		
Probation			Personal Ref. (2)		
Education			A.H.A. (T.B.)		
G.P. (1)			Health Care team		
G.P. (2)			Shire Hall Record		
			Area Record		

2. *Accommodation*: Type of house, neighbourhood, number of rooms, material condition, play facilities, fire precautions, sanitation, water supply, heating, space, etc.

3. *Assessment*: Family background and relationships, special skills and interests, attitude to natural parents, temperament, age of children to be cared for, motivation (including infertility investigations when appropriate)

3. *Assessment* (Cont'd/......)

4. Date of group meetings attended

   Date of personal interviews

5. Recommendation, including restrictions on number of children to be cared for, and any special provisions to be made.

Signed .... Social Worker   Date..........

Approved/Not approved/Deferred..............   Date..........
                                    Area Director

Registered as approved or not approved ....

If refused, date   notified for Committee Report ....

           To file.......................... Date.............
                              Signed

FORM D

NURSERIES AND CHILD-MINDERS REGULATION ACT 1948

Assessment of application to care for a child (Child-Minders)

	Date Sent	Date Reply		Date Sent	Date Reply
Police			Personal Ref. (1)		
Probation			Personal Ref. (2)		
Education			A.H.A. (T.B.)		
G.P. (1)			Health Care team		
G.P. (2)			Shire Hall Record		
			Area Record		

1. Name of Occupier ....

2. Address of Premises ....

   ....

3. Number and description of rooms, and floor area:

   (i) .... (iv) ....

   (ii) .... (v) ....

   (iii) .... (vi) ....

4. Water supply.............. (5) W.C. accommodation.......

6. Lavatory basins............ (7) Drainage ....

8. How are premises heated ...... (9) Fire/Radiator guards ....

10. Any person suffering from tuberculosis or any other infectious disease? ....

11. General condition of premises ....

    ....

    ....

    ....

12. Other remarks..

    ....

    ....

    ....

    ....

Date.............. Signature of Officer........................

FOR OFFICE USE ONLY

Recommendation as to number of children permitted................

Recommendation—Approved/Disapproved/Deferred

If not approved state reason.....................................

....

....

....

Reported to Committee .... Result ....

Certificate issued ....
        or   Entered in Register ....

Notice of Refusal sent ....

Subsequent action ....

....

....

....

....

....

....

....

....

....

....

Regulations 20, 23 and 27
D.   FORM OF UNDERTAKING TO BE SIGNED BY FOSTER PARENTS[1]

We/I, A.B. [and B.B.], of
having on the   day of   , 19   , received
from [the council of the county/county borough of
(hereinafter called "The council")] [*name of voluntary organisation*
(hereinafter called "The organisation")] C.D., who was born on the
                  day of   19   , and whose religious persuasion
is   , into our/my home as a member of our/my family
undertake that—

1. We/I will care for C.D. and bring him/her up as we/I would a child
of our/my own.

2. He/she will be brought up in, and will be encouraged to practise,
his/her religion.

3. We/I will look after his/her health and consult a doctor whenever
he/she is ill and will allow him/her to be medically examined at such times
and places as [the council] [the organisation] may require.

4. We/I will inform [the council] [the organisation] immediately of any
serious occurrence affecting the child.

5. We/I will at all times permit any person so authorised by the
Secretary of State or by [the council] [the organisation] [or by the council
of the county/county borough where we/I live] to see him/her and visit
our/my home.

6. We/I will allow him/her to be removed from our/my home when so
requested by a person authorised by [the council] [the organisation] [or
by the council of the county/county borough where we/I live].

7. If we/I decide to move, we/I will notify the new address to [the
council] [the organisation] before we/I go.

(Sgd.) ....

(Sgd.) ....

Dated..

Note: The Adoption Forms which follow are those for the County Court.
There are similar separate forms for use in applications to the High Court
and the magistrate's court.

Rule 4 (1)

E. ORIGINATING APPLICATION FOR AN ADOPTION ORDER

Form 1

In the   County Court.

No.. . . . .

IN THE MATTER OF The Adoption Act 1958

AND

IN THE MATTER OF The Children Act 1975

AND

IN THE MATTER OF (^{1}). . . . . .a child.

I/We, the undersigned,. . . . .
[and]. . . . . .wishing to adopt
. . . .(^{1}) a child, who
is within the district of this county court,(^{2}) under the Adoption Act 1958
and the Children Act 1975, hereby give the following further particulars
in support of my/our application.

PART I

Particulars of the applicant[s]
1. *Name and address, etc.* Name of (first) applicant in full. . . . .
. . . .
Address (^{3}) . . . .
Occupation. . . . .
Date of birth. . . . .
Relationship (if any) to the child. . . . .
[Name of second applicant in full. . . . .
. . . .
Address (^{3}) . . . .
Occupation. . . . .
Date of Birth . . . .
Relationship (if any) to the child. . . . .]
2. *Domicile.* I am/We are/One of us (namely.. . . . .)
is domiciled in England and Wales/Scotland/Northern Ireland/the Channel
Islands/the Isle of Man.
3. *Status.* I am unmarried/a widow/widower/divorced [*or* We are
married to each other and our marriage certificate (or other evidence of
marriage) is attached] [*or* I am applying alone as a married person and
can satisfy the court that   ] (^{4}).
[4. I am applying alone for an adoption order in respect of my own
child and can satisfy the court that the other natural parent. . . . .
. . . .
. . . .
. . . .] (^{5}).
[5. *Health.* A certificate as to my/our health, signed by a fully registered
medical practitioner, is attached] (^{6}).

PART II
Particulars of the child

6. *Identity, etc.* The child is of the.....................sex and is not and has not been married. He/She was born on the..............day of ....19....and is the person to whom the attached birth/adoption certificate ([7]) relates [*or* was born on or about the ....day of............................... 19...., in........ ....] ([8]).

[7. *Health.* A report on the health of the child, made by a fully registered medical practitioner on the............day of............. 19...., is attached] ([9]), ([10]).

8. *Parentage, etc.* The child is the child ([11]) of.....................([12]) whose last known address was....................................... [*or* deceased] and ([13])... ....whose last known address was... .... [*or* deceased].

[9. The guardian[s] of the child (other than the mother or father of the child) is/are... of... [and.. of.. ....]] ([14]).

[10. *Parental agreement.* I/We attach a document/documents signifying the agreement of the said: .... [and...] ([15]) to the making of an adoption order in pursuance of my/our application].

[11. I/We request the judge to dispense with the agreement of: .... on the ground[s] that... [and.. ....] ([15]) ([16]) and there are attached hereto three copies of a statement of the facts on which I/we intend to rely].

[12. *Care, etc.* The.....................Council [*or*................] of... has/have the powers and duties of a parent or guardian of the child [*or* the parental rights and duties with respect to the child]] ([17]).

[13. *Maintenance.* ....of..................... is liable by virtue of an order made by the.....................court at...........................on the.........day of.............. 19...., [*or* by an agreement dated the.........day of............. 19....,] to contribute to the maintenance of the child] ([18]).

14. *Proposed names.* If an adoption order is made in pursuance of this application, the child is to be known by the following names:—
Surname...
Other names...

Part III
General

15. The child was received into my/our actual custody on the........
day of................19...., and has been continuously in my/our
actual custody since that date (*or as appropriate*) [19].

16. The child has/has not had his home with me/us for the five years
preceding the date of this application.

[17. I/We/One of us (namely..............) notified the..........
Council on the..........day of................19...., of my/our
intention to apply for an adoption order in respect of the child [20].

18. No proceedings relating in whole or in part to the child have been
completed or commenced in any court in England or Wales or elsewhere
[except...
....
....] [21], [22], [23].

19. I/We have not received or given any reward or payment for, or in
consideration of, the adoption of the child or for any agreement to the
making of the adoption order [except as follows:—
....
....] [24].

20. As far as I/we know no person or body has taken part in the
arrangements for placing the child in my/our actual custody [except
....] [25].

[21. For the purpose of this application reference may be made to
.......................of...] [26].

[22. I/We desire that my/our identity should be kept confidential, and
the serial number of this application is........................] [27].

I/We accordingly apply for an adoption order in respect of the child.
Dated this...........day of................19.....
Signature[s].......................................
....

Note: This Form must be filed in duplicate, but duplicates of the attached
documents need not be filed. Every paragraph must be completed or
deleted, as the case may be.

NOTES

([1]) Enter the first name[s] and surname as shown in any certificate
referred to in entry No. 6; otherwise enter the first name[s] and surname
by which the child was known before being placed for adoption.

([2]) The child must be within the district of the county court to which the
application is made.

([3]) Insert the address where the applicant has his home and the place
(if different) where documents may be served on him.

([4]) A married applicant can apply alone only if he or she can satisfy the
court that his or her spouse cannot be found, or that they have separated
and are living apart and that the separation is likely to be permanent, or
that by reason of physical or mental ill health his or her spouse is incapable
of making an application for an adoption order. Any documentary evidence
(including death certificate where relevant) on which the applicant proposes
to rely should be attached to the application. The name and address (if
known) of the other spouse should be supplied.

(^{5}) Enter the reason to be relied upon (that the other natural parent is dead, or cannot be found, or that there is some other reason, which should be specified, justifying his or her exclusion). Documentary evidence, *e.g.*, a death certificate should be supplied where appropriate.

(^{6}) A separate medical certificate is required in respect of each applicant. There is an official form (Form 3) which may be used for this purpose. No certificate, however, need be supplied if the child is the child of the applicant or either of them, or has reached the upper limit of the compulsory school age.

(^{7}) If a child has previously been adopted, a certified copy of the entry in the Adopted Children Register should be attached and not a certified copy of the original entry in the Registers of Births.

(^{8}) Where a certificate is not attached, enter the place including the country of birth if known.

(^{9}) There is an official form (Form 4) which may be used for this purpose. No certificate need be supplied if the child is the child of the applicants or one of them, or has reached the upper limit of the compulsory school age.

(^{10}) If the child is less than one year old on the date of the application, the report should have been made during the month preceding that date. If the child is one year old or more on that date, the report should have been made during the period of six months before that date.

(^{11}) If the child has previously been adopted, give the names of his adoptive parents and not those of his natural parents.

(^{12}) Enter mother's name.

(^{13}) Enter name of father, if known.

(^{14}) Enter particulars of any person appointed by deed or will in accordance with the provisions of the Guardianship of Infants Acts 1886 and 1925, or the Guardianship of Minors Act 1971, or by a court of competent jurisdiction to be a guardian. Do not include any person who has custody of the child only: under section 57 (1) of the Act of 1958 (as amended by paragraph 39 (*d*) of Schedule 3 to the Act of 1975), a father of an Illegitimate child who has custody of the child under section 9 of the Guardianship of Minors Act 1971 (or section 2 of the Illegitimate Children (Scotland) Act 1930) is a guardian, so that his agreement to the adoption is required unless dispensed with, but his identity should be given at entry No. 8 above.

(^{15}) Enter either in paragraph 10 or 11 the names of the persons mentioned in entries Nos. 8 and 9, except that in the case of an illegitimate child the father of the child should be entered only if he has custody of the child by virtue of an order under section 9 of the Guardianship of Minors Act 1971 or under section 2 of the Illegitimate Children (Scotland) Act 1930.

(^{16}) Enter one or more of the grounds set out in section 12 (2) of the Act of 1975.

(^{17}) This entry should be completed where some person or body has the powers and duties of a parent or guardian of the child by virtue of section 24 of the Children and Young Persons Act 1969 or has vested in him or it the parental rights and duties with respect to the child under section 2 of the Children Act 1948 or section 60 of the Act of 1975.

(^{18}) This entry should be completed where some person or body is liable to contribute to the maintenance of the child under a court order or an agreement.

(^{19}) Under section 3 (1) of the Act of 1958, an adoption order cannot be made unless the child has been continuously in the actual custody of the applicant during the three months before the order is made; this is modified by section 12 (3) in the case of a married couple where both are or one is living outside Great Britain (so that a continuous period of at least three months' actual custody with one applicant which includes a period of one month with the other will suffice). In this case the relevant facts shall be stated. *

([20]) Notice does not have to be given if the applicant or one of the applicants is a parent of the child or if at the time of the hearing the child will have reached the upper limit of the compulsory school age.

([21]) The court cannot proceed with the application if a previous application made by the same person in relation to the child was refused unless one of the conditions in section 22 (4) of the Act of 1975 is satisfied.

([22]) Where the application is made by a married couple, of whom one is a parent and the other is a step-parent of the child, or by a step-parent of the child alone the court must, under section 10 (3) or 11 (4) of the Act of 1975, dismiss the application if it considers that the matter would be better dealt with under section 42 (orders for custody etc., in matrimonial proceedings) of the Matrimonial Causes Act 1973.

([23]) State the nature of the proceedings and the date and effect of any orders made.

([24]) Any such payment or reward is illegal except payment to an adoption society or local authority in respect of their expenses incurred in connection with the adoption.

([25]) Enter the name of the local authority, adoption society or individual who has taken part in the arrangements for placing the child in the actual custody of the applicant with a view to his adoption.

([26]) Where the applicant or one of the applicants is a parent of the child, or a relative as defined by section 57 (1) of the Act of 1975, no referee need be named.

([27]) If the applicant wishes his identity to be kept confidential the serial number obtained under rule 5 of the Adoption (County Court) Rules 1976, should be given.

* Now amended to make it clear that there must be six months actual custody when the application is for a provisional adoption order.

F. MODEL LEAFLETS FOR PARENTS
(*Circular LAC* (76) 15)

LEAFLET NO. 1 FOR PARENTS AND GUARDIANS OF CHILDREN WHO ARE BEING
RECEIVED VOLUNTARILY INTO CARE OF LOCAL AUTHORITIES OR VOLUNTARY
ORGANISATIONS

(Name of Local authority or voluntary organisation)
WHERE YOUR CHILD IS
As you know your child..
was received into our care on.....................................
and is being looked after by:
Mr and Mrs..
Address...
....
Telephone Number..

YOUR SOCIAL WORKER:
Your social worker is...
Address...
....
Telephone Number..
If you are unable to get in touch with your social worker, please ask for
....

YOUR SOCIAL WORKER WILL WANT TO:
  help you so don't hesitate to discuss your problems even if they are not
  directly connected with your child;
  discuss and plan with you about what is best for your child while he* is in
  care;
  try to keep brothers and sisters together or at least in close touch with each
  other;
  plan with you for your child's return home.

YOU CAN HELP BY
keeping us informed of your address. The law requires you to do so and your
social worker needs to know where to get in touch with you for your child's
sake. Even if you go away from home for a short time only, it would be
helpful if you would write or telephone to say where you are.

letting your social worker know if there are any important changes in your life
so that you can talk together about how these will affect your child.

telling us all you can about your child so as to help him settle down and make
him feel as much at home as possible. He will want to bring his own clothes
and some of his favourite toys and possessions to remind him of you and his
home. It would be nice for him to have some photographs of his family.

Some of the things you can tell us are:
What school he goes to
What clubs he goes to
Which relatives or friends you want him to keep in touch with
What food he likes or dislikes
Whether he has a special diet
What religious observance, if any, you would like him to follow

Whether he has any bedtime routines such as taking a special toy, having a favourite drink, saying prayers etc.

Whether he puts himself to bed

Whether he wets his bed

What are his favourite things, such as games, television programmes, looking after family pets?

Is there anything he is especially frightened of?

Any other matter you feel is important to him.

KEEPING IN TOUCH WITH YOUR CHILD

Your social worker will let you know how your child is getting on and will make arrangements for you to visit or meet him, will tell you how often visits may be made, at what time etc., and will help with fares if necessary. If you cannot arrange a visit, your social worker will make sure that you hear how he is getting on.

Parents often have mixed feelings about parting from their children and feel awkward about going to see them while they are being looked after by people they do not know very well. Children too may feel upset and confused no matter how carefully it has been explained to them why they are leaving home. They will miss their parents and want to see them but may also feel angry sometimes, because they have been left with strangers, and if they are too young to understand the explanations, they may think they have been deserted. So it is very important for parents to keep in close touch with their children by visiting as often as possible as well as writing and telephoning. This contact helps them to understand that they are still remembered, loved and cared for.

So if you cannot visit yourself, perhaps a close relative or a friend who knows your child well can visit instead and keep the memories of home fresh in his mind. Birthday and Christmas greetings are especially important.

* Note for authorities/voluntary organisations: Although the texts of the models refer to the child as "he", the leaflets should be amended as appropriate for girls or for more than one child.

LEAFLET NO. 2 FOR PARENTS WHOSE CHILD WAS RECEIVED INTO CARE VOLUNTARILY AND IS LIKELY TO REMAIN IN CARE LONGER THAN 6 MONTHS*

PART I

Name of local authority social services department.....................
....
Your social worker is...
Address..
Telephone number...
If your social worker is not available you should get in touch with
....
    Your child...............has now been with us since.............
and seems likely to stay with us for more than 6 months.

    If he is still in care on or after................you must give us 28 days' notice in writing that you want to have him home. The law requires this because children may need a little time to get used to the idea of moving. People looking after your child also may need notice to prepare for these changes and to get his belongings together.

    If you have been in constant touch with your child and with your social worker then it is very likely that your child will be able to return to you before the 28 days have passed, and in some cases almost immediately. At the latest, your child will return to you at the end of the 28 days unless there should be very special and particular circumstances.

    If because of your own circumstances it seems that your child will not be able to go home in the near future, then you and your social worker must continue to talk about the best possible plans which should be made for your child's care. At regular intervals your social worker will consider your child's progress, your own circumstances and make plans and decisions for the child's future. Social workers have a duty to plan for children to return home as soon as this is in their best interest. You will be closely involved in discussion and in the making of plans and decisions.

Important points to remember
    a. While your child is in our care we have a duty to give first consideration to his welfare and interests. If your child is old enough to understand, then we must find out his wishes and feelings about any plans.
    b. For the sake of your child it is important for you to keep in touch with him and with your social worker.
    c. It is essential that we know where you are, so that we can get in touch with you at any time.
    d. Wherever possible all decisions concerning your child will be made with your help and co-operation. If you have any problems or difficulties, we hope that you will ask your social worker to help you.
    e. Your child will not be moved to another address without previous discussion with you except in unforeseen circumstances. In such a case you would be given full information as soon as possible.
    f. If your child has brothers and sisters or if you have other children in care, we shall do our best to keep them together or in touch with each other.

PART II

PROTECTING CHILDREN IN SPECIAL CIRCUMSTANCES

Unexpected difficulties can happen in everybody's life. After a great deal of thought some parents may even feel that they cannot have their child back to live with them. They may therefore make the painful decision that it would be best for the child to be permanently cared for by someone else. In that event the social worker will help parents to consider such a step very carefully and will explain what has to be done legally.

In rare cases children may need protection either from being taken out of care and being placed in a situation which is likely to be harmful, or from being suddenly removed from people who have cared for them for a long time and to whom they may have become attached.

The legal position in such cases is explained below.

PARENTAL RIGHTS

The local authority can take over the rights and duties of one or both parents of a child in their care. The special circumstances in which such a decision could be made are: that the child has no parents or guardian, or that he has been "abandoned" (this means his parents have been out of touch and their address unknown for a year or more); or because of parents' serious illness or disability which make them unable to care for the child, or because of their way of life or their consistent failure to act as good parents. The local authority can also take over parental rights and duties if a child has remained in care continuously for 3 years or more and it is not in the child's interest to be removed from care at this particular time. Parents and children may grow apart from each other during such a long time, and it may be necessary to safeguard the plans that have been made for the child's future.

Parents' legal rights in such a case

If the local authority has to consider taking over parental rights and duties, parents will usually have the opportunity to discuss this fully with the social worker and may agree to this plan. The local authority is required by law to let parents know in writing if parental rights have been taken.

After receiving this official notice parents have 28 days in which to make up their minds whether to object. This has to be done in writing. After the letter has been received the local authority can agree to restore parental rights. If it does not, it must within 14 days of receiving the parents' letter, ask a juvenile court to decide the matter. Parents and the local authority would be entitled to put their case forward in the court. The parents are entitled to be legally represented.

If either the parent or the local authority is not satisfied with the decision the court makes, either of them can appeal to the High Court. In these circumstances parents should be legally represented.

While the local authority has parental rights and duties, it may allow the child to live at home under the supervision of a social worker. At any time parents can apply for their rights and duties to be restored to them and, if the local authority does not agree, parents can ask the court to decide.

Legal advice about these matters can be obtained from

a citizens advice bureau;

a legal advice centre;

any solicitor.

Parents on a low income may apply for legal aid. Any solicitor displaying the legal aid sign will help.

WHEN CHILDREN HAVE LIVED AWAY FROM HOME FOR A LONG TIME

The longer children are away from home, the more attached they are likely to become to the people who are caring for them. What may seem a fairly short time to adults seems a very long time to children. The time may come when they want to remain with those who are looking after them. This does not necessarily mean that they have forgotten their own families.

The law says that if people have cared for a child continuously for 5 years or more, they can start adoption proceedings without the parent's or the local authority's agreement.

Children are sometimes upset by their parents' visits. This may be distressing to the parents, too, and sometimes they feel tempted to cut out the visits or to come less often. But it is far better for children to be able to show their feelings rather than to be hurt and sad because they think they have been forgotten. It is important for parents to tell their children why they are away from home and how long this is likely to last. For your child's sake, do not promise that he can come home before you are sure you can manage.

Sometimes parents cannot visit or meet their children on the day they promised to do so. If this should happen to you, do make sure your child gets a message, either directly or through your social worker or the person caring for him, so that he doesn't feel let down.

PRACTICAL ARRANGEMENTS
Medical Attention
Your social worker will have asked for your consent to routine medical and dental inspection and to immediate medical and surgical treatment of your child if necessary. Your social worker will need to know the name of your doctor, your child's doctor and whether your child takes any medicines or is undergoing any treatment. If your child becomes seriously ill when in care, your social worker will make every effort to get in touch with you immediately to give you the fullest possible information and to get your agreement to any treatment the doctors may advise.

Money Matters
Having a child in care may affect your financial position as you may be expected to contribute to his maintenance according to your income and expenses. If you are receiving national insurance or supplementary benefit, family allowance, child benefit or family income supplement, your allowances may be affected when your child comes into our care. You should tell your local Social Security Office about your changed circumstances.

If you have any difficulties or questions about this, the Social Security Office or your social worker will help to sort them out.

YOUR CHILD'S RETURN HOME
You and your social worker will discuss when it would be best for your child to return to you and you will plan how this can be arranged. Of course you may ask for your child to be returned to you at any time, but we hope you will join us in planning ahead for his return so that he and whoever has been looking after him can make the necessary preparations. The longer a child has been in care, the more likely he is to have settled down in his new surroundings and the longer time he will need to get used to the idea of moving again, to saying goodbye to friends at school, to putting his clothes and belongings together and to saying goodbye to the people looking

after him. THIS IS RECOGNISED IN LAW SO IF YOUR CHILD STAYS WITH US FOR 6 MONTHS OR MORE, YOU MUST GIVE US 28 DAYS NOTICE IN WRITING WHEN YOU WISH TO HAVE HIM BACK. However, it will often be possible for your child to be returned to you immediately or at any rate some time before the official 28 days are up.

This leaflet is intended for general guidance and must not be regarded as a full statement of the law.

* Section 105 of the Children Act provides that the Secretary of State shall lay before Parliament a report on the operation of the sections of the Act brought into operation. So far as time limits are concerned, they may be amended by order approved by each House of Parliament.

G. CHILDREN ACT 1975 TIME LIMIT PROVISIONS (RESTRICTIONS ON REMOVAL)

Decision Points:	CHILD RECEIVED INTO CARE *Children Act 1948, s. 1* 1	2	CHILD IN CARE 3 MONTHS 3	4	CHILD IN CAR 6 MONTHS 5
					section 56
ACTION	DETERMINE reason for reception ASSESS whether short or long stay if possible SELECT suitable placement GIVE and DISCUSS 1st Explanatory Leaflet to Parent GIVE relevant information and guidance to foster parents and residential staff	supervise child, keep in touch with parents keep situation under review	REVIEW mandatory if boarded out REVIEW desirable for all children PLAN for future DECIDE whether it is appropriate to give part or whole of 2nd Explanatory Leaflet to Parents INVOLVE parents, foster parents, residential staff and child as appropriate in plans and decisions	as in column 2 and RE-ASSESS situation if circumstances change CONSIDER whether child will remain in care for more than 6 months	28 DAYS NOTI of intention removal from care now operative DECIDE how prepare for discharge an whether to waive notice REVIEW mandatory f all children i care PLAN for futu DECIDE whether discharge desirable IF NOT consid whether actio possible to as sume parenta rights (or in rare circumstances) to apply for car proceedings

Section 59: Substituting s. 12(1) of the Children Act 1948.
  * This section is not yet in force.
   In reaching any decision relating to a child in their care a local authority shall gi first consideration to the need to safeguard and promote the welfare of the child throug out his childhood; and shall so far as practicable ascertain the wishes and feelings of t child regarding the decision and give due consideration to them, having regard to his a and understanding.

		CHILD IN CARE 3 YEARS		CHILD IN CARE 5 YEARS
6	**7**	**8**		**9**
continue as under column 2 and as under column 5 CONSIDER suitability of placement if circumstances change and possibility of custodianship application	*sections 57 and 41** (1) PARENTAL RIGHTS can be assumed if child has been in care continuously CONSIDER frequency and quality of parental contact DECIDE whether in interest of the child and whether to seek parental consent (2) CUSTODIANSHIP ORDER* can be *applied* for if child has been cared for by applicants for an aggregate of 3 years without parental consent CHILD CANNOT be removed while applications pending except with leave of court	continue as under columns 2, 5 and 6 CONSIDER whether adoption desirable if child boarded out with foster parents and issue not raised previously		*section 29* ADOPTION ORDER can be *applied* for without parental consent. If child has lived with applicants for at least 5 years child cannot be removed while application is pending without the leave of the court

H. GUARDIAN *AD LITEM* REPORT
(*a suggested outline*)

............................Magistrates' Court   Court Ref: ....
                       County
                                            Serial No. ....

                      Date of hearing...........................

Report of guardian *ad litem* on the application of ....
and .... to adopt ....

The Child:

present name and sex.

whether legitimate.

whether related to
  applicant(s).

date and place of birth.

ethnic origin.

baptism; religion.

immunisation; health.

medical certificate.

right to property from
  parent(s); whether insured.

whether old enough to understand
  nature of adoption order;*

if so, wishes and feelings expressed
  to guardian.

whether in care.

history of actual custody throughout
  life.

responsibility for placing.

whether report from placing agency,
  if any, attached.

name by which to be known after
  adoption.

Parentage:

Natural father –

status – 'lawful', husband of
  mother, adjudged putative
  father, (whether awarded
  custody), alleged, not
  named.

name (if appropriate).

date of birth, address,
  occupation, income,
  nationality, religion.

any wishes with regard to
  religious upbringing,
  marital state, previous
  marriages,* whether
  seen, present circumstances.

whether wishes to be heard.*

whether proposes to attend
  hearing, or apply for
  custody.

whether agreement required;

if so, whether given with full understanding of nature of order, and
  given freely.

whether a minor.*

if liable to contribute under
  agreement or order, details.

medical history.*

details of any other children.

(If he had custody but is now
  deceased, names of any relative
  who might wish to be beard by
  the court.)*

interviewed by.

Mother –

full name, date of birth.

whether a minor.*

address, nationality.

occupation, income.

religion, any wishes with

whether understands nature of
  adoption order.

reason for agreeing to adoption.

whether supplied with an
  explanatory memorandum.

regard to child's religious upbringing.

marital status.

previous marriages,* whether documents seen.

custody orders.

whether agreement given freely.

interviewed by.

whether proposes to attend hearing.

medical history.*

other children.

general circumstances.

if deceased, name of any relative who might wish to be heard by the court.*

Applicants:

Male –

full name and date of birth.

nationality; domicile.

occupation; income.

religious persuasion (confirmed, practising).

details of any previous marriages; or of previous adoption applications.

Female –

as for male applicant.

Marriage –

place and date and whether certificate seen.

Children –

details of children of the household.

relationship, if any, to child of present application.

Sole applicant –

if application is by child's father or mother alone, why is the other parent excluded?

if application, otherwise, is by one spouse only, why is the other spouse not a party to it?

assessment of marriage as basis for sound relationship with child to be adopted.

Nature of order –

whether applicants understand nature of order and that it is irrevocable and will render them responsible for maintenance and upbringing. Understanding of child's right to access to birth record at age of 18. Attitudes of relatives to adoption.

Health –

whether applicants have suffered from any serious illness, and whether any history of tuberculosis, epilepsy or mental illness in their respective families. Whether medical certificates satisfactory.

reason for wishing to adopt. Whether written history of child given by agency.

home address, brief description, whether rented or owned, outgoings – rent, mortgage, rates; number of rooms, details of other members of

* These are matters on which the guardian *ad litem* may need to notify the court forthwith. It may be necessary to treat additional persons as respondents, or, in certain cases, for the court to consider whether a parent under a disability should have a guardian *ad litem* appointed to safeguard his or her interests.

household, apart from children of family, garden, play space, furnishings, general conditions, accommodation for child to be adopted.

any rights to, or interests in, property which child stands to gain if adopted.

Referee:

whether responsible person recommending without reservations; whether interviewed personally.

Third Party:

names and addresses of persons taking part in private placing, details of arrangements made.

Reward:

whether made, given, agreed, offered.

Supervision by welfare authority:

date of notification, name of supervisor, whether reports satisfactory, assessment of suitability of applicants for child in question.

Application:

whether statements in application have been verified.

whether any reasons for request to dispense with agreement have been investigated and discussed with parties concerned.

Information to applicants:

have applicants been informed regarding child's baptism, immunisation treatment, insurance for funeral purposes, rights to, or interests in, property which he stands to retain or lose, if adopted.

Other respondents:

is there any other person, not already a respondent, who may wish to be heard as to whether or not an adoption order should be made?

Section 10 (3) and 11 (4)

if these sections apply, what are the relative advantages and disadvantages, to the child, of adoption?

Interim Order:

If there is no legal bar to the adoption, is there any circumstance which might be met by an interim order?

Recommendation:

(if expected by the court)

Refusal of order:

if the order should be refused, should an order be made under Section 17 for committal to care or supervision?

Date of report...

Signature of (or for) Guardian *ad litem* ....

INDEX

285